Remembering
ROADSIDE AMERICA

Remembering ROADSIDE AMERICA

Preserving the Recent Past as Landscape and Place

John A. Jakle *and* Keith A. Sculle

THE UNIVERSITY OF TENNESSEE PRESS / KNOXVILLE

Copyright © 2011 by The University of Tennessee Press / Knoxville.
All Rights Reserved. Manufactured in the United States of America.
First Edition.

Images are from the authors' collections unless otherwise indicated.

Library of Congress Cataloging-in-Publication Data

Jakle, John A.
Remembering roadside America: preserving the recent past as landscape and place / John A. Jakle and Keith A. Sculle. — 1st ed.
    p. cm.
Includes bibliographical references and index.
ISBN-13: 978-1-57233-823-4 (pbk.)
ISBN-10: 1-57233-823-7 (pbk.)
 1. Historic sites—Conservation and restoration—United States.
 2. Historic buildings—Conservation and restoration—United States.
 3. Roadside architecture—Conservation and restoration—United States.
 4. Landscape architecture—Conservation and restoration—United States.
 5. Material culture—Conservation and restoration—United States.
 6. Historic preservation—United States.
 7. Museum techniques—United States.
 8. Landscape protection—United States.
 9. United States—Description and travel.
10. United States—History, Local.
 I. Sculle, Keith A.
 II. Title.

E159.J25 2011
363.6'90973—dc23
2011029286

For Cindy and Tracey

CONTENTS

Preface   xv
Acknowledgments   xxiii

1. The Journey Begins   1
2. Observing Roadside America   29
3. Learning from Roadside America   61
4. Preserving Roads and Roadsides   95
5. Historical Museums and Roadside America   133
6. Experiencing the Past as Landscape and Place   171
7. The Road Continues   209

Appendix   233
Notes   237
Index   273

ILLUSTRATIONS

1.1. Header for "The Great American Roadside"   2
1.2. U.S. 30 at Breezewood, PA, 1988   3
1.3. Dodge Road near 108th Street, Omaha, NE, 1992   5
1.4. Dodge Road near 108th Street, Omaha, 1999   6
1.5. Pavement on the Former Lincoln Highway, West of Omaha, 1989   7
1.6. Vacant Roadside Businesses, Williamstown, KY, 1996   13
1.7. Gasoline Sign, Commerce, GA, 2007   14
1.8. Vacant Gasoline Station, Santa Rosa, NM, 2008   15
1.9. Derelict Highway Cafe, Cecil, OH, 1999   16
1.10. New Restaurant under Construction, Champaign, IL, 1995   17
1.11. West Street, Annapolis, MD, 2006   18
2.1. Rural Road in Illinois, 1915   34
2.2. Postcard View of Lincoln Highway, West of Laurel Mountain in Pennsylvania, c. 1915   35
2.3. Hardware Store with Gasoline Pump at Dewart, PA, c. 1915   37
2.4. Main Street Business District, Wadena, MN, c. 1925   38
2.5. Eighth Street, Coffeyville, KS, c. 1925   39
2.6. Highway U.S. 50, East of Laurel Mountain in West Virginia, c. 1925   39
2.7. Gilmore Family Gas Station, Leroy, IL, 1940   41
2.8. Gilmore Family   42
2.9. Mid-Continental Petroleum Company Roadmap, c. 1940   44
2.10. Advertising Blotter, Dixie Tourist Camp, Kingstree, SC, c. 1925   45
2.11. Advertising Postcard, Trumbull Motel, Troy, MO, c. 1950   46
2.12. Advertising Postcard, B. Lloyd's Pecan Service Stations, c. 1947   47
2.13. Cartoon Parodying Highway Advertising Signs   49

2.14. National Old Trails Highway, West of Troy, IL, c. 1928   50
2.15. U.S. 80 Strip at Gila Bend, AZ, c. 1938   52
2.16. State Route 4 at Edge of Pittsburg, CA, c. 1935   53
2.17. Colorado Avenue, Pasadena, CA, c. 1949   55
2.18. Interstate 70 East of Kansas City, MO, c. 1970   56
2.19. Roadmap Panels, Cities Service Oil Company, c. 1960 and 1965   59
3.1. Cartoon Panels Illustrating Commercial Strip Evolution   64
3.2. Las Vegas Boulevard, Las Vegas, NV, Large Signs, 1983   71
3.3. Las Vegas Boulevard, Las Vegas, NV, Small-Scale Businesses   72
3.4. Modeling the Evolution of a Suburban Strip Corridor   75
3.5. Commercial Land Use Along Previously Residential Thoroughfare, Champaign and Urbana, IL, 1919–89   76
3.6. Changing Land Use along I-474, Bloomington, MN, 1953–76   79
3.7. Shell Gasoline Station, Winston-Salem, NC, 1981   81
3.8. Gasoline Station Building Types Predominant in the United States, 1910–90   83
3.9. A "House with Canopy" Gas Station, Constantine, MI, 1978   84
3.10. An "Oblong Box" Gas Station, Champaign, IL, 1976   85
3.11. A "Canopy with Booth" Gas Station, Chicago, IL, 1992   85
3.12. Vintage Motel 66 on Former Route 66, Tulsa, OK, 1985   86
3.13. Abandoned motel property on U.S. 19, Perry, FL, 2004   87
3.14. Vacant Shopping Center, Dallas, TX, 1989   88
3.15. Westheimer Road near Post Oaks Center, Houston, Texas, 1996   89
3.16. Approach to New York, New York Casino, Las Vegas, NV, 2002   90
3.17. Las Vegas Boulevard, 2002   91
3.18. Golden Gate Casino and Hotel, Las Vegas, 2002   94
4.1. Postcard Rhapsodizing about Sightseeing Bus at Lookout Mountain, TN   96
4.2. Hot 'n Now, Kalamazoo, MI, 2009   97
4.3. Main Street, Old Salem, Winston-Salem, NC, 1973   105
4.4. The Old Coffee Pot, Winston-Salem, NC, 2005   106
4.5. Esso Standard Gasoline Station, Meeting Street, Charleston, SC, 1977   107
4.6. Interior, Historic Charleston Foundation's Architectural Interpretation Center, 1996   108

4.7. Bay Street Construction Site, Charleston, SC, 2000   109
4.8. Meramec River Bridge Deck, Former U.S. 66, Times Beach, MO, 2003   112
4.9. Meramec River Bridge Supports, Former U.S. 66, Times Beach, MO, 2003   113
4.10. Arroyo Seco, Los Angeles, CA, 1968   114
4.11. George Washington Parkway, South of Alexandria, VA, 1968   115
4.12. H. P. Sears Service Station Number Two, Rome, NY, 2007   116
4.13. Vintage Pump at H. P. Sears Service Station Number Two, Rome, NY, 2007   117
4.14. Phillips 66 Gas Station, Creston, IA, 2001   118
4.15. Vintage Pump and Hanging Sign at Phillips 66 Gas Station, Creston, IA, 2001   119
4.16. George Merschdorf's Former Gas Station, Mansfield, OH, 2006   120
4.17. Terry Kinsinger's Former BP Station, Piqua, OH, 2005   121
4.18. Interior of Kinsinger's Gas Station   121
4.19. Terry Kinsinger in Vintage Gas Station Attendant's Uniform   122
4.20. Restored Phillips Station and Garage, Tulsa, OK   123
4.21. Delta Diner, Delta, WI   124
4.22. Lincoln Motor Court, Tulls Hill, PA, 2001   125
4.23. Coral Court, Marlborough, MO, 1994   127
4.24. Coral Court, Marlborough, 1994, with Its Infamous Garage Doors   129
5.1. Postcard view of Lincoln Home, Springfield, IL, c. 1910   136
5.2. South Ninth Street East of Lincoln Home, Springfield, 1971   140
5.3. Mr. Lincoln's Neighbor, "Books, Gifts, and Autographs"   141
5.4. Lincoln home, Springfield, Early 1960s   142
5.5. Eskimo Museum and Gift Shop, Fairbanks, AK, c. 1980   143
5.6. Advertising postcard for Sod House Museum near Moorcroft, WY, c. 1935   144
5.7. Advertising postcard for Longhorn Ranch, Moriarty, NM, c. 1935   145
5.8. Norsk Folk Museum, Oslo, Norway, 2006   145
5.9. Duke of Gloucester Street, Williamsburg, VA, 1964   146
5.10. Entrance to Historic Williamsburg on the South, 1990   147
5.11. Greenfield Village, Dearborn, MI, 1938   148
5.12. Henry Ford Museum, Dearborn, c. 1970   149

5.13. Ford Exposition, Century of Progress Fair, Chicago, 1933–34   150
5.14. Miner Grant's General Store Interior, Old Sturbridge Village, Sturbridge, MA, c. 1950   151
5.15. Pioneer Village, Minden, NE, 1996   152
5.16. Main Museum, South Barracks, Fort Ticonderoga, NY, 1940   153
5.17. Spectators Peer onto "Democracity," 1939   155
5.18. Roadside America, Hamburg, PA, Vicinity, c. 1940   156
5.19. Lincoln Group, Century of Progress Fair, Chicago, 1933   157
5.20. New Mexico Heritage Preservation Alliance's Brochure on Sign Preservation along Route 66   161
5.21. Restored 1932 Phillips 66 Gasoline Station, Cuba, MO, 2009   162
5.22. Gasoline Station Murals, Cuba, MO, 2009   163
5.23. Steamtown National Historic Site, Scranton, PA, 1997   164
5.24. Packard Museum, Dayton, OH, 1987   165
5.25. Packard Museum, Dayton, 1989, Showing One of Henry Bourne Joy's Personal Packards   166
5.26. Pioneer Auto and Antique Town, Murdo, SD, c. 2005, Revealing Historic Main Street Setting   167
5.27. Pioneer Auto and Antique Town, with Antique Cars from Collection Parked on Street   168
5.28. Sign from Douglas, MI, Drive-In Movie Theater   169
6.1. Vintage Gasoline Pump, Studebaker National Museum, South Bend, IN, 2009   173
6.2. Vintage Gasoline Station Re-creation, Antique Car Museum of Iowa, Coralville, IA, 2009   174
6.3. Old World Wisconsin near Eagle, WI, 1982   179
6.4. Sherbrooke Village, Sherbrooke, Nova Scotia, 1985   181
6.5. Postcard View of Heritage Park, Calgary, Alberta, c. 1970   183
6.6. Street Scene, Heritage Park, Calgary, Alberta, 1978   184
6.7. Restored Gasoline Station, Former Route 66, Shamrock, TX, 2003   185
6.8. North Madden Street, Shamrock, TX, 2008, with Its Cluster of Early Roadside Relics   186
6.9. Vintage Gas Stations on North Madden Street, Shamrock, TX, 2008   187
6.10. Reed/Nyland Corner, east of Colo, IA, 2009   188

6.11. Postcard Ad, Chaparral Antique Car Exhibit, Six Flags over Texas, c. 1960   190

6.12. Postcard advertisement, Dogpatch Reptile Garden and Hillbilly Farm, Lake Ozark, Missouri, circa 1960   192

6.13. Pueblo Court, Amarillo, TX, c. 1950   193

6.14. Lincoln's New Salem State Park, Petersburg, IL, 1969   195

6.15. Closed Gas Station, Ola, AR, 2007   198

6.16. Fruit Stand South of Dupont Center, FL, 2002   201

6.17. Signs at Intersection of State Road 204 and I-95, South of Dupont Center, FL, 2002   202

6.18. Postcard Advertisement for General Motors, c. 1955   203

7.1. Postcard View of Cherokee, NC, c. 1950   211

7.2. Postcard View, Eisenhower Center, Abilene, KS, 1957   220

7.3. Coral Court Motel Exhibit, National Museum of Transportation in Suburban St. Louis, MO, 2009   222

7.4. Miracle of America Museum, Polson, MT, 2009   225

7.5. "Gallery" on the Zion–Mt. Carmel Highway in Today's Zion National Park   226

PREFACE

How is early Roadside America to be remembered? Along almost any urban thoroughfare or rural highway in the United States today, there are relics left over from the early days of motoring—something derelict and essentially abandoned, something still standing but substantially modified in reuse, or, more important, something fully restored as if back to its original glory. It might be a gas station, for example, that has been turned into a lawyer's office on a city street near downtown, or it might be a tourist information office located at the edge of a small town. Or, for that matter, it might be lovingly restored as a museum, perhaps by an enthused collector of vintage cars or maybe by a local historical society. Hard—if not impossible—to find, however, are building ensembles variously surviving at the scale of landscape or place. Yes, a building here or there offers a sense of time, a depth, to a contemporary scene. But whole roadsides surviving even from but a few decades back are not to be found. Roadside America by its very nature has been, and remains, ever changeful.

The automobile's historical impact on life in the United States has been most significant and deserves to be well remembered. Perhaps nothing else has made as great an effect on built environment in the United States as automobilty. Use of cars and trucks over the past century has virtually remade American geography, particularly by turning cities inside out and pushing them ever outward through suburbanization, even congealing them together as giant conurbations. Small towns caught in the flux of big city expansion, or otherwise located favorably along highways connecting the nation's metropolises, have been restructured through growth; towns bypassed, on the other hand, have been re-formed more through decline. Central to this process, the commercial strip with its gas stations, drive-in restaurants, motels, and literally every other kind of retail entity has made life convenient for those employing automobiles. But how are Americans to remember how it all came to be, especially if little evidence of automobility's early decades survives and especially on the scale of landscape or place? Will Americans fully understand how the early allure of automobile convenience translated commercially into roadside opportunity? It is doubtful that admiring isolated architectural residuals will fully suffice. Or for that matter, what of viewing old photographs; films or reading travel diaries, short stories, and novels; or even singing old songs that early Roadside America inspired by way of popular culture? We think there ought to be more. We advocate remembering through material culture constituted via landscape and place.

This book is intended for the general reader, especially the reader with an abiding interest in the American past as expressed through evolving landscapes and places. So also might public historians, historic preservationists, and museum curators find interest, since we write to extend their work. We offer straightforward prose, supplemented by a generous use of photographs, to report on Roadside America as a particular kind of landscape or place in the American experience and to pose a line of argumentation regarding how its past might to be better remembered. We deliberately avoid the jargon of social theory (or critical analysis) so fashionable among many scholars in both the humanities and the social sciences today. Offered instead is our personal take on what little survives from the early days of motoring along the nation's streets and highways, why protecting what does survive is important, and how those resources might best be interpreted by way of lasting cultural record. We consider the automobile as technological instrument, the motorist as seeker of roadside convenience, and the roadside entrepreneur as commercial provider of that convenience.

Change has always been a fundamental aspect of life in the United States. And in recent decades new ideas and new technologies, and thus new ways of doing things, have come to the fore with ever-increasing frequency and rapidity. Ours is indeed a world of ephemerality. We see change in our surroundings everywhere. But nowhere, we assert, has change been more apparent than in landscapes and places affected directly by automobile use. It been has especially true of Roadside America, the focus of this book. The internal combustion engine, and all the other technical innovations associated with putting that technology on wheels, wrought a revolution in American life, the effects of which play out through an ever-accelerating restructuring of American geography. It is not just that roadways themselves have changed, but adjacent land uses as well, and, of course, the nature of roadside buildings. Roadside America has been in a state of flux for generations now. Indeed, life lived in the "fast lane" in the United States has been so changeful that many things about the nation's early roads and roadsides tend to be forgotten. Memories are dim and often distorted. For most Americans, one might speculate, there is actually little sense of implicit history.

Change can be confronted in many ways. Some Americans embrace change readily (and many unthinkingly so) as a sign of progress, with that which is new always thought to be somehow better. Others recognize change and abide it, seeking comfort in the face of future uncertainty through what remains of a disappearing status quo. Still others are totally oblivious to change, so normal and thus so expected has it become. An individual's remembering what once was, besides being partial, is always peculiar. No two people remember things just alike, although in every society something of a collective memory lingers, a remembering that individuals can variously relate to should they choose to do so. Collective memories are usually organized around the extraordinary—people, events, or things perceived as having had outstanding social implication or impact. Tastemakers (including corporate advertisers and political leaders, but also writers, artists, and musicians among others) tend to dominate collective remembering.

Remembering U.S. history often proceeds along political or economic lines, with emphasis placed initially on the great leaders of government or business and their accomplishments and then secondarily on ordinary people of everyday circumstances. Americans may prefer highly personalized history, history translated substantially through biography, for example. Less important, perhaps, is remembering the past through built environment, the surviving material culture, such as that of landscape and place. Although Americans very much celebrate "the common man" (certainly in their embrace of democratic ideals), only recently has the material culture of common people in common places come to the fore as having historical importance, including vestiges of what has become the most common kind of place of all—Roadside America.

Relatively recently Route 66 has entered the national iconography of important historic places—along with the likes of Independence Hall, George Washington's Mount Vernon, the battlefield at Gettysburg, and the USS *Arizona* at Pearl Harbor. Historic Route 66, as a relic road and roadside, was not the work of any one person, of course. Its making involved not just individuals, but institutions, some of which were specifically formed in the process of its creation and promotion. Route 66, as it is remembered today, was very much a collective experience rooted in the everyday. It was not just an economic or political accomplishment, although certainly it was both, but, more important, it was an accomplishment that spoke to the cultural aspirations of ordinary Americans. That is why Roadside America deserves careful attention as a source for historical understanding. Roadside America deserves serious attention from historians and others concerned with interpreting the nation's past, if only the recent past of the twentieth century.

Remembering automobility's past may necessarily focus on pioneering inventors and innovating businessmen, such as Henry Ford. It was Ford's Model T, perhaps more than any other motor vehicle, that brought mass automobile ownership to the nation, an accomplishment based on his manufacturing cars with standardized parts and his breaking down factory work into specialized tasks along moving assembly lines. He also innovated marketing, with a franchised Ford dealer being established in nearly every small town of any size across the country and, of course, in big-city neighborhoods and suburbs. Other manufacturers and their leaders, such as General Motors' Alfred Sloan, followed suit. But Sloan also emphasized styling, making the automobile a status symbol and a focus of lifestyle as well as a means of transport.

Mass automobility wrought widespread demand for improved roads. And good roads in turn led to an emergent economy of roadside selling, starting with gasoline, overnight accommodations, and food. But eventually roadside commerce came to dominate all retailing, with roadside locations providing intervening opportunities to sell and to buy. No longer, for example, did customers have to access congested downtown or Main Street business districts to find what they needed or thought they wanted. Today's brick-and-mortar retailers operate mainly out of big-box stores and shopping centers that are fully road-oriented and generously provided with convenient parking-lot surrounds; otherwise goods are ordered over the Internet and delivered to a customer's home by delivery truck. Substantially fostered by Roadside America, a consumerist society expanded, and success in the United States was redefined in terms of what one bought and consumed. Corporate dominance rose through the "branding" of commodities. An "experience economy" of highly customized products and services evolved, and social values were symbolized along the nation's roadsides through distinctive signage, store architecture, interior store decor, and product packaging. Emphasis on appearances made roadsides into landscapes of desire.

Is the consumerist revolution not as important to remembering our nation's past as our establishing national independence or our making the constitution work or our preserving the Union? What of our fighting tyranny abroad? Consumerist landscapes of the past, especially those spawned through automobility, are as significant as any other kind of historical place for understanding what we as a people have become. They reflect the market as it grew. And it was the market of an essentially free enterprise system that sustained the nation's successes and failures. The market is what we argue about (or over) when we debate national issues, for example health care or energy conservation, arguments that rage as we prepare this book for publication. What our nation became in the twentieth century has evolved in a market substantially reoriented toward the automobile.

Remembering Roadside America invites storytelling. As with the auto industry itself, the building of highways and the establishment of roadside services brought heroes and heroines to the fore. Highway building in the United States congealed around such names as Fisher, Joy, MacDonald, and Moses. The history of Roadside America is remembered through names such as Rockefeller, Getty, and Phillips in the petroleum industry, Hilton and Marriott in the hospitality field, and Sanders and Kroc in the quick-service food business. But remembering roads and roadsides should also embrace the stories of common or ordinary people, especially as they learned to be consumers. And material culture, we suggest, is essential to that end, especially relic material culture, as rare as it might be in many localities today. Memory potentially hinges not just on the relic pavements and antiquated rights-of-way of various sorts of streets and highways, but likewise on the various kinds of garages and gas stations, cabin courts and motels, and diners and drive-ins that lined those thoroughfares.

What follows is our coming to grips with the problem of how best to remember and understand Roadside America, along with proposing at least a partial solution. Our purpose is not to explore the topic exhaustively, but to raise awareness by making observations, and, of course, by asking questions. We begin by reviewing the automobile's impact on the nation's built environments, elaborating, at the same time, the important concepts of landscape and place. We examine, as well, the extent to which cars, roads, and roadside commerce have indeed impinged on American cultural awareness, especially through literature, painting, still photography, cinema, and music, especially song lyrics. Early-twentieth-century highway development in the United States, and the concurrent rise of auto travel, especially auto tourism led to a demand for roadside services. Out of that demand, of course, came Roadside America. Of interest is just what motorists of the early twentieth century actually experienced in confronting the nation's new highways. How did historians and other scholars, halfway through the twentieth century, come to document Roadside America's rise? More important, what did early critics of Roadside America have to say? And how did those perceptions change?

With the rise of the historic preservation movement in the United States, there was a focus not just on the work of public and private organizations, but also on what individuals (car enthusiasts among others) and what they achieved in celebrating the nation's evolving car culture. What might preservation-minded people do today to aid our remembering of America's early roads and roadsides? Consider the nation's museums, especially the outdoor history museums, all of which support much of the nation's collective remembering, certainly that involving residual material culture. Supporting these museums is a great start.

What aspects dominate the telling of U.S. history in the nation's outdoor museums today? Unfortunately roads and roadsides figure relatively little. Need that be? An outdoor history museum focused on the rise of automobility and specifically on the rise of Roadside America might contribute to an understanding of our history. We seek to bring our many strands of thought together by outlining the themes that an actual museum focused on roadside history might explore.

That such a museum does not yet exist we take to be problematical. What then might one be like and how might it function? Answers are at least hinted at in many popular entertainment and educational venues very much extant today: antique car festivals, vintage-car museums, and, of course, roadside restorations, including dated gas stations, motels, and drive-in restaurants refit or re-created with degrees of historical accuracy.

Ours is a call to remedy what we consider to be serious neglect. It is not just a call to embrace roads and roadsides as important strands in the nation's story, but to do so through the instrument of material culture presented not just at the scale of machines and architecture but at that of landscape or place. There is a growing predisposition among Americans today to embrace road and roadside history in a direct, physical sense—to embrace an important kind of environmental history at the scale of actual past environment.

If Roadside America has been, and remains, fundamentally ephemeral, perhaps even epitomizing ephemerality in the material sense, then an outdoor museum of roadside history may not be just another venue for remembering the past, but a very necessary one for conserving what is left—a venue of last resort. But, more important, if American roadsides of the past, even of the relatively recent past, are to be experienced firsthand, then a suggestive "Roadside America" may need creating—something that the simulation of an outdoor museum might best accomplish. The "open road" of fast cars on good roads has come to symbolize values that are fundamentally American: freedom of mobility and individual control over travel, for example. The car has come to symbolize success. Perhaps more than anything else one might own, cars and their use have become very much a social status declarative. Such understandings are easily subsumed in nostalgic longings where, for example, the past is selectively made out to be a simpler or less complicated place, or a place more romantic or more exhilarating than the present. It is the sort of thinking around which "heritage" is easily assumed and where much actual, knowable "history" is denied. Thus what sorts of understanding might a museum of the American Roadside bring to the fore? And what sorts of misunderstandings might it seek to avoid and to what purpose?

ACKNOWLEDGMENTS

Without shared information from reliable personal recollections and/or archives familiar to a few alert local residents, the authors would not have been able to complete the research behind this book. We are beholden to all. In addition we wish to thank Carol Ahlgren, Minneapolis City Planning Department, Minneapolis, Minnesota; Scott Berka, Colo Development Corporation, Colo, Iowa; Pat Burg, Illinois State Museum, Springfield, Illinois; Dave Geisler, Pioneer Auto Show and Antique Town, Murdo, South Dakota; Esley Hamilton, Saint Louis County Parks and Recreation, Clayton, Missouri; Arthur Krim, Cambridge, Massachusetts; Jeff LaFollette, state director, Iowa Lincoln Highway Association, Ogden, Iowa; Karen Lane, Fairbanks Convention and Visitors Bureau, Fairbanks, Alaska; Heather MacIntosh, Preservation Action, Washington, D.C.; Paul Daniel Marriott, Paul Daniel Marriott and Associates, Washington, D.C.; Kevin J. Patrick, Indiana University of Pennsylvania, Indiana, Pennsylvania; Michael Romero Taylor, National Park Service, Santa Fe, New Mexico.; Tim Townsend, Lincoln Home, National Park Service, Springfield, Illinois; and the staffs of the Abraham Lincoln Presidential Library and Illinois State Library, both in Springfield.

We are grateful for the University of Tennessee Press's fine work on this volume, including the assignment of constructive readers. Their critical comments were very useful. We are grateful as well to Kerry Webb and Gene Adair on the press's staff, and to freelance copyeditor Bill Adams for his judicious and careful work.

CHAPTER ONE
THE JOURNEY BEGINS

> Automobile in America,
> Chromium steel in America,
> Wire-spoke wheel in America,
> Very big deal in America!
>
> **From "America," *West Side Story*,
> lyrics by Stephen Sondheim**

Our collaboration as authors, which now continues in this, our eighth book focused on the history of Roadside America, began in the summer of 1973, along a stretch of the Old National Road (U.S. 40) in downstate Illinois.[1] Keith A. Sculle, a historian and preservationist, having just been appointed a historic sites surveyor for much of the central part of Illinois, and John A. Jakle, a brand new assistant professor of geography at the state's largest university, were away from their offices, thinking about how history might be "read" from ordinary landscapes and places. Built environment, after all, can provide information relevant to understanding the past, just as do archival and other documents, the traditional bases for historical understanding. And suddenly, there it was—a building rendered in Greek Revival style. It was not a bank, a house, or a church—something of nineteenth-century origin that might be so styled architecturally. It was instead a gasoline station, a structure of modern early-twentieth-century origin that had been fabricated in a factory at some distance and then assembled on the roadside. Vacant, it looked quite forlorn. Indeed, within a few years it was torn down. But what did it mean?

That building had us thinking about Roadside America and its importance in the history of the nation. In developing a dependency on motoring over the past century, Americans fundamentally changed their nation's geography, creating built environments that were not just automobile-convenient in design and use, but fully automobile-oriented. Change was most apparent along the margins of the nation's highways where enterprising business people sought not only to sell goods and services to motorists, but to intercept consumer dollars short of traditional retail destinations. After World War II, spawned outward from virtually every town and city in the United States, were what Americans tended to term "commercial strips." Within the nation's big cities, commercial thoroughfares born in the streetcar era were reconfigured for auto convenience. Roadside America was born.

Flying high above Kansas one evening in the gathering dusk, essayist John B. Jackson noted below a typical farm town out of which, like the tail of a comet, stretched a long, sinuous line of lights: "lights of every color and intensity, a stream of concentrated multicolored brilliance." They were not only of "fleeting beauty," but they expressed, he said, a vital "new force in American life."[2] Whether

Figure 1.1. Header for "The Great American Roadside," an article anonymously written by James Agee and illustrated by John Steward Curry. *Fortune* 10 (Sept. 1930): 53. It was with this essay that Roadside America was first identified and celebrated as a new type of landscape, or a kind of place, in the American experience.

called "roadsides" or "strips," this aspect of America's geography (especially its urban geography) was very much in the process of being fundamentally transformed. Indeed, by the 1960s commerce in most U.S. towns and cities had already been substantially oriented to the new strips. It was not just gas stations, motels, fast food restaurants, and such built to cater to motorists, but all manner of commercial infrastructure. All kinds of urban development were involved: shopping centers, office buildings, factories, and, of course, residential subdivisions. It was everything that today, for better or for worse, we associate with suburban sprawl.

Roadside America, however, has proven to be ever so changeful, with a continuous and rapid metamorphosis. The *Great American Roadside* was what James Agee called it in his unsigned 1934 essay in *Fortune*, an article lavishly illustrated by Charles Stewart Curry (fig. 1.1).[3] It was, he said, a new kind of American frontier fully inviting to commercial pioneering. And, as he emphasized, it was fully rooted in American restlessness. It was something ever-changeful. Roadside buildings were constantly being modified if not replaced altogether as businesses came and went, and, more important, as land uses changed (fig. 1.2).

Figure 1.2. U.S. 30 at Breezewood, Pennsylvania, 1988. Here a roadside landscape thrives along the former Lincoln Highway, America's first marked transcontinental auto road. It is the nearby interchange with the Pennsylvania Turnpike that leads to the exciting visible activity here. Much that is depicted in this photograph is now gone, replaced several times over by new things. The Sohio brand of gasoline and the Howard Johnson's Restaurant chain have now disappeared from U.S. roads.

Indeed, ephemerality was actually programmed in. Roadside buildings have always tended to be lightly constructed with little if any pretense to permanence. Thus today relatively little survives from the early decades of the 1920s or 1930s in most localities, perhaps a gas station here or a cabin court or drive-in food stand there; but nowhere does a vintage commercial strip survive in its entirety. Roadside landscapes seemingly come and go even before a sense of history—a sense of pastness—can attach.

Automobility

America's embrace of the automobile, and the important changes in landscape and place that accompanied it, is of fundamental historical significance. The term *automobility*, popularized in the 1960s, has to do with the collective beliefs and attitudes, as well as the accumulated material culture, associated with mass motoring. It is an umbrella term covering the automobile's centrality to life in the United States through most of the twentieth century and into the twenty-first.[4] Regarding the material culture of Roadside America, it is important to ask the following questions. Lacking tangible examples at the scale of landscape, will Americans in the future appreciate how and why Roadside America evolved as it did? Will they appreciate how radical the very creation of Roadside America really was? In a broader sense, will they be able to visualize the steps by which landscape and place in America, and thus life in America, was changed so drastically by auto use?

Classical Roadside America was very much in its twilight years, the geographer Darrell A. Norris noted, in the mid-1980s. Forces operating against permanence, he wrote, included "concentration and redistribution of traffic flow, obsolescence of taste and its related technology, the changing scale of the minimally visible business, and powerful inducements to the agglomeration and expansion of highway commercial premises." A Darwinian model of changing roadside commerce was not farfetched, he argued. "Random mutation, national selection, environmental adaptation, and competition all have quite strong parallels in the evolving species along Via Americana." A fossil record of sorts still existed, most notably along stretches of old highway bypassed by new construction and in small towns and big city neighborhoods notably lacking in economic vigor. But much of the nation's "roadside legacy" had already been "destroyed, stolen, or altered beyond recognition." Classic Roadside America faced certain extinction (figs. 1.3, 1.4, and 1.5).[5]

What ought to be done about this "twilight landscape?" One organization, the Society for Commercial Archeology, was already organized to celebrate the kitsch of Roadside America, its members immersed in documenting roadside history and celebrating roadside architecture relics.[6] Others, however, actively rejected Roadside America's significance, although largely on aesthetic grounds, involving themselves, for example, in various initiatives to "regulate, contain, and eliminate," using Norris's terms, what was considered roadside blight, especially the tacky buildings, the overabundance of exuberant signage, and the extravagant waste of space. Most Americans, of course, were completely ambivalent. So ordinary and so commonplace had Roadside America become that people hardly thought about such things one way or another. Of course, cars, roads, and roadsides did come to feature prominently in American arts and letters, so very fundamental had motoring become to life in the United States. Roadside America was rising as an important metaphor in the realm of imaginative expression. "These insights," Norris asserted, stemmed from "primal

Figure 1.3. Dodge Road near 108th Street, Omaha, Nebraska, 1992. Dodge Road, which evolved as a classic commercial strip after World War II, became the principal axis for Omaha's suburban expansion westward, with gas stations, motels, and other roadside services leading the way. Very quickly, however denser land uses took over, including the shopping centers and office complexes pictured here in the distance.

Figure 1.4. Dodge Road near 108th Street, Omaha, Nebraska, 1999. With accelerated development, traffic volumes on Dodge Road soared, causing gridlock, especially during morning and evening rush hours. Shown here is an elevated roadway that is under construction. It is designed to speed up commuting traffic and to pass over local traffic, mainly shoppers.

and conflicting themes of freedom and isolation, haven and vortex, the familiar and the unknown, direction and futility, even life and death." They spoke to the U.S. experience with "mythic power."[7]

Automobility and indeed landscapes of automobility derived from deep-seated American values. Motoring brought degrees of geographic mobility to an already highly mobile nation, but amplified it as never before. Car use also spoke to social mobility, car ownership developing very much as a badge of social status. Motoring brought a kind of freedom. It helped move women out of the household and into the marketplace, for example. But mainly automobility greatly accelerated change, not only along the nation's highways, but everywhere. In 1850 animals accounted for roughly 70 percent of the nation's total "horsepower," and animal power in total was rivaled only at a great distance by that of steam and water. By 1880, however, it was down to 45 percent, and to 29 percent in 1900. With the coming of the automobile, its contribution by 1920 had collapsed to less than 5 percent. By the 1930s horsepower equivalents to the national total of 1850 were being added to the economy every ninety days.[8] Some 85 percent of it was attributable to cars and trucks.[9]

Figure 1.5. Pavement on the former Lincoln Highway, west of Omaha, Nebraska, 1989. At one time Omaha's Dodge Road was part of the Lincoln Highway. Pictured here is an old section of that road just north of where it turned toward Fremont, Nebraska. Today's Dodge Road (U.S. 6) continues in a straight line westward toward the state capital at Lincoln, a six-lane limited access freeway. The brick pavement shown here is marked as a historic byway.

In 1908 there were approximately 200,000 automobiles in a nation of some 90 million people. The introduction of Henry Ford's Model T the next year wrought a revolution, its price declining from $950 in 1910 to $290 in 1924. Whereas it took the average worker twenty-two months to buy a Ford in 1909, by 1925 it required only three. Motoring, previously the reserve of the well-to-do, was turned into a middle-class preoccupation. Motor vehicles outsold carriages and wagons for the first time in 1914. There were some 2 million cars and trucks operating on American roads two years later, with 8 million in 1920 and 10 million in 1923.[10] The auto industry became a giant. It consumed in 1929 some 85 percent of the rubber produced in the nation, 67 percent of the plate glass, and 19 percent of the iron and steel. The number of workers employed in making, selling, and servicing motor vehicles that year stood at an estimated 1.5 million. By 1950 there were some 45 million cars and trucks on the nation's roads. In 2000 there were 221 million.[11]

At first the automobile was mainly a thing for pleasure, and the road trip was very much a part of middle-class affluence. For factory workers in the 1920s, increased wages and the reduced workweek came hand in hand with expanded vacation time. Some 29 million Americans, more than a third of the nation's population, took pleasure trips by car in 1927.[12] Quickly, however, cars became essential for commuting, shopping, and many other activities, especially in and around cities. What began as a vehicle to freedom in leisure time became a necessity for everyday life. Motorcars and trucks clogged city streets, making mass transit exceedingly slow. With downtown districts congested, stores began to open branches out in the suburbs, making living in the suburbs all the more attractive. As suburban subdivisions multiplied, the spatial reorganization of metropolitan America accelerated, with roadways playing a key role.[13]

Increased volume and usage of cars and trucks meant better roads were needed. But improved streets and highways only invited still faster and larger motor vehicles. New roads were built to underpin suburban growth. Dual-lane separation and limited accessibility defined whole new categories of road, and the new high-speed turnpikes and freeways even penetrated to the very centers of American cities. Not just cars in motion, but cars at rest needed accommodating, so parking lots began to fragment downtowns. Indeed, by the 1960s streets and parking lots together consumed more than one-third of the real estate in most of big city's central business districts.[14] Off-street parking very much came to characterize retailing in the suburbs, most especially in shopping centers with their large parking lots. Improved roads tied rural America firmly into an increasingly metropolitan nation. In 1915 there were some 276,000 miles of paved road in the United States with 9.0 motor vehicles per mile. In 1930 there were some 694,000 miles of paved road with 38.5 vehicles per mile. And by 1950 there were some 1,936,000 miles of paved road with 25.4 vehicles per paved mile.[15]

Automobility asserted itself in the United States by stages, phases of collective "automobile consciousness" as the historian James J. Flink termed it. Before 1910 cars were largely sporting and recreational devices for the nation's affluent elites. From 1910 to World War II, car use dramatically expanded, generating a car-based culture across the breadth of U.S. society. Not owning a car became sign of deprivation. It is important to note that new opportunities for consumption and thus self-absorption were spawned. The car was understood as an important symbol of progress and of modernity. After World War II, automobility assumed a dominance across the United States, not just as a transportation system, but as a fundamental basis for achieving a modern life style. "Auto-convenience," "auto-accessibility," or "auto-orientation," call it what you may, came fully into ascendency.[16]

The notion that auto ownership and auto use enhanced personal freedom was perhaps the most important idea sustaining automobility's rise. The urbanist Lewis Mumford questioned that belief, although he admitted that motoring did seemingly serve to enlarge egos otherwise shrunken by modern technology's overall implications. Through acceleration of speed and the individual's ability to maintain fast movement over long distances, human mobility was indeed substantially enhanced, at least when combined with improved streets and highways free of traffic congestion. That, of course, was the rub. The car was but part of a system, one defined not just by cars, but also by roads and their adjacent land uses. It was quite paradoxical that as automobiles became faster, their speed potential was more than offset by the increases in time necessary to negotiate traffic congestion and the greater distances to be negotiated between destinations as stores and other venues became increasingly spread out, especially in sprawling suburbs. Additionally, as alternative forms of transport declined, such as mass transit, automobility, through a diminished range of choices, actually wrought less rather than more freedom of action.[17]

The car was also part of a social system, and society and geography mirrored one another. Geography, it should be emphasized, does not just reflect society. Rather geography (defined especially in terms of human spatiality—the way people structure landscapes and places and make location decisions) is fully inculcated in social behavior. Places, including those of Roadside America, are structured in ways that invite normative activities and behaviors. In their classic study of Muncie, Indiana, or "Middletown," conducted in the 1930s, the sociologists Robert and Helen Lynd recognized the already-strong symbolic relationship between family life and cars. Even those households that scrimped on food, clothing, and/or quality of residence sought to own cars. Car use changed family dynamics. It affected many "social habits," including those of courtship, for example.[18] Everyday driving created a new "automobile psychology," another study concluded, one closely related to consumption, in general, which had become the dominant influence in modern life's restructuring.[19] Automobility promoted false consciousness about how individuals related to society at large. Motoring tended to reinforce individualist ideology, the notion that people were best valued as autonomous actors. Many observers argued that community was devalued.[20]

Motoring not only changed how Americans traveled, but how they idealized travel. Motoring brought the exhilaration of speed, a sense of control over movement, and the suggestion of convenience, not only in originating and terminating trips, but in attending intervening opportunities along one's way, just what the American roadside was created to encourage. The car was a kind of "self-mover," offering a sense of autonomy. As such, motoring encouraged degrees of isolation. The car was a "vehicle of separation," although group cohesion might be greatly reinforced when, for example, a family motored together, especially on a vacation trip.[21] Cars became increasingly comfortable with enclosed car bodies, improved suspension, and, of course, heaters and eventually air conditioning. If barriers of glass and steel were not enough, car radios came to offer a kind of sound barrier further separating inside from out.

Cocooned in one's car with the road fixed firmly in view ahead, motorists could travel largely oblivious to passing scenes, especially on the nation's new freeways. The passing landscape, when it was noted, was absorbed largely as a visual thing, with the changing view a means of experiencing, understanding, or comprehending. Travel by car offered the quick takes of rapid serial viewing. That explains, of course, the primal character of roadside selling, embracing, as it did, exaggerated and often quite garish signage and easily interpreted buildings, themselves often covered with signs and always strategically positioned for ready visibility.[22]

Before automobility, and even before the coming of canals, steamships, and railroads, the average person rarely traveled far from home, not more than a radius of perhaps a dozen miles or so on a regular basis. Affluent persons, of course, tended to travel more, not just in repeating circles near home, but over long, straight-line distances well away from home. With the rise of mass motoring, however, the ordinary person could engage in and indeed amplify both sorts of travel. Automobility brought places "closer" together in terms of time required to travel. Thus was geographical space seemingly "compressed." Automobility made possible the greater separation of home and work, an important factor underlying the rise of modern suburbia. But, as was the case before the auto age, not everyone was equally served. The decentralization of people and economic activity rendered public transportation systems inefficient and brought their decline. Those dependent on public transport were thus significantly disadvantaged, a social cleavage between haves and have-nots marked substantially by race/ethnicity and class differences. Suburbanites, largely affluent whites through the 1970s, were blessed with steadily rising incomes and could substitute longer commuting distances (but not travel time) for larger and higher quality residences at relatively affordable cost.[23]

Automobility came to underpin accelerating change in built environment. We tend to think of physical structures as somehow permanent. But along America's roadsides, especially, impermanence prevails. Roadside America remains essentially a commercial or capitalistic enterprise, with capitalism, by its very nature, an engine (if not the engine) of creative destruction. Creative destruction of landscape and place is fundamental to the recycling of capital in a capitalistic economic system. Rounds of investment, first in technological innovation, and then in technology's application to restructuring built environment, require destroying, or at least altering, the old to facilitate new rounds of innovation in the realization of surplus value.[24] The result is constant disjuncture between what landscapes and places are in a physical sense and the meaning of landscapes and places, which is constantly being negotiated anew in the face of change. As Roadside America changes, so do the perceptions of it change. Memories change.

Landscape and Place

As the automobile came to symbolize new social realities, so did roads and roadsides. Both are fully symbiotic as kinds of places, both in function and in what they symbolize. Places nest in landscape, that is, one's environmental surround, especially as visualized.[25] Landscapes may be thought of as having physical actuality, but the landscape concept also carries a traditional implication of something seen or viewed, whether natural or human made. Place, on the other hand, is wherever and whenever a focal point of meaning is recognized in one surroundings.[26] Recognition of place is fundamental to human life as lived. All life, it can be argued, "takes place." Place experience is a sort of medium through which everyday activities as well as life's exceptional involvements are anticipated, embraced, and remembered. Place making produces built environment. A landscape is like a palimpsest, a surface on which previous layers of place making are partially scraped off as others are applied, and the entirety is always waiting to be read through seeing.[27]

Places are variously cued visually. Of course, places have physical location and physical extent. They occur variously as loci in geographic matrices of human intentionality. Places contain behavior and are also where that behavior is remembered. Places are defined at various geographic scales that sometimes relate to one another hierarchically. Often, but not always, places are structured in a physical sense. Thus they have seemingly permanent boundaries with points of access and egress and temporality as well as spatiality. They open and close, most often in daily, weekly, annual, or even longer cycles. They have duration.

Places are centers of meaning. To identify a place is to create a social construct, one variously conducive to interaction with others or in some instances avoidance of others. Beliefs and attitudes attach to places, which invite a range of behaviors variously thought appropriate and potentially useful. Codes of conduct anticipated on the basis of past experience are seen to apply to various kinds of places. Places that are physically structured as built environment are specifically programmed to invite and sustain normative ongoing activities and even specific kinds of behavior. According to intentions of the moment, people insert themselves into or extract themselves out of places through appropriate behavior. Thus is place conceptualization emotionally charged rather than strictly rational. Of course, the people in a specific place or the kinds of people that normally characterize it, along with their usual activities and behavior, carry the primary load when it comes to place assessment. Secondary to this are the props or furnishings used in that activity and in that behavior.

The roadside constitutes a kind of landscape. Clustered within are various places: gas stations, motels, or drive-in restaurants, and all other sorts of venues, commercial or otherwise. Each kind of place tends to be distinctively structured according to its function. Each tends to communicate through bundled cues: physical structuring and furnishing, but also the normal activities that sustain functions and the kinds of people so engaged in those functions. The satisfactions to be had are cued to the customer. Building shape, building mass, size of footprint, architectural styling, and signage, for example, all serve to identify overtly a place as a specific kind of social setting having distinctive purpose.

In U.S. landscape experience, what made the modern roadside special was quite straightforward—people arriving and leaving various venues by motor vehicle, and doing so both with convenience and dispatch. Enabling a motorized lifestyle, the roadside became a technically sophisticated environment, one meant to sustain transiency. It was a kind of "stranger's path" where people from beyond a locality might briefly feel at home and then, as appropriate, move on.[28] In social sense the roadside was quite modern. Roadside America was and is a place of rapid change. Improved cars and trucks and rebuilt roads, or the totally new roads replacing them, the growth of large corporations, changes in the marketing and distribution of products and services, and mere fad and fashion, especially as these played out in ever-changing advertising schemes, all wrought changes concentrated spatially or geographically as never before. Roadside America not only comprised landscapes and places of transiency, but landscapes and places ever in transition (figs. 1.6, 1.7, 1.8, 1.9).

Sudden, cataclysmic destruction is not what modern economy is all about. Most change is incremental, some of it very superficial. Cosmetic upgrading was important right from the beginning along the American roadside. With gas stations it might be face-lifts through new signs and new color schemes

Figure 1.6. Vacant roadside businesses, Williamstown, Kentucky, 1996. Traffic flow has been diverted from U.S. 25 (the old Dixie Highway) to the I-75 freeway nearby. Left behind is a highway cafe and a vacant teepee-shaped gasoline station—rare architectural legacies from the 1930s.

Figure 1.7. Gasoline sign, Commerce, Georgia, 2007. An anachronism reminiscent of when the Standard Oil brand spread across the United States, the gasoline station which it once announced is long gone. Branding was essential as chains of similar gas stations, motels, and fast-food restaurants came to dominate Roadside America, mainly through franchising. Like everything else along the American Roadside, logos appeared, were altered, and then replaced in cycles of seemingly inevitable change.

applied with periodical regularity. Or change might be somewhat dramatic: small buildings enlarged through add-ons, or replaced altogether by larger structures, for example buildings very differently sized, massed, and/or styled. Change might come through disinvestment, as building maintenance might be reduced and repairs postponed in the face declining profits, for example. Or gas stations might be closed, and their sites given to other uses with different kinds of buildings predominating altogether.

Over the long run, change has come to Roadside America, as with all other landscapes and places, through life cycles of birth, maturation, and eventual death, with new ways of doing and being inevitably displacing the old. The old thrives only through constant adaptation, although the old can survive, at least for periods of time, through sheer neglect. Outright dereliction—things seemingly fossilized in decay—may occur, especially where a highway has been displaced by new road construction or where, for whatever reason, economic energy has been drained from the locality that was served. But where traffic continues to

Figure 1.8. Vacant gasoline station, Santa Rosa, New Mexico, 2008. Astride old U.S. 66, a woeful sentinel of the 1960s sits neglected. "Happy Motoring" the sign says.

flow and where customers and other users continue to be attracted, roadside change continues apace, often bringing new degrees of sameness over large areas—the same yet new places are created seemingly everywhere. Today, for example, old gas stations in all their diversity have largely disappeared, replaced by new convenience stores, all looking pretty much alike from locality to locality (figs. 1.10 and 1.11).

Decade by decade new rounds of roadside investment have indeed produced look-alike landscapes and places nationwide. Consequently, it might be argued, much of Roadside America has become overly predictable as built environment. Perhaps it is because investment capital has increasingly been channeled locality to locality through widely shared financial incentives, zoning laws, building codes, and other restrictive encouragements conducive to uniformity place to place. It could be argued that today's Roadside America lacks much of its earlier quirkiness. Indeed, much of the kitsch is gone. As the critic Jane Jacobs argued about urban places generally over time: "every place becomes more like every

Figure 1.9. Derelict highway cafe, Cecil, Ohio, 1999. Relics bring a sense of time-depth to landscape and place. Things on the brink of utter ruin forcefully symbolize loss—the past abandoned as if unwanted.

other place, all adding up to Noplace."[29] It was what the geographer Edward Relph called "placelessness."[30] There is, of course, no such thing as placelessness. But there is "commonplaceness"—places so common and thus so predicable as to generate little concern, little emotion, and thus little sense of edification for users. They are too easily "read" and thus excite little interest. Encroaching sameness is certainly one incentive for remembering and reevaluating the past, if not for preserving relics that survive from the past.

Memory

Memories form around words used to capture and hold down ideas. They are formed visually according to what people remember seeing, either firsthand or through pictorial imagery. Also they form around sounds. Regarding place, perhaps nothing offers stronger memory cues than odors—the smell of gasoline, for example. Who is not reminded of some specific car or truck, or of some specific motoring experience, through an unexpected whiff of gasoline? Who over the age of fifty is not reminded of vintage gasoline stations and the refueling and the servicing of cars that once centered in such places. There was the ring of the station bell as cars approached the pumps. There was the air pump where

Figure 1.10. New restaurant under construction, Champaign, Illinois, 1995. This restaurant may have lived to see old age, or perhaps it fell as a casualty of roadside change.

small boys inflated bicycle tires and inner tubes, and, better still, the soft-drink cooler (soda pop in the American South).

How are places remembered? Pierre Nora may be correct that "memory attaches itself to sites, whereas history attaches itself to events."[31] Certainly the historical study of place-oriented memories opens an opportunity to test such assertions. Memory, of course, can be individual and private and yet very likely to well up or form around memories that are fully societal or culturally embedded. Collective memories invariably form around myths that are socially created (and often ideologically based) and perpetuated by persuasive arbitrators of taste acting in their own self-interests.[32] Nonetheless it is the stories that we tell ourselves about our past, whether personal or public, that enable us to construct and maintain a sense of identity. Such storytelling in fully interwoven into life's "symbolic interactions" whereby meaning—place meaning included—is constantly being negotiated through communication with others. Variously, as we interact with others, we change the past, or what the past is seen to represent or mean. The remembered past is not an actuality—a reality that no longer exists—so much as a set of negotiated understandings that well up substantially as collective understanding.[33]

Figure 1.11. West Street (formerly U.S. 50), Annapolis, Maryland, 2006. Roadside America, whether new or largely reconfigured, tends toward homogeneity. The businesses, their goods and services, the buildings containing them, their architectural design and styling, and their signage all seemingly add up to many eyes as "Everywhere U.S.A."

Memory is a process of selecting and organizing what we consider in the present to be significant about the past, with significance in the present a partial function that we anticipate as useful for the future. Most that might be remembered is simply forgotten. Life would be unlivable if all aspects of the past constantly intruded through memory. As the planner Kevin Lynch noted, people dispose of old things (the physical remnants of past landscapes and places, for example) for the same reason that they dispose of memories. What is forgotten has simply become irrelevant to their ongoing lives. Both individuals and people in society generally necessarily select and create a useful past, thus making it part of a living present. Of course, some people, as some societies, do a better job than others, being more diligent in their appreciation of the past.[34]

What is the value of old things in landscape? Lynch noted that relics of landscape and place generally get saved, albeit often in modified form, when they in fact retain their usefulness. They also get saved when their scarcity as old things gets appreciated. Old things lend contemporary context—a kind of time-depth through suggestion of how things got to be. They make visible, in other words, something of the processes of change operative in a landscape or in a place. In this regard they focus as they jar remembering, something that traditional forms of historical documentation (particularly the written word) perhaps can not do as well. They serve as immediate cues to remembering. It was a sense for the recent past, Lynch argued, that was most significant. An understanding of what he called "near continuity" was emotionally more important than knowing about a distant time, irrespective of how exotic or romantic the far past seemed. "We should seek to preserve the near and the middle past," he wrote, "the past with which we have real ties. A humane environment commemorates recent events quickly, and thus allows people to mark out their place in time quickly."[35]

Remembering the past often leads to celebrating a sense of pastness that is hardly rooted in what actually might have been—actual history in other words. When hinged on a strongly felt contemporary or future need, celebrating the past can produce not historical awareness so much as a false sense of what might be called "heritage." Heritage speaks not to the past as it was, so much, but to the past as people might wish it to have been. Such an assertion assigns contemporary social or cultural agendas in the name of an imagined past, making that past more persuasive regarding one or another imagined future. "Heritage activists use the past to find roots, to affirm identities, claim legacies, to celebrate collective bonds, and to traduce rivals." And too often, as historian L.P. Hartley surmised, the pursuit of heritage promotes acrimony.[36] The past remains a "foreign country," the historian turned geographer David Lowenthal argued, but one "domesticated for contemporary causes."[37] Thus is the past filtered and sanitized for one or another contemporary agenda.[38]

Even the least jaundiced views of the past can embrace misconception through one or another bias in one's approach to history. Lowenthal noted four kinds of popular historical preconception: the idea of a timeless past that until recently was largely devoid of change, or at least significant change; the idea that the past actually mirrors the present in reflecting eternal and universal causes for change; the idea that the past was unprogressive and thus stagnant of redeeming virtue; and, finally, the idea that one's own past (or the past of one's community) fully deserves to be, for some beneficial purpose, sharply distinguished from that of others. All of these orientations are present-centered and thus potentially distorting, he argued.[39] Such distorted approaches are especially visible in U.S. history museums and in outdoor museums, which too often attribute present modes of thought and action to the past.[40] Additionally, outdoor museums have a way of sanitizing the past thus making displays palatable to contemporary sensitivities. The place of the past in any landscape, "museumscapes" included, is as much a product of today's prevailing beliefs and attitudes as of past history.[41]

Much remembering is outright nostalgic, a search not for factual understanding regarding the past so much as a search for comforting feelings supportive of the present day.[42] Nostalgia valorizes positive aspects of the past, countering negative aspects that can then be conveniently ignored. Nostalgia may serve to strengthen what many scholars call "sense of place": the feeling that one is affectively bonded to and thus fundamentally connected with a place. It is a kind of attachment to place where one feels comfortable if not "at home." Such feelings of place-rootedness strongly reinforce personal if not collective identity.[43]

Cultural Icons

The stories we tell one another about our collective past resonate powerfully in the books we read, the movies and television programs we view, the art we look at, and the songs we sing, among other forms of cultural expression. For Americans today cars and roads loom large. Roadsides, on the other hand, have tended to play mainly a subsidiary but important role. What cars, roads, and roadsides mean to Americans is reflected in their consumption of popular culture, if not fine art. It is through cultural icons created by novelists, cinematographers, and others that the collective remembering of Roadside America substantially forms.[44]

Automobiles appear throughout American literature in diverse ways, variously reflecting the personal aspirations of the characters portrayed and the storylines that those aspirations are seen to drive. The car, besides standing on its own as a symbol of success, if only for its owner's ability to afford it, also has spoken of opportunity, if only to get away from the humdrum of life in breaking ordinary routines.[45] While providing enclosure and security in travel, cars also have offered autonomy of control and a kind of liberating freedom, as we have said, especially through the siren song of adventurous motoring, of the "open road." Cars have provided the raw sensation of speed and thus the exhilaration of moving quickly over long distances, but, more important, cars have empowered the individual in doing so. Their use invited self-reliance as challenges on the road were met and overcome.

Highways stretch through literature in diverse ways also. But basically they represent a path ahead, one largely unknown and thus challenging. Both the road and written narrative are linear, inviting storytelling that is fully chronological in structure. Typically sustained in the telling is a protagonist's epic quest, one often colored by the carnivalesque and even the picaresque. Attention is drawn to how experience is reshaped. The highway's enabling narratives are formed, the essayist J. N. Nodelman observed, through the unfolding of conflicting visual cues along the roadside and "the traveler's wider yet inchoate sense of moving physically and perhaps conceptually between one place and another."[46] Most road narratives expand by stages that reflect the nature of travel itself: predisposition to journey, trip preparation, departure, outward movement, turnabout, homeward movement, return, and trip recollection.[47] "A recurring heroic deed in modern America," wrote Ronald Primeau, "is the automobile journey with its call to adventure on the open road, its initiation rites of trials, threshold crossings, conflict, return, and resurrection."[48] Most road narratives involve ordinary people seeking variety and difference, if not the extraordinary, as a means of confirming self-worth. But it is not just the road itself but the roadside that fully entices the traveler. There they "enter the sacred space along the highway," Primeau mused, "where they discover adventures and endure trials that are educative, healing, and expansive."[49] Most memorable, perhaps, are the stories of down-and-out characters—characters anxious or angry and thus in need of healing or recovery—with social protest being fully implicit.

Automobile travel has figured prominently in American fiction since the beginning of the twentieth century. Automobile road narratives, however, differed markedly from prior travel literature, especially that focused on exploration and migration. Danger seemingly lurked everywhere for early travelers out and beyond the settled frontier of the American West, for example. But, once the West was largely developed, adventurous travel there was harder and harder to come by. It had to be deliberately sought out. For early motorists the uncertainties of punctured tires or broken axles on western roads was noteworthy, but as cars and roads improved and as roadside services became available even along sparsely populated roads, breakdowns hardly justified epic storytelling. And yet the novelty of motoring remained, even as it became increasingly dependable, comfortable, and predictable. Sinclair Lewis was among the earliest fiction writers of early twentieth century America to embrace motoring as a means of developing characters and storylines. In various novels, but especially in *Free Air*, he explored the automobile's effect on middle-class Americans through the lens of Roadside America.[50]

But it was John Steinbeck who, by treating America's down-and-out, brought a sense for the epic back into road literature. In *The Grapes of Wrath*, Steinbeck's ill-fated Joad family, tenant farmers displaced by dust-bowl conditions in Oklahoma, make their way along the legendary Route 66 toward a promise of good fortune in California.[51] The Joads are badly treated in the highway's primitive migrant camps. Many of the highway's commercial services were priced beyond their reach. Central to the story, especially in the movie version, is a Hudson sedan with its back half torn off and refitted with a truck platform. Carrying thirteen family members and all their possessions, the car/truck lumbers westward, a buffer between the Joads' impoverishment and hopelessness. It is in fact the family's home. Ironically the Hudson—their supposed salvation—marks them as impoverished, thus opening them up to exploitation and abuse. Steinbeck's writing stood not just as a protest, but as a call for social reform.

The quintessential road book, however, remains Jack Kerouac's *On the Road*, a protest against an American establishment perfectly capable of ignoring, if not abusing, the down-and-out and, for that matter, anyone who seemed somehow different.[52] *On the Road* explores the fervent relationship between the storyteller, Sal, and his often outrageous and fully exasperating friend Dean Moriarty. As with most road narratives, road and roadside do not force what character and plot development there is so much as facilitate it. Yet metaphorically the seeking of the open road in *On the Road* provides a perfect context for what does transpire—not just a throwing off, but an active embrace of alternative ways of thinking, doing, and being. As its characters take advantage of the anonymity of the roadside as a "strangers path" to experiment, so the narrative itself was experimental, originally written as a free-flow 125,000-word narrative on a 120-foot-long scroll of paper, the linear manuscript very much like the road itself.[53]

Where better to explore the becomingness of change than in Roadside America's landscapes and place of transiency and emphemerality? Where better to explore the more deviant aspects of life, with their moral and ethical implications, than in roadside settings of relative anonymity? Such novels as Vladimir Nabokov's *Lolita* or John Updike's *Rabbit Redux* and *Rabbit, Run* are very much embedded in the untoward of Roadside America.[54] Humbert Humbert and Lolita flit from drab motel to drab motel. Rabbit Angstrom drives in search of comfort. Because his liaison with Ruth had once opened up Rabbit's life and stultifying marriage, he thinks Ruth's street will surely open onto "a brook, and then a dirt road and open pastures." But instead "the city street broadens into a highway lined with hamburger diners, and drive-in sub shops, and a miniature golf course with big plaster dinosaurs, and food-stamp stores and motels and gas stations that are changing their names, Humble to Getty, Atlantic to Arco."[55]

America's roadsides came to figure importantly in cinema. As with most novels and short stories, most films used Roadside America not to drive character and plot development so much as to provide convenient context, contributing thus to storyline plausibility. Sometimes the intent was to signify a condition, for example, the symbolizing of "modernity" through automobility.[56] Often it was a mere showcasing of modern technology so as enhance a film's novelty. So it was with many of the silent films produced by Max Sennett's Keystone Film Company, including all of his Keystone Kops films with their many chase scenes and many of the Charlie Chaplin and Harold Lloyd films based around auto-oriented stunts. Throughout the remainder of the twentieth century, chases tended to dominate use of road scenes both in the movies and on television.[57] One of road cinema's most compelling aesthetic aspects involved the use of cameras placed inside or outside a moving vehicle, on another vehicle close by, or at a distance, perhaps on a helicopter, for example. No matter what drivers do, or how they are filmed doing it, cars and trucks are an ubiquitous presence in modern America and are necessarily included in the depicting of society at large.

Road films have tended to follow simple surefire plots. Characters take to driving away from trouble thus to confront various adventures. Ultimately, however, their driving serves to solve some kind of problem. Basic American myths are reinforced, such as those concerned with "rugged individualism." It was what many a moviegoer aspires to personally but yet is contented to embrace only vicariously as a movie watcher. The cultural studies aficionado Corey K. Creekmur put it thus: "Born too late for the pioneer projects of blazing trails, extending natural frontiers, or just lighting out for the territory, modern Americans hit a road not only already taken, but paved, ramped, mapped, and marked by the commercial sites of mobile mass culture: the motel, the roadside diner, the filling station, and the drive-in movie theater. For those traversing this ground for purposes other than leisurely sight-seeing, the road points towards a promising future or leads away from a dead-end past." But only the slightest redefinition of perspective could shift the purpose of a road trip from "seeking a desired goal into flight from a desperate origin."[58] An important subgenre of the road trip film has concerned fugitives, often in pairs, seeking escape and safety or, conversely, excitement and even danger; key examples include *Bonnie and Clyde* (1967) and *Thelma and Louise* (1991).[59]

Perhaps no road movie has received as much attention as *Easy Rider* (1969), a film about two bikers making their way westward across the United States, meeting in the process a spectrum of characters from hitchhiking hippies to redneck truckers. Of course, the film spotlights "biking," which for most Americans was a novel means of travel. It is quite different from driving a car, given the rider's perception of speed and acceleration, apparent vulnerability to the road, and apparent closeness to the passing scene. In most earlier road movies, roads and roadsides had served to depict a coherent America, a nation of essential national unity. Thus did highway and roadside homogeneity, from locality to locality, provide a kind of uniformity of vision. But *Easy Rider* deliberately emphasizes differences—regional, racial, ethnic, class, and gender. The United States is not only viewed in a different way here, but viewed as a nation of differences. Diversity was valorized as an aspect of American popular culture.[60]

Images of landscape and place in the early days of television, with its black-and-white pictures on small screens, tended not to communicate well with viewers. Shots on screen were largely restricted to indoor, room-scale locales, if not to close-up portraiture-like images of performers. Especially with the coming of color, but also with the coming of large-format screens, television programming moved outdoors (or "on location") to depict landscapes and places more fully. *Route 66*, the weekly television series, was important in this regard. The show was structured as an anthology of road adventures. The program's characters, Tod Stiles and Buz Murdock, discovered much of that adventure in Roadside America, not along the actual U.S. 66 highway, but along highways the length and breadth of the nation. The program was television's response to Steinbeck's *Grapes of Wrath* and Kerouac's *On the Road*, but it also anticipated movies such as *Easy Rider*. Like those iconic works, *Route 66* grew out of events and national preoccupations of its time. The use of road and roadside encounter as a storytelling device, and the thematic trope of escape and discovery, illuminated a singular search for social meaning in a rapidly changing America, and much of that change was driven by a rapidly accelerating automobility.[61]

Route 66 built on preceding television fare filmed outside of television studios, especially westerns and detective shows where the fuller depiction of landscape and place as a means of fully establishing a context for action initially evolved.

With detective shows the automobile chase became almost mandatory, and Roadside America became an action backdrop. But *Route 66* further socialized the road quest as an important cultural invention. It helped focus attention on Roadside America as an important new kind of built environment, one fully laden with artistic possibility and even newsworthy. Thus Charles Kuralt launched his regular "On the Road" essays at CBS News.

The 1960s also found John Steinbeck back on the road with *Travels with Charley in Search of America*.[62] By then Roadside America was firmly established in our lexicon of distinctive landscapes or place types along with nature (including wilderness), the frontier, the family farm, the small town (with main street), the metropolis, and the big-city suburb. With the building of the new interstate freeways, however, roadside observers, whether on television or in literature, took increasingly to the bypassed back roads of the nation to search for fundamentally American things.[63]

Not only did Roadside America, broadly viewed as landscape and place, take on iconographic implication, but so also did many of the specific elements typical of Roadside America—including places defined more at the architectural scale. The cabin court, or motel, was celebrated in *It Happened One Night* (1934) and the highway café in *Bus Stop* (1956), by way of example. Recently the Disney Corporation's cartoon feature *Cars* (2006) employed a full spectrum of vintage roadside icons from gas stations to drive-in restaurants to drive-in movie theaters. Nonetheless it was perhaps more in the graphic arts of painting and photography that roadside architecture came to be appreciated earliest. Indeed, artists and photographers have long embraced cars, roads, and roadsides as worthy topics for depiction, which John Sloan's *Hill, Main Street, Gloucester* (1916), Thomas Hart Benton's *Boom Town* (1928), Alfred Stieglitz's *Hand on Wheel* (1933), Walker Evan's *Joe's Auto Graveyard* (1936), Edward Hopper's *Gas* (1940), Edward Ruscha's *Standard Station, Amarillo, Texas* (1963), and Andy Warhol's *White Car Burning* (1997) all serve to illustrate.[64] Photo books have been especially important to roadside discovery and celebration, including the many retrospective volumes focused on the work of Depression-era photographers, Walker Evans included, working for the Farm Security Administration, which was overseen by A. Roy Stryker.[65]

Car, road, and roadside came to figure importantly in music, and iconographic images reverberated through song lyrics but also through sheet music and record album covers. Early on, automobility loomed importantly in popular tunes produced commercially by Tin Pan Alley, including ragtime, jazz, the blues, big-band dance music, and, of course, rock and roll and even the folk revival of the 1960s. Rock and roll in fact was fully incubated through car and road connections. Rock and roll stemmed from many sources, combining as it did "the primitivist vitality of black blues with the agrarian, pastoral flavor of white country-western music," as the historian Warren Belasco put it. But rock and roll also embodied the "open road" spirit, especially of rebellious youths who were questing or searching. Down the road, Belasco argued, lay a new kind of American frontier ready for adventure, opportunity, and self-discovery.[66]

Popular music of all kinds tends to celebrate interpersonal relationships, especially the romantic kind—the love song, in other words. When it came to cars and driving them down highways, it was mainly a matter of males attracting females. It held true from *In My Merry Oldsmobile* ("Come away with me, Lucille") of 1905 to Maybelline ("As I was motivatin' over the hill, I saw Maybelline in a Coup de Ville") of 1955. Much of the self-discovery along the open road, song lyrics seemed to suggest, was not so much about adventuring and experiencing life alone, but with special others. To many in their audiences, musicians fully epitomized "road life," constantly motoring, as most of them did, from one gig to another in one city or town to another. "On the road again. Just can't wait to get on the road again. The life I love is making music with my friends," as Willie Nelson put it in 1979.[67]

* * *

Through the twentieth century, automobiles, roads, and roadsides figured increasingly in how people conceptualized themselves both as persons and as Americans. With automobility becoming so pervasive in U.S. life, how could it have been otherwise? Cars and highways, however, have probably resonated the strongest. The car was something to own and to use in personalizing life. The highway variously symbolized not only release, but potential fulfillment. The American love affair with the open road was first and foremost one of cars speeding down highways from some kind of past to some kind of future. What lay beside the highway—gas stations, motels, drive-in restaurants, and the like—serving immediate needs. Roadside America provided opportunities to interact with others, although generally only superficially as anonymous strangers as people were constantly engaging and disengaging one another. Roadside America fostered societal fluidity beyond the social stabilities of home, school, church, and workplace. In that regard the open road was liberating in a social as well as a geographic sense. Roadside America was also materially fluid and constantly changing physically.

Ephemerality may very well be a quintessential variable in the larger American scheme of things. Ours has always been a nation championing change—change assumed in general to be progressive. Nothing has accelerated change in the United States quite like automobility. Nowhere has that change registered more forcefully than along the American roadside. If not quintessentially American, then roadside landscapes and places in the United States might be considered quintessentially modern. Early in the twentieth century, a new kind of modern technology was set loose to run its course. Pioneered in the United States, roadside phenomena such as gasoline stations soon spread worldwide. The roadside has certainly served for a century or more as a new kind of frontier where decidedly American values joined to modern technology could play out in innovative, and often very profitable, ways for commercial interests. But in embracing fluidity, Roadside America underwent constant metamorphosis. The "past" did not last long.

CHAPTER TWO
OBSERVING ROADSIDE AMERICA

With the coming of mass motoring, Americans in ever-increasing numbers answered the siren song of the open road, not so much as migrants moving to new places or as business people traveling for work, but more as motorists making use of increased affluence and leisure time to explore the nation's highways as a form of recreation. Slowly but surely, however, motoring of all kinds came to congest the streets and roads and to affect American roadsides, especially the locations of automobile-convenient businesses. Thus was Roadside America created, a highly ephemeral world characterized by slow but constant change.

The quintessential signature of automobile-influenced roadsides quickly evolved: widely spaced buildings, low in profile and set back from rights-of-way in parking-lot surrounds; bold signs announcing driveways at curbsides, and even buildings themselves covered by signs; and then, on occasion, sign like buildings, with iconic structures (sometimes called "ducks") whimsically shaped like lighthouses or windmills or some such thing to attract attention. On previously rural roads outside of towns and cities, and then within them as well on major traffic arteries, commercial strips steadily evolved: thoroughfares where automobile convenience (or automobile orientation) came to dominate business dealings. Although such change came incrementally, a revolution nonetheless was underway, one that would seemingly overnight, at least in retrospect, fully reinvent urban development in the United States.

There had always been roadside commerce, but not necessarily in places organized around rapid vehicular traffic. Early in the twentieth century, commercial streets in towns and cities were organized mainly for pedestrians and slow-moving, horse-drawn vehicles, and in larger urban places for streetcars also tended to be slowly paced. Along commercial streets, stores with narrow frontages closely clustered. Often of multiple stories, they were set perpendicular to rather than parallel with traffic flow. Signs were designed mainly to attract customers who walked, not just signs placed on building facades or projected out over sidewalks, but those placed in show windows alongside merchandise displayed for the lingering pedestrian to browse. Sidewalks were usually improved, and streets were usually paved, except, perhaps, in the smallest of urban places. Before 1910 motorcars and trucks tended to fit right in whether they were moving up and down streets or parked at curbside. Automobiles in small numbers required no special accommodation. They were not a problem. Most American assumed it would always be that way.

In the countryside most roads were unpaved, and rural roadsides for the most part remained quite unimproved. Fences and hedges, often ill-kept, hemmed in road traffic. On main roads utility poles marched endlessly, their wires tending to dominate visually. In many parts of the United States, the earliest modern rural highways closely paralleled railroad rights-of-way, themselves fully utilitarian to say the least. Road margins, however, were largely devoid of commerce, save for the occasional vegetable or fruit stand or other farm-related enterprise or perhaps, at a key intersection, a general store or tavern. Before 1910 motor vehicles might attract attention for their novelty, but they did not stimulate anything revolutionary regarding land use adjacent to rights-of-way except in urban places. That, however, would not last for long.

Improving America's Roads

What motoring did stimulate was road improvement through what came to be called the Good Roads Movement. With the coming of railroading, the nation's rural roads had for the most part been left to languish under the aegis of county or township road commissions acting for municipalities that were usually quite impoverished and geared only to meeting limited local needs. Much road maintenance was done through corvée labor, where property owners of a jurisdiction agreed to work on road rights-of-way in lieu of paying property taxes. Lacking in almost every locality, once the auto age dawned, were intercity highways that could facilitate long-distance motor travel. In many localities farmers actually opposed road improvement despite the benefits that might accrue in their moving crops to market. The belief was widespread that road upgrades mostly benefited big-city, auto-owning elites. For locals such improvements brought mainly higher taxes. Additionally, fast cars on fast roads were a safety hazard for those in horse-drawn vehicles. Farming and motoring seemed to be in fundamental conflict.

> The smooth, free rush in the winey breeze,
> By open field and by tangled brake,
> By curving roads where the stately trees
> Are mirrored deep in the placid lake,
> Past town and village, by farm and stream,
> Through peaceful valley and rugged glen,
> Is life that rivals a poet's dream—
> Till one encounters the wayside hen![1]

The Good Roads Movement grew with only limited federal involvement, although Congress did establish in 1893 the Office of Road Inquiry located in the Department of Agriculture, its purpose being to conduct research on road-building methods and road materials and to provide local governments with information conducive to improving farm to market travel. At about the same time, the U.S. Post Office (now the Postal Service) also made limited funds available for postal route improvement in rural areas. In 1919 the renamed Office of Public Roads and Rural Engineering became the Bureau of Public Roads with a much enlarged program dictated by the Highway Act of 1916, the legislation that established the federal-aid program whereby federal monies were made available to the states for highway building. To obtain federal road-building subsidies, however, participating states were required to organize highway departments and to do master planning not only for intercity travel, but also for interstate highways as well.[2]

Nonetheless it was the privately financed road associations (markers of and promoters of "named" highways) that initially fostered comfortable long-distance motoring. The Lincoln Highway Association led the movement, and the Lincoln Highway between New York City and San Francisco became the nation's first marketed transcontinental auto route. Literally hundreds of highways were named and marked between 1912 and 1925. Established east-west, for example, were the National Old Trails Highway (Baltimore to Los Angeles), the Old

Spanish Trail Highway (St. Augustine to San Diego), and the Pikes Peak Ocean to Ocean Highway (New York City to Los Angles). Established north-south were the Atlantic Highway (Fort Kent, Maine to Miami, Florida), the Dixie Highway (connecting the Straits of Mackinac in Michigan to Miami in Florida by various routes), and the Jackson Highway (Chicago to New Orleans) among others. Highway associations sought to attract motorists to specific routes, acting as a kind of chamber of commerce, not for a specific town or city, but for all locations along a given highway. Not only did highway associations mark roads, they also published maps and guidebooks to facilitate navigation. They also lobbied with state and county highway officials to improve routes.[3] The Lincoln Highway Association raised funds for highway construction, actually building long stretches of highway in the American West as well as so-called ideal miles in each of the traversed states to demonstrate the potential for modern highway travel.[4]

The Bureau of Public Roads, renamed the Public Roads Administration, was transferred in 1939 to the Federal Works Agency. In 1949 it resumed its former name as part of the Department of Commerce. Beginning with the Highway Act of 1921, which enlarged the federal aid system to some 7 percent of the total rural road mileage then existing in the nation, the federal government began to assume a truly dominant role, although actual road construction remained fully the purview of the states. Highway standards nationwide were set by the American Association of Highway Officials (AASHO), which effectively put an end to the "named highway" era when it proposed that federally subsidized roads be numbered rather than named. The Highway Act of 1944 established the secondary road system, directed more toward the farmer's needs in rural America. But it also made road-building subsidies available for expressways and other urban road projects. In 1949 federally subsidized roads included some 34,799 miles of rural highway, 2,882 miles of city street, and 2,319 miles of city-bypass road.[5]

The Highway Act of 1956 established the Highway Trust Fund, a kind of perpetual-motion machine designed to funnel federal gasoline tax monies exclusively into highway building. As previously, federal spending was to be supplemented by a smaller amount of state spending, with most of the funds coming from gasoline taxes collected at the pump. The 1956 act also established a new interstate-highway system to be composed of dual-lane, limited-access freeways, what is now officially known as the Dwight D. Eisenhower National

System of Interstate and Defense Highways. Design of the "interstates," as they popularly came to be called, followed that of the numerous toll highways already established in various states, starting in the early 1940s with the Pennsylvania Turnpike and Connecticut's Merritt Parkway. The toll highways in turn owed much to earlier boulevard and parkway development, including the Bronx River Parkway in New York's Westchester County completed in 1923.[6]

Encountering Roads and Roadsides

America's freeways could hardly have been foreseen when motorists ventured forth on the nation's very primitive roads early in the twentieth century. It is useful to consider what journalists, authors of travel books, and other writers had to say about the nation's roads and roadsides decade to decade, if only to chart the changes that federal road subsidies fostered nationwide. Also useful are examples of how roads and roadsides were pictured whether in snapshots, postcards, or advertisements. Slowly Americans became aware that new things were "afoot."

Early motoring out and away from the nation's major cities was wrought with difficulty, although in the Northeast bicycle enthusiasts, acting through such organizations as the League of American Wheelmen, had successfully lobbied for hard-surfaced roads around the fringes of major cities. But, in outlying precincts and elsewhere, rural roads tended to be notoriously poor: dusty in the dry heat of summer, all but impassable in wet weather (most of them quickly turning into mud), and very difficult to traverse in winter snow and ice. Pictured in 1915 is an Illinois road after a summer's rain (fig. 2.1). Even in dry weather, ruts left in roadways after heavy summer rains discouraged easy driving. James Flagg, writing in 1925 of the Lincoln Highway in Nevada, perhaps with some exaggeration, complained: "The ruts were so deep we had to drive a little to the right or left of them . . . in order not to scrape the poor car's abdomen entirely off. Between the ruts was a continuous deep hue two inches wide that I discovered was the trail of the crank case nuts of many cars!"[7]

It required many years for the nation's "named highways" to become anything more than marked routes. Indeed, many of them were never actually marked, remaining merely "paper trails" published on road maps with good intentions. In 1915 Effie Gladding's party on the Lincoln Highway was "guided by the red, white, and blue marks; sometimes painted on telephone poles, sometimes put

Figure 2.1. Rural road in Illinois, 1915. From S. E. Bradt, "The Benefits and Burdens of Better Roads," *Illinois Highways* (Oct.–Nov. 1915): 148.

up by way of advertisement over garage doors or swinging on hotel signboards; sometimes painted on little stakes, like croquet goals, scattered along." Like Flagg she complained of poor road conditions. At one location in the East, cars were being driven along the road's margins, the road itself being an impassable muddy quagmire. At another location in the West: "We have to be watchful for chuck holes made by the infatigable gophers or prairie dogs. They often burrow in the ruts of the road. Our guide leaflets, furnished us by garages along the route, are full of warnings about 'chucks.'"[8] Yet a year later Austin Bement, secretary of the Lincoln Highway Association, could report that the Lincoln Highway across New Jersey was entirely hard-surfaced. In Pennsylvania only eighteen miles were

Figure 2.2. Postcard view of the Lincoln Highway, west of Laurel Mountain in Pennsylvania, circa 1915.

dirt. In Ohio four out of every five miles were either concrete or brick. Wyoming, Utah, and Nevada, however, had no hard-surfaced stretches whatsoever.[9]

The Lincoln Highway received substantial publicity. Its many benefits were trumpeted. The road did not just enable motorists to get to places faster and in comfort, as important as that was. The road was also a means of seeing the United States (fig. 2.2). It was a means of sustaining Americanism. With just a little hyperbole, travel writer Newton A. Fuessle wrote, "Teaching patriotism, sewing up the remaining ragged edges of sectionalism, revealing and interpreting America to its people, giving swifter feet to commerce, gathering up the country's loose ends of desultory and disjointed good roads ardor and binding them into one highly organized, proficient unit of dynamic, result-getting force, electric with zeal, [the road] is quickening American neighborliness, democracy, and civilization." He added, "It will lead you like no other guide, through the startling wonders of American physical geography, with all its marvels of placid lowland and tumbled mountain ranges, forest, farmland and prairie, valley and dreaming river, lake and hills, cool seashore and savage desert."[10]

Linking a series of historic routes (the Old National Road, the Boone's Lick Road, and the Santa Fe Trail), the National Old Trails Highway was promoted in similar terms and for similar purposes. "People are demanding of Congress," Charles Henry Davis, president of the National Highways Association, wrote, "the construction not only of the National Old Trails Road, but likewise National Highways in the length and breadth of these United States of America, which will secure the benefits—social, moral, commercial, industrial, material, educational, and personal—in the progress and uplift of the American people."[11] Based in Kansas City, Missouri, the National Old Trails Association was a commercial proposition, but one which partnered with the Daughters of the American Revolution, which saw it as a patriotic cause. The road, Davis asserted, would serve to "bind the States together in a common brotherhood, and thus perpetuate and preserve the Union."[12]

Eastward from Cumberland, Maryland, the route (originally the Old National Road) had been hard-surfaced with macadam in the nineteenth century, and it had remained reasonably fit and thus passable for long-distance motoring. As one traveler reported in 1908: "The National Road possesses a distinctive individuality. From 60 to 80 feet wide, with two sometimes three lines of telegraph and telephone poles, there is not the least chance that the tourist will lose his way." The road completely overshadowed "the puny little roads" that branched off from it. Additionally, unlike most other roads, at least in the eastern United States, it was perfectly straight for up to ten miles at a stretch.[13] As on the Lincoln Highway across Pennsylvania, which followed the historic route of the Pennsylvania Road laid out during the Revolutionary War, old taverns stood begging for revival. "A hundred Cumberland Road taverns will be opened, predicted historian Archer B. Hulbert, "and bustling landlords welcome, as of yore, the travel-stained visitor. Merry parties will again fill those tavern halls, now long silent, with their laughter."[14]

Early motorists found few services near newly marked automobile routes, save at the centers of towns and cities. Especially important in early cross-country driving were the garages, restaurants, and hotels along small-town Main Streets or located immediately off those streets. Gasoline, sold in tin containers, was available in various places: drugstores and hardware stores, for example, as well as garages. Pictured is the front of a hardware store in Dewart, Pennsylvania, with locals standing beside an early gasoline pump (fig. 2.3). Availability of gasoline, lubricating oils, and other motoring necessities in small towns was fully expected. Rural people were actually in the vanguard of automobile ownership, especially in the prosperous Midwest. In 1923 farmers owned some 30 percent of the automobiles in the United States while constituting some 44 percent of the population. But, as the editors of *Motor Travel* reported, "The ownership of motor cars is proportionately heaviest in the villages from 1,000 to 5,000, which have but 9 percent of the United States' population, yet use 20 percent of the total motor cars."[15]

In the smallest of places, garages were often converted livery stables. Large "boxlike structures of graying unpainted wood, with oversized doors to permit carriages to enter," was how historian Lewis Atherton remembered them.[16] But in larger towns they were often purpose-built and usually located at the edge of downtown, as pictured here in Wadena, Minnesota (fig. 2.4). The novelist Mary King in *Quince Bolliver,* set in fictional Good Union, Oklahoma, during the oil boom of the 1920s, pictured her hero walking down the town's Main Street: "He came to a garage. 'Hotshot Motor Hospital. You Wreck 'Em We Fix 'Em.' The front of the garage and the gasoline pumps were bright orange. The workshop . . . had been given a prime coat of aluminum paint that glittered like steel in the morning sun. At one side of the building was an unfenced vacant lot piled with parts of discarded cars: old chassis, broken axles, wheels, fenders, radiators, worn tires."[17] Hamilton Basso described a similar scene in his novel *Court House Square* set in the American South. The African American doorman at the town's

Figure 2.3. Hardware store with gasoline pump at Dewart, Pennsylvania, circa 1915.

Figure 2.4. Main Street business district, Wadena, Minnesota, circa 1925.

leading hotel walks down Main Street toward the railroad tracks. "It was a street of garages and automobile showrooms, gasoline tanks like rows of robot sentinels with tubular, pistol-fitted arms, the new cars behind the plate-glass windows staring with round glassy eyes."[18]

In cities the numerous garages, restaurants, and hotels competed for the motorist's dollar. Invariably located in or around the edges of downtown early on, these sorts of enterprises were not located out along peripheral highways until after World War I. Motoring, driven both by mass automobile ownership and widespread highway improvement, brought economic revival not only to small-town Main Streets but especially to downtown business districts, both in small and large cities (fig. 2.5). For example, booster clubs and other civic organizations organized investor syndicates to build new hotels, with financing based on the general affluence of transients who now arrived more often by car than by train. The dining rooms, ballrooms, and other venues in the new hotels also served local residents as community centers of sorts. A new generation of hotels, with modern amenities such as en suite bathrooms, but also with auto entrances and parking garages, characterized a rather vigorous period of hotel building roughly between 1910 and 1930.[19]

Figure 2.5. Eighth Street, Coffeyville, Kansas, circa 1925. Courtesy of Lake County Discovery Museum/Curt Teich Postcard Archives.

Figure 2.6. Highway U.S. 50, east of Laurel Mountain in West Virginia, circa 1925.

Roads paved in concrete or surfaced in asphalt or other sealants slowly displaced dirt and gravel on the nation's federally subsidized highway network. The new roads defined a new kind of travel aesthetic. The novelist Sinclair Lewis captured the essence of the new reality in his 1921 novel *Oil!* "The road ran, smooth and flawless, precisely 14 ft. wide, the edge trimmed as if by shears, a ribbon of grey concrete, rolled out over the valley by a giant hand," he wrote. "The ground went in long waves, a slow ascent and then a sudden dip; you climbed, and went swiftly over—but you had no fear, for you knew the magic ribbon would be there, clean of obstructions, unmarred by bump or scar, waiting the passage of inflated rubber wheels revolving 7 times a second." It was, Lewis asserted, a fully engineered world capable of capturing and holding attention: "the magic ribbon of concrete laid out for you, winding here and there, feeling its way upward with hardly a variation of grade, taking off the shoulder of a mountain, cutting straight through the apex of another, diving into the black belly of a third; twisting, turning, tilting inward on the outside corners, tilting outward on the inside curves, so that you were always balanced, always safe" (fig. 2.6).[20]

Evolving Roadside Commerce

Writers of travel books tend to emphasize travel destinations. Keepers of travel diaries, on the other hand, enthuse as much over the adventures (and misadventures) of getting there. In the case of motorists early in the twentieth century, the logistics of driving, keeping to the road, and stopping by the wayside figured prominently. Emphasized by all, of course, were the differences observed from place to place, with the unusual to be found here and there, if not the exotic. But normal and typical things also entered into the storytelling. People noticed both old and new things such as features in landscapes and places that stood out both as relics of the past and as novelties that were fully suggestive of an emerging future. In this regard, evolving commercial roadsides spoke forcefully, particularly when gas stations, cabin courts, and other roadside features clustered as a new kind of urban form, the commercial strip.

It might be argued that motoring for pleasure went through a series of transitions early in the twentieth century. At first motorists confronted not only primitive roads, but a general lack of services, especially where distances between urban places was great. A kind of "pioneering" was required: a "living off the land" that saw early auto tourists, especially in the American West, tending to their own needs by typically eating by the roadside through the day and camping beside the road at end of the day. Then services began to appear at the fringes of towns and cities and even in the countryside, especially at the junctions of major highways. As in the towns, gas stations, motels, and highway cafes led the way. All of it was initially small in scale—"mom-and-pop" operations where husband and wives, with perhaps the help of an employee or two, handled everything. Pictured here is Charles L. Gilmore's gasoline station beside U.S. 150 at the edge of Leroy, Illinois (fig. 2.7). Gilmore sold seed and other farm supplies and, as indicated by the gas pumps, Monarch brand petroleum products. He was also a part-time farmer, and the station was located on a corner of his small acreage. His wife poses with their grandchildren, as the business was very much a family affair (fig. 2.8). Essential as well as highly personalized services were extended to travelers at such places. Accordingly motoring became less a "masculine" challenge of man against road and machine, and more a "feminine" embrace of comfort and security.[21]

A roadside culture emerged that was at once anonymous, with strangers engaging and disengaging episodically, but it was also one that was, superficially

Figure 2.7. Gilmore family gas station, Leroy, Illinois, 1940.

Figure 2.8. A Gilmore family picture posed at their gas station, Leroy, Illinois, 1940.

at least, highly personalized and familiar. Impersonal corporations and their minions supplied critical products and services (gasoline and lubricating oil, for example, in the case of gas stations), but business itself was for the most part conducted in a "down home" manner, and a kind of democratic conviviality prevailed. Some of this "spirit of helpfulness and good-fellowship," as one traveler phrased it in 1925, was fully reassuring to strangers away from home.[22] John Steinbeck found it in an Ohio restaurant traveling with his dog Charley in the 1960s. "The waitress in a roadside stand said good morning before I had a chance to, discussed breakfast as though she liked the idea, spoke with enthusiasm about the weather, sometimes even offered some information about herself without my delving. Strangers talked freely to one another without caution."[23] Roadside America was not just about business, but also about socialization. It was not just something physical in the sense of material landscape, but it was also something social, that is, a kind of place for socializing.

Nonetheless it was James Agee, in a 1934 article for *Fortune,* who brought evolving roadside commerce to public attention.[24] Many others joined the chorus in celebrating the new thing, not so much for its socialization, but for its money-making implications. The motor tourist, wrote the editors of *Concrete Highways and Public Improvements,* "may camp by night or patronize hotels along the way.

He may cook most of his meals on a portable gasoline stove, or eat from lunch counters and hotel restaurants. Regardless of how he lives, he leaves many dollars behind him as he goes along."[25] *Fortune* calculated that the average U.S. family on tour (3.5 persons) drove some 234 miles a day, spending a week to get some place and a week getting back. They spent about seven dollars a day: "One dollar forty for transportation costs, which include gasoline, garaging, and accessories bought en route. One dollar forty of it goes for lodging. One dollar forty-seven cents goes to restaurants and to eating places of all types. One dollar seventy-five cents of it [the] wife takes good care of: this goes in exchange for linens, lotions, goggles, kodak films, postcards, bead, baskets, pottery, blankets, antiques, balsam cushions, and so on ad lib., ad infinitum. Forty-two cents more goes into candy, ice cream, hot dogs, and similar roe. And fifty-six cents of it goes to theatres and to places of amusement."[26] Not all of it, of course, was spent on the roadside, but, perhaps, most of it was.

In commercial strip development, gasoline stations invariably led the way. The gas station epitomized roadside commerce in that physically it was the most fully auto-oriented. It was designed to be readily noticed and to be both quickly and conveniently accessed by motorists, as the accompanying road-map cover fully illustrates (fig. 2.9). By the mid-1920s oil corporations were well advanced in creating trade territories symbolized by chains of look-alike gas stations carefully styled architecturally, attractively color-coded, and fully signed for ready customer recognition—what came to be called place-product packaging.[27] Place-product packaging coordinated not only what gas stations looked like, one company to another, but the specific products and services each company offered. Likewise station attendant uniforms were carefully rationalized, and as well as how attendants were to approach and serve customers—preferably speedily and with good cheer. Gasoline stations quickly proliferated. "More than a million and one half gasoline pumps are dispensing gasoline to the nation's motorists today," celebrated the editors of the *Stanolind Record* in 1940, the employee magazine of the Standard Oil Company of Indiana. "Were a highway built to skirt the earth at the equator and all these pumps placed on it," they speculated, "a motorist driving along the superhighway would pass a pump every 100 feet . . . and then find enough pumps left over to stretch out 3,000 miles more." Almost 12 percent of the total retail trade of the United States was being transacted at gasoline stations.[28]

The motel, which grew out of the auto campground, was another contributor to strip development. Through the 1920s localities across the nation established

Figure 2.9. Cover illustration, Mid-Continental Petroleum Company roadmap, circa 1940.

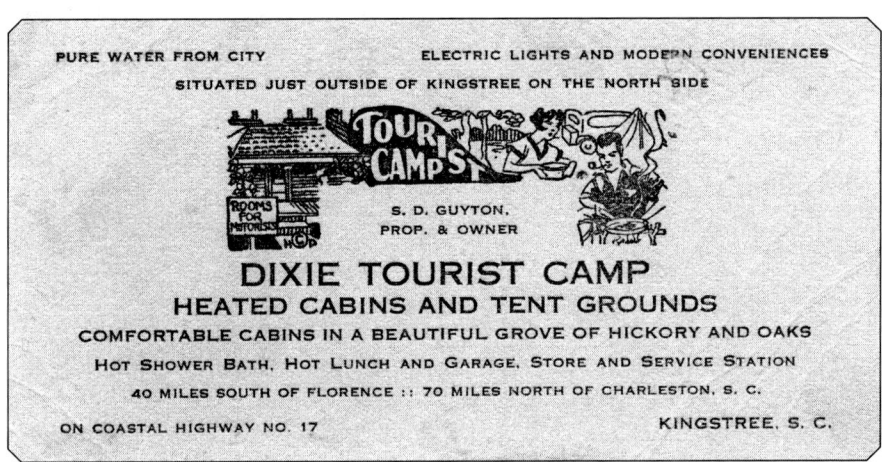

Figure 2.10. Advertising blotter, Dixie Tourist Camp, Kingstree, South Carolina, circa 1925.

campgrounds, in part to stimulate local business, but also in self-protection. Roadside camping was problematical, a "trail of trash and swill," as essayist George H. Lorimer put it in an article in the *Saturday Evening Post*, characterizing many a highway margin. "Never camping in the same place, [auto tourists] never had to camp on their own garbage heap. They searched . . . for the spot . . . where stream and trees and flower were most enticing—and fouled it, hacked it, trampled it, burned it, destroyed it utterly, leaving behind their greasy papers, their empty cans and miscellaneous filth."[29] Effie Gladding had the impression that the Lincoln Highway across Nevada "could be marked by whisky bottles if by no other signs."[30] By concentrating campers in one spot, litter, among other problems, could be limited. Many campgrounds began to charge. Others began to provide small cabins for a larger fee. Thus was the foundation set for privately run cabin courts, tourist courts, motor courts, and finally motels (figs. 2.10 and 2.11).

Sinclair Lewis, also writing in the *Saturday Evening Post*, wondered why place-product packaging (although he did not call it that) had not yet come to characterize the nascent motel industry. "Somewhere in these states," he wrote, "there is a young man who is going to become rich. He may be washing milk bottles in a dairy lunch. He is going to start a chain of small, clean, pleasant hotels, standardized and nationally advertised, along every important motor route in the country." When he completed his work, Lewis asserted, "he will be in the market for European Chateaux as fast as retiring royalties have to give them up."[31]

Figure 2.11. Advertising postcard, Trumbull Motel, Troy, Missouri, circa 1950.

Completing the classic roadside trilogy was the highway-oriented restaurant, initially a mere roadside stand, then a highway café (often bundled in with a gas station and/or a motel), and eventually (but only in the larger places initially) a classic drive-in eatery with carhops. Sinclair Lewis, commenting again, found food offered along the nation's roads to be notoriously bad: "Fried steaks—fried chops—fried Hamburg steak—coarse fat chunks of fried bacon—hash fried to solidity—fried sausage meat—fried potatoes—scrambled eggs black with grease from the pan."[32] But others found roadside eating to be one of the great joys of traveling. As food preferences shifted locality to locality, the traveler had enjoyed the variety. "No longer are we in the Frankfurter belt," reported James Flagg, a journalist from Indiana. "The hot dogs have ceased from bubbling and their kennels are no more. The barbecued pork and ham sign has taken the place of the familiar 'Hot Puppies' of the East."[33] Important also were the tourist-oriented highway stops that specialized in baskets, rubber snakes, and balsam cushions. But, as James Agee marveled, they also made regional delicacies available, like the pecans grown and favored across the American South (fig. 2.12).

As roadside businesses proliferated, criticism followed. The nation's new highways, many of them in very scenic areas, were being despoiled along their margins, critics said. The humorist Irvin Cobb thought little of what U.S. 1 had

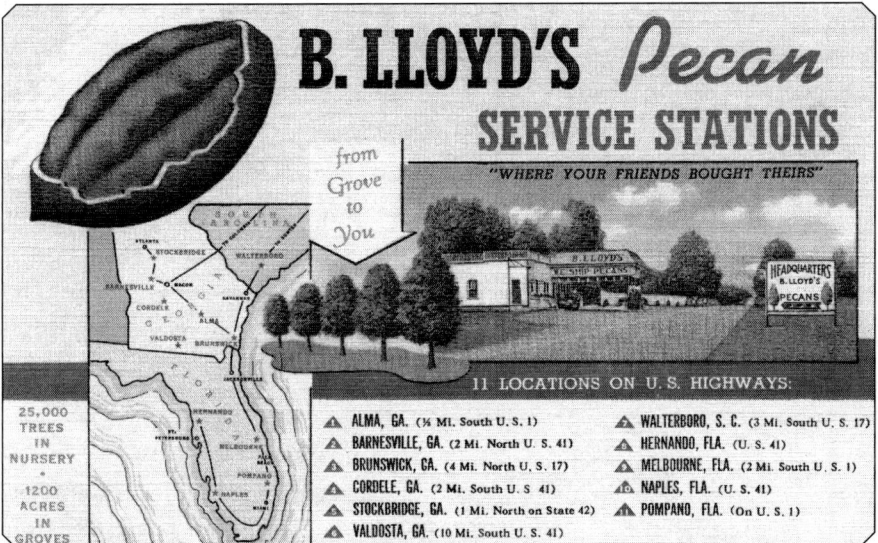

Figure 2.12. Advertising postcard, B. Lloyd's Pecan Service Stations, circa 1947. Courtesy of Lake County Discovery Museum/Curt Teich Postcard Archives.

become in Connecticut. "Cars without number go skyshooting through, by day raising pillars of grit, by night tainting the air with reeks of gasoline and lubricating oils. From end to end they closely are enfiladed by filling stations, repair stations, tea-houses, road-houses and lunch-stands, these last invariably being open-fronted to the world and the dust."[34] With such thinking the de-meaning of Roadside America began.

But not all agreed. The English writer J. B. Priestly, traveling across the desert Southwest, marveled at the new commerce. "Here along these western highways, with their fine surfaces, careful grading and banking, elaborate signs, their filling stations, their auto camps, their roadside eating-houses and hotels, their little towns passionately claiming your custom in a startling sudden glare of electric signs, is brand-new busy world." With signs shouting Gas, Hot and Cold Drinks, and the like spelled out in paint by day and by neon at night, very soon something like it would surely characterize "road life" all over the world, even penetrating Africa and Asia. "There was rapidly coming into existence a new way of living—fast, crude, vivid—perhaps a new civilization, perhaps another barbarian age—and here were the signs of it, trivial enough in themselves, but pointing to the most profound changes, to bloodless revolutions," he wrote. "This new life was simply breaking through the old like a crocus through the wintry crust of earth." It was in the United States that it was "most multiplied and clearest."[35] Priestley's is an often quoted observation, but an important one. The new roadside, as an expression of modernity, would surely spread globally. It was fully functional as an embrace of speed and convenience. In an age dominated by the automobile, it was fully pragmatic. Nothing would stop it.

The most-heated criticisms were leveled at roadside advertising. Besides "the windrows of luncheon boxes and sardine tins and paper bags and wrapping paper and discarded newspapers and the miscellaneous filth of countless thoughtless tourists" and the "doggeries and crab-meateries and doughnuteries and clammeries and booths that dispense home cooking on oil cloth and inch-thick china in an aura of kerosene stoves frying onions and stale grease," not to mention the "forest of telephone and electric light poles and tangles of wires," there was the signage that made America's main highways into a kind of "Billboardia," wrote journalist Kenneth L. Roberts.[36] Numerous sign counts were made to demonstrate the nature of the problem. Driving the 167 miles between Philadelphia and Pittsburgh on U.S. 30 (the former Lincoln Highway) in 1936, 2,017 stand-alone signs could be counted, or twelve to the mile. One-quarter of them were large billboards. Not included were the on-premise or point-of-purchase signs at gasoline stations and other roadside venues. "Thus on your loveliest mountain road, curving around the hills and through the forests, winding along the streams, rising to the summits with their far-flung views . . . the traveler who seeks relief from commercial cares . . . will meet instead a constant relentless bombardment of advertising at the rate of 8 to 10 assaults per minute."[37]

Cartoons appearing in newspapers and popular magazines mocked what was thought to be an all-too-common highway scene (fig. 2.13). Such lampooning was more than a little overdone, however. For one thing most advertising was located at the margins of cities and towns, and not in open country. And highways peripheral to urban places were already quite utilitarian. In many rural areas, main roads paralleled railroad rights-of-way, which were hardly scenic. Such was the case along the stretch of the National Old Trails Highway (the Old National Road) east of St. Louis in Illinois (fig. 2.14). Billboards seen in the far distance detract little from what was a very utilitarian scene to begin with.

The nation's brief flirtation with scenic parkways was in part a response to evolving roadside commerce, including its advertising. "Few will disagree that

Figure 2.13. Cartoon parodying highway advertising signs. J. N. Darling, "Why We Go to Europe for Beautiful Scenery," *New York Herald-Tribune*, reprinted in Roadside Bulletin 1 (circa 1933): 6. Courtesy of Jay N. "Ding" Darling Wildlife Society.

Figure 2.14. National Old Trails Highway, west of Troy, Illinois, circa 1928.

a beautiful highway precludes such things as ugly signboards, or advertising stickers on poles and trees; multi-colored petrol service stations; smelly and greasy garages; cheap refreshment stands and restaurants, equally smelly and greasy; and the awful conglomeration of shanties and sheds, the nameless piles of junk and debris that seem to accumulate along highways," wrote one journalist.[38] The cure was to exclude commerce from highway margins altogether, turning roadsides in long linear parks. The cure was, in other words, the treatment of roads and roadsides as works of landscaped art. "The appeal of the countryside," argued one commentator, "is no longer to be that of nature, alone and unaided. Landscape art, here and there very simple, here and there very elaborate, will add a human touch, a new appeal, not in skyscrapers that tower hundreds of feet and ornament the sky, but in varied fascinating roadsides which extend to the horizon for hundreds of miles across the landscape. And thus the traveler will find that everywhere in the country, just as everywhere in the city, the human spirit expresses itself."[39]

The landscaped parkway was, of course, a notion that found only limited application. "A completely landscaped highway is perhaps a desirable ideal," wrote the planner J. M. Bennett, "but the cost of proceeding on such a scale is prohibitive and it savors of the impractical because motorists in reality see a very small part of the detailed landscape as they pass. Furthermore, the intensive maintenance necessary for such a development is practically impossible."[40] What Bennett did not mention, of course, was the rapid rise of commercial strip development beyond the edges of small towns and cities all across the United States. There roadside real estate was simply too valuable to be sustained as landscaped landscape.

Commercial Strips

Commercial strips shared much in common from one location to another, although distinctive differences generally characterized strips that were marginal to small towns as opposed to those marginal to big cities. Inside cities, as well as beyond their margins, strips evolved out of pre-automobile urban thoroughfares that had been previously oriented, as often as not, to streetcar lines. Gas stations were usually the pioneers of land-use change, often being located at intersections on lots that had been occupied by houses along what were previously fully residential blocks. Where streetcar-oriented business was located, traditional commercial buildings were joined and then slowly replaced over time by auto-convenient businesses.

In small towns garages and then gas stations popped up in and around Main Street business districts and then at the margins of town along major highway approaches. Then farm-implement dealers and auto dealers that required large parcels of land joined in. Finally, other businesses followed, especially new chain stores that were corporately owned or franchised to locals. These merchants sought more space than was generally available in traditional downtown business areas in order to accommodate what was becoming increasingly essential—off-street parking. But peripheral locations were also capable of intercepting customers on their way into town, well before they reached traditional downtowns. Pictured here are nascent commercial strips outside Gila Bend, Arizona, and Pittsburg, California, respectively (figs. 2.15 and 2.16). Towns were "spreading out in a new way," wrote Sherwood Anderson, "the old tight close life" was being " broken up by the coming of the new big paved highways." "Rivers of cars flow through the towns. At night the headlights of the cars make a moving stream of light . . . the streets are lined with tourist houses and tourist camps have been built at the town's edge. On summer nights as you lie on your bed in your house in the American town, you hear the heavy rumble of goods trucks."[41]

Figure 2.15. U.S. 80 Strip at Gila Bend, Arizona, circa 1938.

By the 1950s Main Street had become an obsolete model for small-town commercial development. The essayist John B. Jackson wrote of the changes taking place in county-seat towns out on the high plains, towns where Main Street was rapidly losing its vitality. "The hotel is empty, many stores are empty, the depot is empty. The decline in the number of customers is one reason; another reason, which holds good in prosperous regions too, is that modern farm equipment and its servicing takes up a great deal of space, and consequently that important aspect of small town business has often moved out to the highway where there is plenty of cheap land. And the chain store supermarket has followed suit, and so has the new restaurant, and the new motel has been built out there as well." Taking the viewpoint of the approaching motorist, he wrote, "The nearer you get to town the thicker the signs and billboards become, then service stations, trailer courts, used car lots, supermarkets and motels appear. On dirt roads bulldozed through alfalfa fields stand rows of identical tract houses, all perched on fill held in place by a scanty growth of grass. The climax to the whole strip development is 'Towne and Country Plaza,' a stylish 300,000 square foot shopping center recently built by a Chicago firm, and almost entirely tenanted by chain stores."[42]

Figure 2.16. State Route 4 at the edge of Pittsburg, California, circa 1935.

Highway strips that were peripheral to big cities were longer and contained more businesses. There was usually a greater variety of businesses present, and business premises were often larger; both these aspects befitted a larger trade territory. Tom Wolfe, in his classic book *The Kandy-Kolored Tangerine-Flake Streamline Baby*, described Riverside Drive in North Hollywood, California. "It's like every place out there: endless scorched boulevards lined with one-story stores, shops, bowling alleys, skating rinks, taco drive-ins, all of them shaped not like rectangles but like trapezoids, from the way the roofs slant up from the back and the plate-glass fronts slant out as if they're going to pitch forward on the sidewalk and throw up."[43]

Many suburban strips specialized: for example, as an "automobile row" (with car dealers) or as a motel row. Las Vegas, Nevada's motel row out along U.S. 91 evolved into the granddaddy strip of all: Las Vegas Boulevard, known as "The Strip." Wolfe has his hero cruise down the Las Vegas Strip in his hot rod, a street "where the neon and the par lamps—bubbling, spiraling, rocketing, and exploding in sunbursts ten stories high out in the middle of the desert—celebrate one-story casinos."[44] Driven by legalized gambling, many of the strip's motels had morphed into giant hotels with gambling floors and night clubs and surrounded by large parking lots. Closeness to Hollywood (with its fantasy world of entertainment bizazz) influenced strip architecture. Closeness to Los Angeles guaranteed customers. Closeness to Hoover Dam brought in cheap electric power to light a nighttime sign extravaganza.

Not only the one at Las Vegas, but literally every commercial strip underwent constant change: old buildings were replaced by new ones, often with different functions, where strips thrived. Where they did not, then building disinvestment, underutilization, and even abandonment was often evident. Nothing depressed the vitality of a commercial strip faster than having traffic diverted away through, for example, new highway building, especially freeway construction. By the 1970s most metropolitan areas in the United States had derelict strips where old motels sold rooms by the week or the month, where old gas stations served as marginally profitable muffler or tire-recapping shops, or where old shopping centers might contain rummage stores and other marginal businesses or in fact be totally boarded up.

No where was change more evident than along central-city thoroughfares. Early on, in order to accommodate automobiles, streets were widened, sometimes by moving buildings back on their lots. Streetcars were eliminated so that more automobiles might be accommodated, including those parked at the curb. Buildings, especially on corner lots, might be demolished, especially for gas stations. Over time many buildings might be torn down not for new automobile-oriented business buildings, but merely for parking lots. Where once the facades of buildings coalesced rather like small-town Main Streets, these strips began to look fragmented, more like suburban strips. Even downtown streets became striplike. Such was the case with Pasadena, California's Colorado Avenue as early as the 1930s (fig 2.17).

Previously residential boulevards were rarely spared auto impact. "Once it was a proud thoroughfare, and it bore a proud name," Erling D. Solberg wrote of many a former residential show street in the United States. "Every fourth building, once very likely the home of a prosperous family, seems now to have a sign, *Tourists*. Every third house, perhaps with a false front, has a sign: Beer, Pizza, Groceries, Aunt Minnie's Café, Joe's Hot Dog Shoppe, Ice Cream, Soft Drinks. Others offer insurance, real estate, used cars. The rest are stores that seem to have no business." "Equally depressing," he added, "are recurrent blocks of weed-grown vacant lots—vacant except for billboards clamoring for your attention."[45]

Figure 2.17. Colorado Avenue, Pasadena, California, circa 1949. Courtesy of Lake County Discovery Museum/Curt Teich Postcard Archives.

The "New Road" Versus the Old

Unfettered commercialization of highway margins invariably reduced road efficiency. Roadside business not only added to traffic volumes, but cars and trucks leaving and entering a highway interfered with smooth traffic flow. Advertising signs for their part distracted motorists not only by slowing traffic as they paused to gawk, but by causing traffic accidents, critics claimed. At the edges of many cities, failure to curb commerce at the curbside produced traffic tie-ups not unlike those in downtown business districts, leading many highway departments eventually to build bypass roads, including urban freeways. Just before and then immediately after World War II, the building of four-lane divided highways headed outward from cities and linking them together as well proceeded apace, to be supplemented in the 1950s by the continued building of limited-access tollways, and then, of course, the construction of interstate freeways.

The new freeways, with their multiple traffic lanes, wide median strips, broad shoulders, and entrance and exit ramps at intervals represented a new kind of road (fig. 2.18). Adjacent real estate could not be directly accessed. Commerce, therefore, was restricted to interchange locations where one or another variation

Figure 2.18. Interstate 70 east of Kansas City, Missouri, circa 1970.

of the commercial strip evolved, sometimes oriented to a crossroad and sometimes oriented to a parallel side road. John Steinbeck commented on freeway driving in North Dakota: "These great roads are wonderful for moving goods but not for inspection of a countryside." There were "no roadside stands selling squash juice, no antique stores, no farm products or factory outlets." "When we get these freeways across the whole country, as we will and must, it will be possible to drive from New York to California without seeing a single thing."[46]

Other than at the interchanges commercial Roadside America was eliminated, except for the billboards, in most states. Visually landscape was pushed back well away from the road. The passing scene became something to be glimpsed at great distance, and at high speeds a driver's eyes necessarily focused on the road ahead. John Steinbeck put it this way: "You are bound to the wheel and your eyes to the car ahead and to the rear-view mirror for the car behind and the side mirror for the car or truck about to pass, and at the same time you must read all the [road] signs for fear you may miss some instructions or orders."[47]

George R. Stewart, in his 1950s cross-country survey of the United States along U.S. 40, commented on the stretches of four-lane pavement he encountered in Indiana. They represented what he called "dominating" highway. As a motorist, he was more conscious of the highway than the passing scene.[48] He might have been *in* the landscape, but he was no longer really *of* it. Following Stewart's route some thirty years later, the geographers Thomas and Geraldine Vale commented on the I-70 freeway that had essentially replaced U.S. 40 across the state. "The wide right-of-way, the absence of roadside businesses, the massive cuts and fills, and the ever-present chain-link, barbed wire, or woven fence all contribute to the lack of intimacy between road and setting. The land beside a freeway seems far away, cut off from the pavement hurrying travelers to distant destinations."[49] Such roads did more than that. Their engineering actually changed landscape, or at least land form, with hills being cut down and valleys filled and the ground seemingly leveled into a flat plain.

The essayist J. Todd Snow differentiated between various kinds of "old road" and the modern "new road." Old roads, he wrote, were definite places, paths that connected locations at a distance, but that also gave access to what was immediately at hand. They were trajectories along which things directly accrued. Landscape was something immediate and not something seen only at a distance. Old roads encouraged social interaction with people: travelers more intensively interacted with locals and with one another. The "new roads," epitomized by the interstate freeway, did not facilitate these interactions. With broad rights-of-way and limited access, they tended to turn motorists in on themselves, as the surrounding landscape seemingly was pushed away. It was a sensation that was amplified through the exhilaration of greatly enhanced speed.[50]

Roadside commerce was eliminated. But even where roadside services were found clustered at freeway interchanges, things were not the same. Speed seduced there as well, reducing social contact. As the novelist Larry McMurtry wrote, "The development of credit-card gas pumps, microwaves, and express motels has eliminated the necessity for human contact along the interstates. It is now possible to drive coast to coast without speaking to a human being at all: you just slide your card, pump your gas, buy a couple of Hershey bars, perhaps heat up a burrito, and put the pedal to the metal."[51] The interstates severed landscape apart. "The landscape as a whole is a continuous interwoven background within which structures are enfolded," wrote John Brookes, "but the new road cuts through this as a strong dividing line." The old roads had been part of the landscape, "twisting and turning to inflect to the patterns of the land as they went."[52]

At first readily embraced for the novelty of time-saving convenience, freeway travel quickly lost its allure for many motorists, especially those traveling to see and know their surroundings. Motor touring was always about reaching desired destinations, but it was also about "getting there." Freeway driving, however, substantially leveled down that kind of experience. Freeway driving discouraged interest in the passing scene, so distanced was it. Slowly, however, former ways of motoring enjoyed revival. Driving back roads, or the "Blue highways" (as colored on road maps, as the author William Least Heat Moon dubbed them), provided relief, even assuming nostalgic implications.[53] It was what generated revival of iconic Route 66. Stretches of that old highway, of course, have today become important tourist destinations. In disparaging the loss of U.S. 66 soon after the number had been decommissioned, the historian Thomas W. Pew wrote, "No more home-made apple pies, real milk shakes, real coffee; no more place to skinny dip in the Colorado on a hot afternoon, farms with fruit stands run by the youngest kid in the family; advertisements reading 'Chew Mail Pouch' on the sides of barns; no more Burma Shave rhymes, Giant Snake farms, Teepee motels and 'rooms for rent.'"[54]

The nation's freeways were about speed, especially about "making time." The change could be seen in how petroleum companies advertised their services on road map covers. The Cities Service Oil Company even changed its brand name to Citgo, with the emphasis thus placed on the idea not just of going, but of going fast. Through the mid-1960s the company's map graphics emphasized quick roadside service, and the roadside itself was pictured as a kind of place. But then map advertising disemboweled motoring from its surroundings save for the road depicted as a kind of raceway (fig. 2.19). The getting there, not the being there, was what was emphasized, and speed was made the common denominator.

Motoring had always carried such implications. In the 1920s James Flagg had wondered about motorists, even those traveling for pleasure, who madly drove in an "inescapable impulse to keep going—to keep up the pace, and not to be able to stop." Touring, he thought, ought to involve tarrying here and there with degrees of relaxed contemplation. "The continuous motion forward begets a habit of mind," he wrote, "and the mere thought of stopping, except from exhaustion, is repugnant." Perhaps, it was something inbred in people who were always busy, and, as characterized the United States, traditionally mobile. The national bird, he quipped, instead of being the eagle, ought to be "the squirrel in the cage."[55]

Roads and roadsides have changed fundamentally over the course of the past century, as have their meanings, at least as regards Americans and their experiencing of landscapes and places, especially those that are road oriented. Primitive automobiles and roads enticed motorists to adventure, if not for fun and pleasure pure and simple, then for empowerment through speed and convenience. Better

Figure 2.19. Roadmap panels, Cities Service Oil Company, circa 1960 and 1965.

cars and trucks invited highway improvement that in turn wrought still better vehicles and still better highways in cycles of mutual reinforcement. Motoring broadened to embrace everyday travel and not just pleasure tripping. Roadsides did not escape unchanged. Indeed, a wholly new urban form was born: the commercial strip—a sprawling, spread-out kind of linear business district intended at first mainly for retailing goods and services to motorists, but then for retailing goods and services generally.

The American roadside quickly became an engine for economic growth. Particularly important, real estate speculation and development was stimulated, especially in suburbia. It was there that highways most quickly turned into commercial strips, providing transportation infrastructure for the creation of residential subdivisions and indeed every other kind of real estate promotion. Corporate enterprise was favored, and the "mom and pop" pioneers of early roadside commerce were largely displaced in retailing, along with other small business operators. Today they function as proprietors within corporate franchising schemes or as mere employees of corporate chains. If ordinary citizens have been empowered by Roadside America, it has been primarily as consumers. However, with their consumption of all things automotive (with modern motoring's emphasis on personal speed and convenience, in other words), most Americans probably do feel themselves empowered, at least bodily, through enhanced mobility.

Over time automobility wrought highly homogeneous built environments nationwide—one road and one roadside looking very much like another. Having seen one commercial strip, it was increasingly argued, one had seen them all. Perhaps the sameness of car-dominated habitats was not truly progressive. What about sustainability? Would Roadside America even last? Might it prove to be but a passing form of American self-indulgence, one fostered by cheap petroleum, weak land-use regulation, overemphasis on private property rights, and the valuing of the strictly utilitarian?

CHAPTER THREE
LEARNING FROM ROADSIDE AMERICA

When the editors of *Fortune* commissioned "The Great American Roadside" in 1934, enthusiasm for unfettered automobility was high. James Agee gushed with more than a little optimism. The nation's nearly 1 million miles of improved highway constituted "the greatest road the human race [had] ever built," he wrote. Roadside America, where Americans "paused to trade," was, he argued, "incomparably the most hugely extensive market the human race has ever set up to tease and tempt and take money from the human race."[1] But two decades later *Fortune*'s enthusiasm for the new highway-oriented marketplace had considerably dampened. There had been unanticipated implications, both geographic and social. Automobility indeed had wrought a market revolution, but in ways not fully anticipated, especially as to how Roadside America would look.

The editors of *Fortune* commissioned a report, published in book form as *Exploding Metropolis*.[2] Its anonymous authors were charged with assessing transportation planning in New York City and its surrounding region, but also with assessing the automobile's impact on the nation's landscapes and places in general, using the specific lens of its largest metropolis. The federal highway program, coupled with federal housing policies (especially mortgage insurance programs administered by the Federal Housing Administration and the Veterans Administration), was creating disorder, or so journalist William Whyte emphasized in the book's introduction. There seemed to be little desire to control or direct urban growth through meaningful planning, especially at the regional scale. Favored instead, a laissez-faire attitude was considered conducive to "vast, inefficient urban sprawl."[3] The automobile was at the heart of it all.

The federal government harbored no coherent vision for regional growth. Like the state legislatures, which, it seemed, had never had much use for cities, Washington consistently favored country over city in its highway and housing programs. The FHA was partial to the suburban homeowner, and its rules encouraged architecture that was ill suited for city housing, or so Whyte thought. Flying over any major metropolis could be "an unnerving lesson in man's infinite capacity to mess up his environment." Aesthetically the result was chaotic. "It takes remarkably little blight to color a whole area," he argued. "Let the reader travel along a stretch of road he is fond of, and he will notice how a small portion of open land has given amenity to the area. But it takes only a few badly designed developments or billboards or hot-dog stands to ruin it."[4]

In 1969 Edmund K. Faltermayer, also an editor at *Fortune*, published *Redoing America*, another indictment of the nation's planning (or lack thereof) regarding auto-oriented landscapes and places. "We are building a cheap, disposable environment containing hardly any man-made places that people can love and feel and identify with," he wrote.[5] As the suburbs sprawled, central-city neighborhoods languished. Through neglect they were turning into slums. Foreigners who came to the United States expecting to see thriving cities found instead littered streets, vandalism beyond belief, forests of ugly telegraph poles and wires, decrepit mass transit systems, unkempt parks, and eroding downtowns. Beyond the cities they saw "countryside being devoured by monotonous new suburban housing and by shopping centers whose graceless buildings are little more than merchandise barns; highways splattered with enormous billboards and hideous drive-in establishments that shriek for the passing motorist's attention." And the mess was getting messier, he worried.[6]

To Faltermayer the causes were obvious: the values of the nation's frontier past—namely exaggerated individualism, a profound disrespect for nature, a naive belief in the inexhaustibility of the country's resources (including most especially land), and a bias against cities—were raising their ugly heads. "Our troubles," he wrote, "were complicated after World War II when the middle class, increasingly motorized and yearning for a suburban life-style, spilled far beyond the confines of the big cities, into a hodgepodge of suburban jurisdictions ill-prepared for the influx. In this state of near anarchy, new settlements were flung across the landscape in haphazard fashion and new commercial ugliness spread wildly along roadsides, in a process that is still going on." The result, he said, were "noncommunities" that were "not only chaotic looking, but also notoriously inefficient."⁷ [handwritten: Do you think unorganization yields non-communities?]

The most pervasive form of ugliness and inefficiency, however, was the "commercial-strip highway," lined, he wrote, with its "jumbled assortment of roadside businesses." Suburban strips had resulted from "a total lack of planning by sleepy farm communities that failed to anticipate the postwar deluge of suburbanization, or which engaged in competitive 'grubbing for ratables' with neighboring towns by simply strip-zoning their main thoroughfares for commercial or industrial activity and then letting haphazard, automobile-age construction lay waste the landscape." Here and there a shopping center might make good use of the land, he admitted, but the interstices between them were invariably filled up with indifferent-looking stores, "each surrounded by its ugly asphalt pool of parking space."⁸ Unfortunately most Americans were oblivious to it all, "numbed," as they were, by overexposure to it. Many simply accepted it "as an inevitable manifestation of the exuberant, competitive American spirit that keeps our economy humming."⁹

Fortune's 1930s promotion of the "Great American Roadside" was essentially reversed. Instead Roadside America was made symbolic of what had been going wrong in the 1950s and 1960s, specifically in regard to automobility's still largely unfettered impact on evolving landscape and places, especially around the nation's largest cities. Suddenly Roadside America, and particularly the commercial strip, was thrust front and center into several debates. What ought (or ought not) American cities be? How should they function? And what was (or was not) aesthetically pleasing about built environments generally?

Roadside Aesthetics

When many Americans thought about commercial strips, especially those of large cities, it was often in terms of visual chaos, a way of thinking imaginatively captured by the cartoonist R. Crumb in his "A Short History of America," a series of twelve cartoon panels published in 1979 (fig. 3.1).¹⁰ Roadside America had substantially come to be associated with makeshift buildings covered by exuberant signs and ubiquitous utility poles among other things readily distasteful to many. To critics commercial strips were just plain ugly. [handwritten: Does our generation still believe this?]

The sociologists Christopher Tunnard and Boris Pushkarev were especially critical. Commercialization of the roadside was so visually aggressive and [handwritten: Do we question the buildings in something similar?]

Figure 3.1. Cartoon panels illustrating commercial strip evolution. R. Crumb, "A Short History of America," *CoEvolution Quarterly*, no. 24 (winter 1979–80). These three panels depict a road at the edge of the city during the eras of horse-drawn transport, streetcars, and then automobiles, with the coming of exaggerated advertising signs shown as belonging to the last. Courtesy of R. Crumb.

ubiquitous a feature, they wrote in *Man-Made America: Chaos or Control?*, that it had indeed come to be considered typical, and even inevitable, in the urban fringes of cities. It comprised "everything from billboards to drive-in movies, from gas stations to motels, from diners to truck terminals, from farm fruit stands . . . to discount department stores, from junk yards to dine-and-dance." Land adjacent to main highways was too expensive for residential use and thus usually went into commercial use, as towns, in search of a tax base, were all too eager to aid and abet the process. Unfortunately, vehicular movement and the commercialized road margin were incompatible. "Both speed and capacity are reduced and accidents rise," they noted. But mainly it was the "lack of visual order" that was bothersome.[11]

The architectural critic Peter Blake, in *God's Own Junkyard: The Planned Deterioration of America's Landscape,* wrote, "Our suburbs are interminable wastelands dotted with millions of monotonous little houses on monotonous little lots and crisscrossed by highways lined with billboards, jazzed-up diners, used-car lots, drive-in movies, beflagged gas stations, and garish motels." Bad architects could be blamed for only some of the vandalism, but there were many others that could and should be blamed also. "Some of our latter-day vandals are 'little people'—tradesmen and shopkeepers trying to make a modest living—people without ties to the landscape or townscape in which they live, people whose eyes have lost the art of seeing. And still others among our latter-day vandals are all the rest of us—all of us who no longer care, or no longer care enough."[12]

Also at work, of course, was unregulated private profit: "profit from speculation with land, profit from manipulating land and buildings, and profit from the actual construction and subsequent lease or sale of buildings"—buildings built, in other words, solely "for the purpose of making a fast buck faster." "The laws and codes and commissions that exist for the avowed purpose of helping create better cities are utterly ineffectual," he argued, "and they are seemingly intended to be so; the policies that govern taxation and financing actually encourage and handsomely reward the builders of bad buildings and penalize the builders of good ones."[13]

Ian Nairn, the editor of *Architectural Review,* also saw commercial strips as intrinsically chaotic. Buildings along the typical strip, he wrote in *The American Landscape: A Critical View,* were not only "overly ordinary," but, loosely spread out in a linear array, they were poorly related, if not totally unrelated, to one another. By and large Roadside America failed to add up to anything meaningful. "Townscape," he wrote, "depends on two things: relationships and identity. Relationship means making the parts of the environment fit together—the supermarket, the gas station, the car lots; identity is the recognition and enhancement of the specific needs and qualities that make one place different from another." Roadside America, in contrast, was largely a "mindless mixing up of . . . man-made objects without pattern of purpose or relationship." It was "goop." Its "archetype" was "man treating the landscape as a set of ruled squares and then filling them with low density muck."[14]

The geographer Peirce F. Lewis decried various categories of landscape blight in the United States. "America is getting uglier," he asserted. It was appropriate that scholars ask why, as well as try and do something about it. "I would suggest that we tackle the problem of visual blight soberly as we would any other professional matter: by describing the phenomenon carefully, by naming its parts, by locating its habitat, and by trying to identify its origins and behavior." Visual degradation was at its worse, he wrote, "beside the roads where most people travel." Blight occurs, he argued, because it is financially profitable to do so, and our political institutions contain few mechanisms for preventing it, let alone encouraging something else. As a nation, he added, we embraced unrestrained technological applications that pretended progress, little anticipating, in our enthusiasm, unintended negative consequences. Americans did it more out of habit rather than out of necessity. "There is nothing in the essential chemistry of petroleum products, for instance, which requires motor fuel to be sold amid whirling plastic signs, foil wrapped multi-colored tires, cannibalized cars, half an acre of ill-tended asphalt, and the syndrome of *schlock* that we have come to associate with gas stations across America."[15]

Negative criticisms leveled at Roadside America during the 1950s and 1960s were rooted more in "cultivated tastes"—aesthetic values rooted in the realm of art and academic scholarship rather than in the vernacular of American popular culture, which involved artisan craftsmanship and popular thought. From earliest colonial times, ordinary Americans had embraced, mostly through necessity, the functional and utilitarian values in the creation of tools, buildings, and indeed whole landscapes. Everyday practicality tended to triumph over stylishness as dictated by one or another social elite. In the art of making places, John A. Kouwenhoven pointed out, Americans tended to be better engineers than architects. They were good at maximizing utility while minimizing costs, although admittedly such proclivity frequently reduced architectural styling to a rather low common denominator.¹⁶ By extension to the roadside, Americans were much better at building highways then they were at lining them with what might be considered tasteful architecture.

The United States evolved out of a frontier past. Wilderness, by whatever definition, was humanized, first, or so the historical record seemed to say, through the establishment of farms, and only then through the rise of towns and cities where the bulk of the nation's population came to reside in the twentieth century. Yet what constituted beauty in landscape remained very much rooted in the "middle landscapes" of the nation's pastoral past. Thus were suburban subdivisions invariably laid out to look romantically pastoral, houses ("ranch houses" after World War II) built on sprawling lots landscaped in ways fully suggestive of a rural picturesque. Nonetheless many of the suburban ideals being put into place originated not with what ordinary Americans once did living in rural areas, but with what aristocratic Europeans had once done with their estate gardens and landscaped parks. It was, in other words, substantially elitist, and America's affluent classes were the first to "escape" to suburbia.¹⁷

Whatever its roots, the imagery of the typical twentieth-century suburban subdivision was essentially pastoralism in disguise. It was symbolism adopted to make housing estates more tasteful and thus more acceptable as a form of modern commodification. On the commercial roadside, however, there was little pretense in that regard—not much effort was made to disguise what it was. Vernacular impulses rooted more in doing rather than in pretending were allowed to fully prevail. When design pretension did come to the fore, it took its cues mainly from popular amusements rather than from refined culture. Much of the criticism leveled at Roadside America stemmed from that practice. The "training, refinement of mind, tastes and manners" of professional architects and landscape architects was missing, as one critic put it.¹⁸ Popular culture in the United States tended to ignore, if it did not wholly reject altogether, the cultivated conceits of practiced stylishness. In the essayist Stewart Alsop's opinion, "Out of the frontier past has grown a subconscious consensus that there is something manly about messiness and ugliness, something sissified about whatever is handsome, or well ordered, or beautiful."¹⁹

Embrace of the picturesque—and even the beautiful—did not leave U.S. highways totally untouched. During the 1930s, and then again in decades after World War II, parkways were built in various parts of the United States, many of them administered by the National Park Service. Roads in the national parks were landscaped so as not to detract from park scenery, and commercial enterprise was either excluded or carefully concentrated and was largely screened from view.[20] So also were attempts made to control billboards, especially along the new interstate freeways with the Highway Beautification Act of 1965.[21] That act left commercial strips largely unaffected, however. As one observer put it, "The bill curtails billboards along the 225,000 miles of federally supported roads but allows them in commercial and industrial areas—which is where most of them are anyway."[22]

The idea that commercial strips, among other kinds of twentieth-century urban landscapes, were essentially "placeless," was initially promoted by the geographer E. Relph. *Placelessness* was the term he used, although he might better have called it, as we have stated elsewhere, *commonplaceness*. Suburban subdivisions and commercial strips were all so alike from location to location that they excited little special notice, he said. They were so predictable that they were easily ignored. Of course, no landscape is placeless. A landscape may excite little sense of one's being in a distinctive place, but that does not mean it has little meaning—that it does not exist as a place inviting to kinds of behavior or as a setting for kinds of activity. Certainly many roadside landscapes were (and are) overly simple. "The simple landscape," Relph wrote, "is the landscape that declares itself openly, presents no problems or surprises, lacks subtlety." "Ambiguities, contradictions, and complexities" are insufficient to excite search for deep meaning.[23] A roadside may be, as Ian Nairn put it, "a strip with no tease."[24]

Roadside Functionality

Initial criticism did not give much consideration to how U.S. roadsides functioned. If critics were concerned with how Roadside America looked, that concern largely ignored how Roadside American was looked at. They were not very interested with how motorists experienced roadside places as visual display. Thus little attention was given to how commercial strips functioned or to the role that visualization played in that functioning. Rejecting narrow focus on aesthetics, new voices began to be heard, prime among them earliest on was John B. Jackson, founder of *Landscape*, a literary magazine dedicated to describing and understanding America's human geography. The magazine was influential with scholars, especially cultural geographers, but also with members of the design disciplines, including architects, landscape architects, and planners.

Jackson's writings brought vernacular culture to the fore, and his focus on ordinary landscapes and places and what made them work was especially significant.[25] Landscape was not something merely to be looked at in a search for tastefulness. Rather it was very much how places worked that counted and who it was who worked in them and why. As ordinary human or cultural landscape was not created as a work of art, it ought not to be assessed as such, he argued. Cultural landscape was "the temporary product of much sweat and hardship and earnest thought," he wrote, and "we should never look at it without remembering that, and we should never tinker with landscape without thinking of those who live in the midst of it," he argued. "What the spectator wants or does not want," he said, should be of relatively "small account."[26]

Several of his writings stand out as especially informative regarding Roadside America. In a 1965 essay, "Other Directed Houses," he admitted that some roadside drive-ins, diners, souvenir stands, and such were often eyesores. Yet there was often fleeting beauty also, and most always usefulness. He asked how much more might be said or asked of most other things. If indeed Roadside America was something that needed taming, we as a nation needed first to understand it and to develop an appreciation for it. And there was much to learn. "We know (and seem to care) far too little about the variety of businesses which comprise it. Why is it that certain enterprises proliferate in certain areas and not in others? Why are some of them clustered together, and others are far apart? Which of them are dependent on the nearby town and city, which of them depend on transients?"[27]

The ability to attract attention was central. Convenience of access was important. But promise of personal reward or pleasure was also involved as businesses played on customer expectations. "We must accustom ourselves to the fact that the basic motive in the design of these establishments—whether they be motels or drive-in movies or nightclubs—is a desire to please and attract the passerby." On the strip, he wrote, the "austere ambitions of the contemporary architect to create a self-justifying work of art has no place" Every business "had to woo the public—a public, moreover, which passes by at forty miles or more an hour." Thus it was that Roadside America had come to foster "other-directed" architecture.[28]

Jackson's essay refuting the basic tenets of Peter Blake's *God's Own Junkyard* is particularly revealing. Unfortunately, he said, there remained a cleavage between aesthetic and social approaches to understanding landscape. There were those who judged Roadside America as visual spectacle. There were those who, on the other hand, judged it "as a place for living and working." The former did treat landscapes as "works of art." What followed was the notion that landscapes needed curatorial oversight and that kinds of threatened landscape needed saving. But landscape, Jackson argued, took care of itself, accordingly to peoples' needs, aspirations, and intentionality.[29]

Landscape was insinuated in human socialization. Landscape was formed by, but also fully implicated in the forming of human society. It needed to be understood and assessed accordingly. "The billboard and the utility pole, for all their insulting ugliness and ubiquity, have little or no effect on the landscape. They irritate the passerby, they irritate those compelled to see them day after day; but in no appreciable manner do they interfere with the inhabiting or exploiting of the landscape, or with its biological well being," he argued. What they do express, and very bluntly so, is what advertisers and utility companies think of us: "we matter as consumers only."[30]

Jackson promoted a new disciplinary outlook, including what he called the study of "odology"—in essence the study of roads and road journeys. The most important "odological" development of the twentieth century, he maintained, was that the road had evolved from a path connecting places into a kind of place itself.[31] Jackson actually preferred the term *way* to the word *road*. The latter implied, he said, a reductive emphasis on physical features. A *way* suggested to him not just a material entity, but cultural or social forces also, forces that shaped human activity or behavior, including human perceptions.[32]

Acquainted with Jackson and aware of his thinking, the architects Robert Venturi, Denise Scott Brown, and Steven Izenour wrote their influential and now-classic *Learning from Las Vegas*.[33] Working from the premise that "chaos is an order we have not yet discerned," they undertook, along with their students, to examine the most exuberant of all roadsides, the Las Vegas Strip.[34] The idea was to assess the strip not so much as architectural form as architectural communication. They found two types of order on the strip: an obvious visual order of street elements and a more difficult visual order of buildings and signs. As for the latter, they identified three message systems: first, "heraldic signs"(or actual sign boards), especially those located at the curbside to advertise nearby building functions; second, "physiographic" signs where messages were implied through the size, shape, fenestration, and other physical aspects of buildings themselves; third, "locational signs" whereby buildings were seen as spaced, for example across organized spaces such as driveways and parking lots. To read or interpret these sign systems, one really had to be driving, since they best communicated at speeds around 45 miles per hour (fig. 3.2). Las Vegas Boulevard was not, when they looked at it, very successful as a pedestrian place. And it was as pedestrian places that landscapes were assessed by most critics.

What they discerned overall was a certain rhythm whereby large casinos were spaced at intervals with lesser things, such as gas stations and fast-food restaurants, but also with drive-in wedding chapels and the like, arrayed in-between (fig. 3.3). All buildings large or small tended to be inflected toward the road, with their side elevations as well as their facades given special treatment since buildings tended to be seen on the oblique as motorists drove toward them. The casinos were also introduced to view by their large porte-cocheres, made readily accessible to motorists by broad driveways, and with the convenience of parking immediately at hand in large parking lots; the whole readily symbolized ready access.

Additionally they examined the overt symbolism of the buildings themselves, differentiating two general building types: what they called "the duck" (so

Figure 3.2. Las Vegas Boulevard, Las Vegas, Nevada, 1983. Large signs announce casinos distributed at intervals along "The Strip," with each casino entrance elaborated by a large porte-cochere with adjacent parking lot, thus symbolizing convenient accessibility. The big casinos bring a kind of rhythm to the street, at least for motorists passing down the street at relatively high speeds.

Figure 3.3. Las Vegas Boulevard, Las Vegas, Nevada, 1983. Gas stations, fast-food restaurants, and other small-scale businesses fill the intervals the casinos, amplifying the sense of rhythm through contrast of scale.

named for the celebrated roadside duck of Long Island) and "the decorated shed." Where the architectural systems of space, structure, and program were submerged or distorted by an overall symbolic form, the resulting "building-becoming-sculpture" was a duck. Where systems of space and structure were directly at the service of the program and ornament was applied independently, then it was a decorated shed. What they sought, of course, was not just understanding as to what made commercial strips symbolically and functionally impelling, but design cues that they, as architects, might take away. What resulted was innovative thinking on then-contemporary modern architecture, with its embrace of buildings with stripped-down geometric simplicity void of stylistic ornamentation. When ornaments for buildings were abandoned, Venturi, Scott Brown, and Izenour argued, modern architects unconsciously created buildings that were ornamental themselves. In contrast to what had dominated landscapes and places previously, their buildings communicated as ducks.[35] What needed saying, of course, was that much of that change had first come about along U.S. roadsides. Additionally, commercial strips, epitomized perhaps by Las Vegas Boulevard, were a vernacular form. They were not worked out by any one designer or by designers working in concert, although once zoning and building codes and other governmental controls were set in place, it could be said that some overarching controls were indeed operative.

John B. Jackson called commercial strips "auto-vernacular landscapes."³⁶ They were landscapes created largely through serendipity to accommodate the auto as distinguished from the pedestrian. They were machine spaces and not people places. However, that did not mean that places along the strip did not carry profound social implication, at least once motorists got out of their cars or their trucks or off their motorcycles or motorbikes. It hardly meant that Roadside America lacked humanized spaces. Take gas stations, he argued. "Having worked in a gas station, I am aware of a very definite sense of place in many of them and of a sense of fraternity that can develop in even the least sightly of roadside installations. In spite of my weakness for truck stops and service stations, I hesitate to think of them as the modern equivalent of the 'moral unit.' Still, they are places where strangers come together and where they often turn for help, advice, and companionship." He fostered the idea that society was not based on territoriality or position, but on "shared interests and mutual help."³⁷ Commercial strips not only held design lessons, but insights into human sociality.

"Many elements of the American cultural landscape exhibit morphological regularity underscored by economic forces, yet infused with cultural values," reminded the geographer Darrell A. Norris in his study of strip development at interstate highway interchanges. Reinforced was the fact that Roadside America's was not just auto-oriented, but well rooted in serving motorist convenience. Motorists approaching commercial strips at interchanges, he thought, invited a kind of "time and motion" analysis. Motorists tolerated lengthy deviations from exit ramps, he concluded, if a long pause or overnight stay was envisioned; but they did not tolerate it when only refilling a gas tank, using a restroom, or getting a quick snack. The consecutive sequence of exit establishments therefore should be gasoline stations first, followed by eating establishments, then stores, and finally lodging facilities, he concluded. Such, however, was rarely the case. "Roadside homogeneity in American culture is a common assumptive slur which does not survive close scrutiny," he emphasized. Commercial clusters at freeway exits did tend to follow norms of form, scale, composition, and structure, but in detail the repertoire was endless. "It bore witness to unmistakable variation that continued to pervade and enrich American mass culture."³⁸

Created at many interstate interchanges were commercial agglomerations that fully represented a new kind of place. They were townlike, but not towns.

And there was no town nearby. As places they were mainly nameless and thus seldom considered to be places.³⁹ One exception was Breesewood, Pennsylvania, where, on the old Lincoln Highway (today's U.S. 30), where traffic was (as it continues to be) exchanged with the Pennsylvania Turnpike (traffic moving east and west to Philadelphia and Pittsburgh, respectively) and I-70 (connecting Washington, DC, to the southeast; see fig. 1.2). Breezewood stood, according to the essayist Craig Whitaker, as "one of the purest examples in America of the synergy between motorists and merchant." It was as large as a small town but had no mayor, no police department, and no residences. "It's just one long street whose only purpose is to sell to passing travelers," he wrote.⁴⁰

Roadside Change

Just how roadsides in general, and commercial strips specifically, came into being and then changed over time had begun to excite a wide range of scholars by the 1960s. Attention was given variously to central-city strips (which evolved along streetcar lines, for example, but eventually made auto-convenient), suburban strips (which evolved fully auto-oriented along peripheral highways in previously rural areas), and eventually freeway-interchange strips (including those isolated well beyond towns and cities). Strips invariably developed incrementally, the result of large and small decisions spread across numerous players—property owners, business owners, and government officials, among others. Over time a street's personality could be altered radically.

Before 1960 academic concern with commercial-strip development in and around cities was focused mainly on economic issues related to real estate development and the market reach of businesses, as opposed to issues of architectural form and function.⁴¹ Small-town strips, particularly those arrayed together along specific highways, also began to be examined, with the focus being on identifying the structural forms associated with different kinds of businesses and their geographic distribution along highways.⁴² In subsequent decades concern broadened to consider the changing spatial makeup of commercial strips over time. The journalist Grady Clay, then the editor of *Landscape Architecture*, identified stages through which highway-oriented commercial strips typically evolved, using a case study from suburban Louisville, Kentucky, one that had undergone consider highway realignment over time (fig. 3.4).⁴³ The geographers Richard L. Mattson and John A. Jakle relied mainly on city directories and

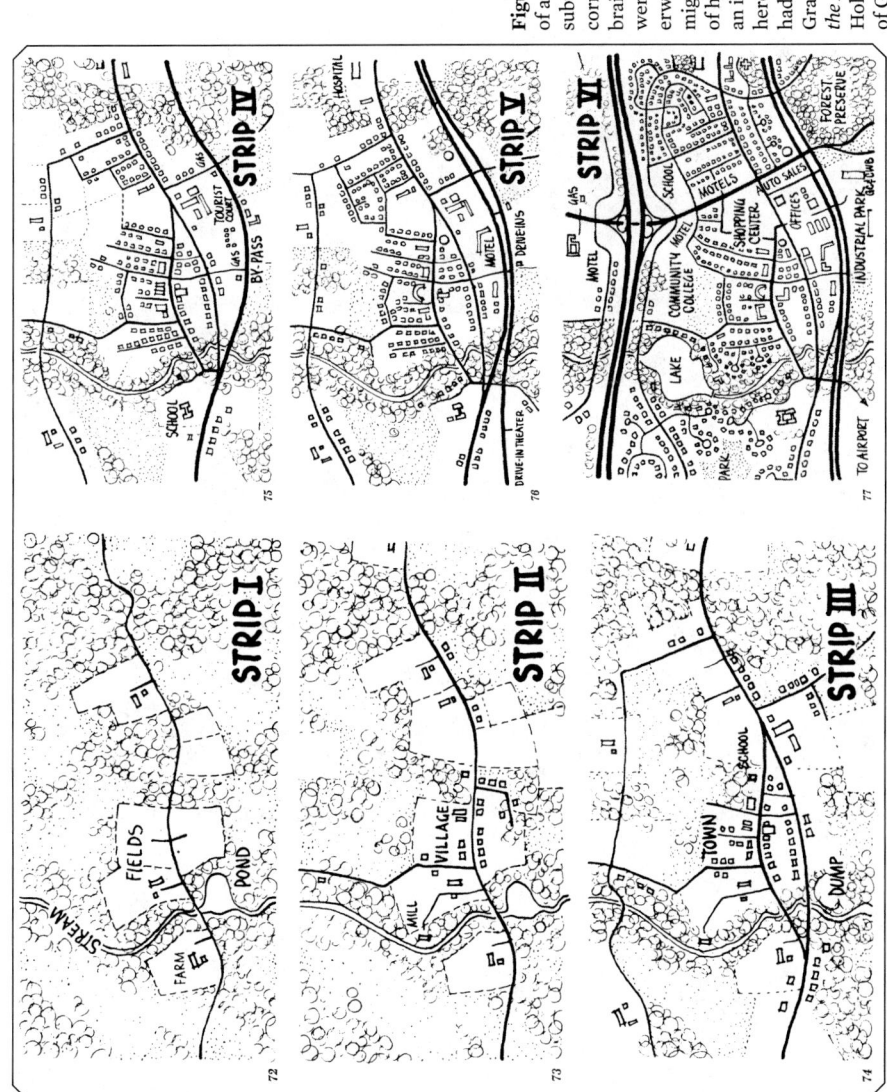

Figure 3.4. Modeling the evolution of a suburban strip corridor. In the suburbs of large cities, highway corridors often took on the form of a braided stream as original roadways were shortened, realigned, or otherwise modified. Strip development might cling to bypassed sections of highway or cluster nearby at an interchange when, as modeled here, a parallel interstate freeway had replaced an earlier road. From Grady Clay, *Close-Up: How to Read the American City* (New York: Henry Holt & Co., 1973), 93–94. Courtesy of Grady Clay.

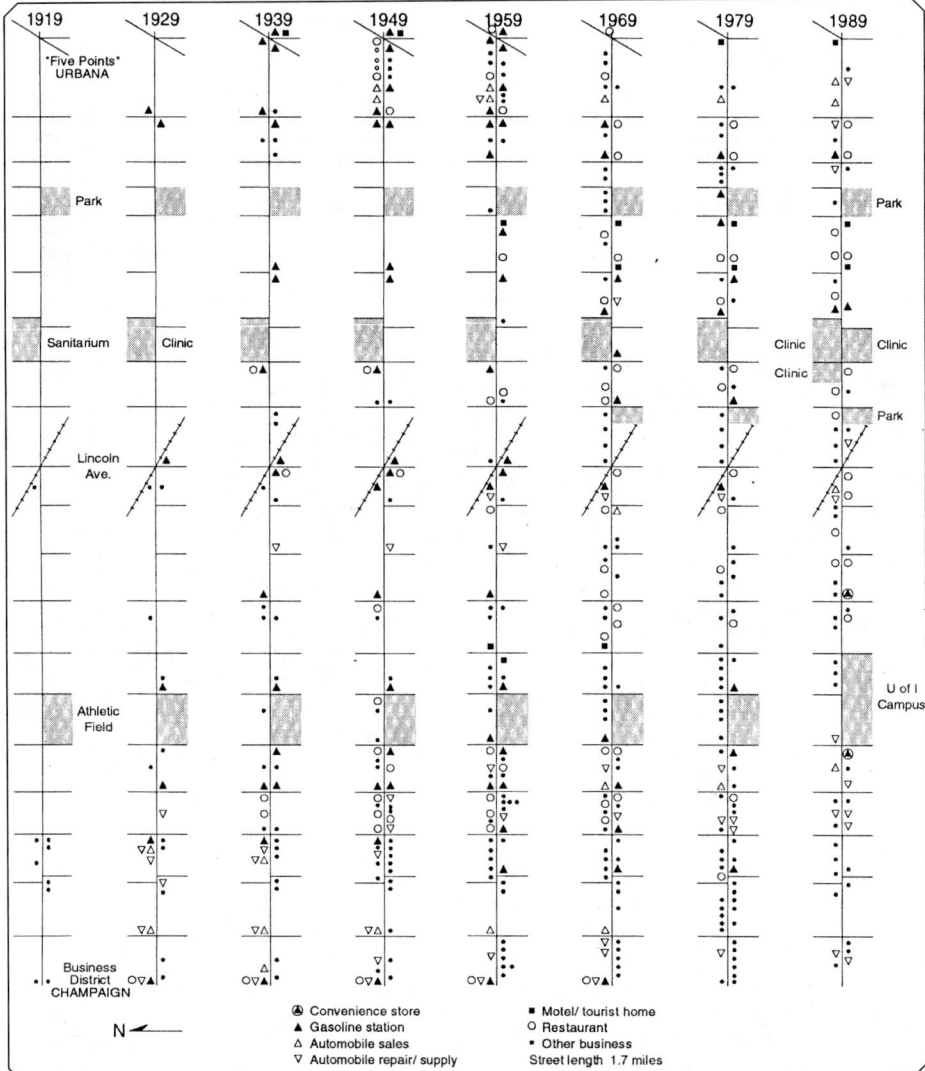

Figure 3.5. Commercial land use along a previously residential thoroughfare, University Avenue, Champaign and Urbana, Illinois, 1919–89. From Jakle and Sculle, *The Gas Station in America* (1994), 211. Courtesy of Johns Hopkins University Press, Baltimore.

insurance maps to explore structural change along an in-town commercial strip connecting the downtowns of Champaign and Urbana, Illinois. They focused on the role that gasoline stations and other types of businesses played in pioneering strip development along what had originally been a residential boulevard (fig. 3.5).[44] The architectural historian Richard Longstreth emphasized historical photographs as a source for understanding changing strip development, using photos of various Los Angeles boulevards between the two World Wars.[45]

Historical case studies, however, remained few in number, perhaps because most scholars, like most Americans, saw commercial roadsides as being very much the same from one place to another. Perhaps they saw the changes that were taking place as being essentially the same everywhere. Strips are assumed to be standardized places, the journalism professor Richard P. Horowitz admitted. True motorists driving long distances often measured their progress by standard strip stops, one "tankful" apart, he said. But most commuters and shoppers had their favorite places "to fill up, grab a gallon of milk, or buy a burger." "They take turns stopping for the office doughnuts at a drive-up window on the way to work. Salespeople have favorite phones or mailboxes to use from their cars or motel rooms that are their homes on the road. Families frequent the mall for back-to-school clothes." "No strip is as striking as an unfamiliar one," he concluded, "one where you have not yet staked out routines and favorites."[46] No two strips contained the same mix of roadside venues. There was always variation in how they were arrayed, and even some novel juxtapositions. There was always some differences in apparent sameness.[47]

Horowitz looked at the Coralville, Iowa, strip just west of Iowa City, and interviewed business proprietors and their employees. Variation entered strip development if only through business decision making. He called for scholars to explore how it was that national food and fuel franchisers, for example, selected locations. Horowitz thought the following criteria were critical: traffic count (at least 15,000 to 20,000 cars in a 24-hour period), local speed limit (minimum of 35 mph), available front footage (at least 125 feet), land cost (preferably low), visibility (corner sites preferred), sign and other land-use restrictions (no restrictions preferred), accessibility to motorists (two-curb openings on undivided road preferred), immediate market (subdivisions nearby dominated by two-income families ideal), and other businesses already established (preferably complementary businesses rather than those that were competitive).[48] Location decisions also hinged on how corporations themselves functioned. But by what rules did retail chains expand? If by franchising, what were the territorial rights extended to individual franchisees? What was expected from local bankers or other local lenders regarding the financing of startups? How dependent were franchised outlets on central commissaries or other corporate facilities? Also important, a locality's tastes and preferences were ascertained through market surveys.

It was mainly through the place-product packaging of franchisers—their distinctive building designs, color schemes, and logos, most especially—that gave commercial strips such look-alike implications. Relatively few chains operated nationwide. In the restaurant field, of course, the signs of McDonald's and Subway were seemingly everywhere. But most chains had only a regional reach. They overlapped with one another locality to locality, creating very subtle differences in the look of commercial strips from locality to locality. Franchises were "kits," journalist Phil Patton observed: "assemble-it-yourself systems of products, finance, location, service, architecture, and advertising." "The more flexible, the more neatly packaged and replicable the kit, the more successful the franchise."[49] But no one kit fit all. And every strip had a different mix of kits at work, and never the same ones year to year as franchisers and franchisees came and went.[50]

Franchising very much underpinned America's evolving consumer culture. With inflated discretionary spending (beyond the necessities of housing, clothing, and food that is), to be a consumer in the United States took on new meaning. New styles of life emerged. "Prosperity meant a shift from purely utilitarian to symbolic goods," Gary Cross emphasized. Fashionable home furnishings, fashionable clothing, up-to-date appliances, and especially new cars could express new versions of oneself, of one's community, and, additionally, new understandings of past and future, he wrote. "Through their packaging, display, and advertising, consumer goods came to embody a distinct and eventually dominant alternative to political and even religious visions of American life."[51] Needless to say, Roadside America, especially out on the commercial strips of suburbia, figured prominently.

The geographer Thomas J. Baerwald, looking at the I-494 freeway corridor south of Minneapolis, Minnesota, identified phases by which a whole new kind of downtown had evolved, including development of the nation's largest shopping

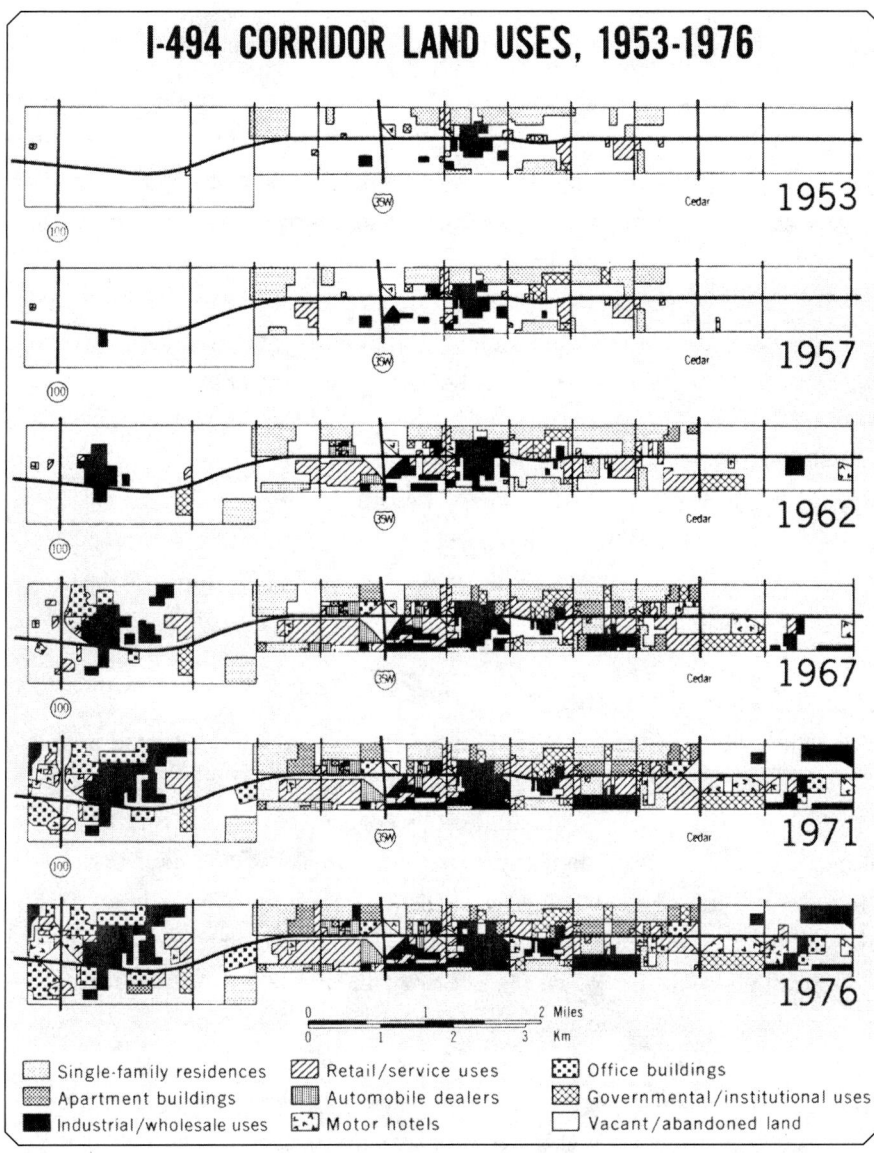

Figure 3.6. Changing land use along I-474, Bloomington, Minnesota, 1953–76. In a Minneapolis suburb a freeway corridor has spawned urbanization that is highly reminiscent of a traditional big-city downtown and its immediate surround—retailing, wholesaling, and light industry are concentrated together. From Thomas J. Baerwald, "The Emergence of a New 'Downtown,'" *Geographical Review* 68 (July 1978): 312. Courtesy of the American Geographical Society.

mall, the Mall of America (fig. 3.6). "The suburban freeway corridor," he wrote in 1978, "now houses a complete mix of the business establishments regularly frequented by the geographically mobile middle- and upper-class residents of the modern metropolis. Light industrial plants, warehouses, and office buildings along the freeway employ breadwinners; homemakers shop at large supermarkets and regional shopping malls; and motor hotels, bars, restaurants, nightclubs, and sports complexes attract those in search of entertainment."[52] Alternative business districts, or "Edge Cities" as journalist Joel Garreau called them, were rapidly rising (quite literally with skyscrapers) around the nation's largest cities.[53] As clusters of office buildings, hotels, and large shopping centers, they were invariably freeway-oriented. The historian Peter G. Rowe's *Making a Middle Landscape* contains a concise overview of shopping-center and shopping-mall development through the 1980s.[54] But for specific case studies one turns to the work of the architectural historian Richard W. Longstreth, especially his *City Center to Regional Mall: Architecture, the Automobile, and Retailing in Los Angeles, 1920–1950*.[55]

Roadside Architecture

With the commercial strip established as something worth appreciating, if only for its centrality in twentieth-century urban development, an extensive literature emerged to focus on the buildings of Roadside America. Especially influential was Chester H. Liebs's *Main Street to Miracle Mile: American Roadside Architecture*, published in 1985. Liebs looked carefully at different kinds of commercial strips, especially "taxpayer" strips (which evolved along central-city streetcar lines in the early days of motoring) and the new "miracle-miles" (fully auto-oriented strips that came later in the suburbs). More important, he focused on various kinds of businesses (including gasoline stations, motels, restaurants, putt-putt golf courses, and drive-in movie theaters), tracing the rising popularity of different architectural styles. He emphasized architectural styling rather than building type.[56] For Liebs most roadside structures represented "a marriage of architecture and advertising, a blend of building and sign."[57] Roadside architecture was meant for "speed reading."[58] → Consistency? Target always looks like Target

Other writers variously emphasized architectural styling, building type, business function, and cultural meaning. Most authors sought to trace historical evolution, including how roadside elements actually fit into roadside landscapes. Scholarly articles and books accumulated, along with coffee-table picture books directed more to general readers. Writing focused on gas stations, motels, roadside restaurants, and roadside signage.[59] Diverse other topics included, drive-in movie theaters, supermarkets, car dealerships, and even on parking lots.[60] Roadside tourist attractions were also treated.[61] Books focused on the history of specific corporations central to roadside selling were important as well.[62] Treatment of roadside architecture was invariably included in books dealing with specific highways, and books on Route 66 led the way.[63] Other highways of note included the Dixie Highway, the Lincoln Highway, the old National Road, and the Yellowstone Trail.[64] Many photography books were devoted to various highways or just highways in general.[65]

Much of the writing on roadside architecture emphasized "ducks" rather than "decorated sheds" (figs. 1.6 and 3.7). That was especially true of coffee-table books that tended to emphasize roadsides of the past rather than of the present day. Often combining historical photographs (including postcard art) and historical advertising images with contemporary photography of old things, authors tended to stress the unique or the exotic in roadside buildings. Although not intended as scholarly works, these books add up to a most valuable literature. They offer a concise summation as to how Roadside America evolved. Those books printed in full color especially remind us of how Roadside America once attracted attention.

Figure 3.7. Shell gasoline station, Winston-Salem, North Carolina, 1981.

However, with emphasis on the unique or the unusual, relatively little attention was given to what actually typified roadsides in the past or, for that matter, typified contemporary roadsides. "Ducks" were common really only for a short time—during the 1920s mainly. Financing was difficult to obtain for unique structures that were not readily reusable, at least for purposes other than an original business program. A restaurant shaped like a lighthouse made a poor dress shop, and, of course, was likely not located appropriately. Bankers until recent decades thought in terms of generic architecture, that is, buildings capable of housing any kind of business, and they thought primarily in terms of traditional business streets with their look-alike storefronts. Corporate America, the petroleum companies for example, quickly found traditional architecture of little value, including the numerous garages erected in business districts in the years just before and after World War I. Much preferred for retailing, the specialized structure communicated something about the products and services available. For petroleum companies it was the standardized gas station, although what constituted standardization changed over time.

It was the decorated shed, in other words, that won out in Roadside America. But there were sheds and then sheds. In gas-station design a range of standardized building types can be identified through the twentieth century (fig. 3.8). They were part of an emerging architectural vernacular that emphasized form as much as styling, if not more so. Yet most authors writing on roadside architecture have emphasized styling or ornamentation over form. Liebs gave full elaboration to style, dealing with all the widely accepted historical styles, including nineteenth-century revival styles, such as Greek Revival, and on to more recent styles, such as twentieth-century Art Deco and Streamline Moderne. But he also tackled motifs that seemed to be emergent at the time of his writing, calling them "looks": the environmental look, the old building look, and the high tech look.[66]

In twentieth-century gasoline retailing three building types assumed primacy over time; each form reflected an important shift in industry marketing strategy, shifts that can not be understood solely in terms of architectural styling.[67] The "house with canopy" station reflected a time of very cheap gasoline when companies needed a small, and thus inexpensive, building type that would be acceptable along urban thoroughfares, especially those in residential areas (fig. 3.9). Gas stations needed to fit in. The "oblong box" station, on the other hand, reflected the economic downtown of the Great Depression. With gasoline

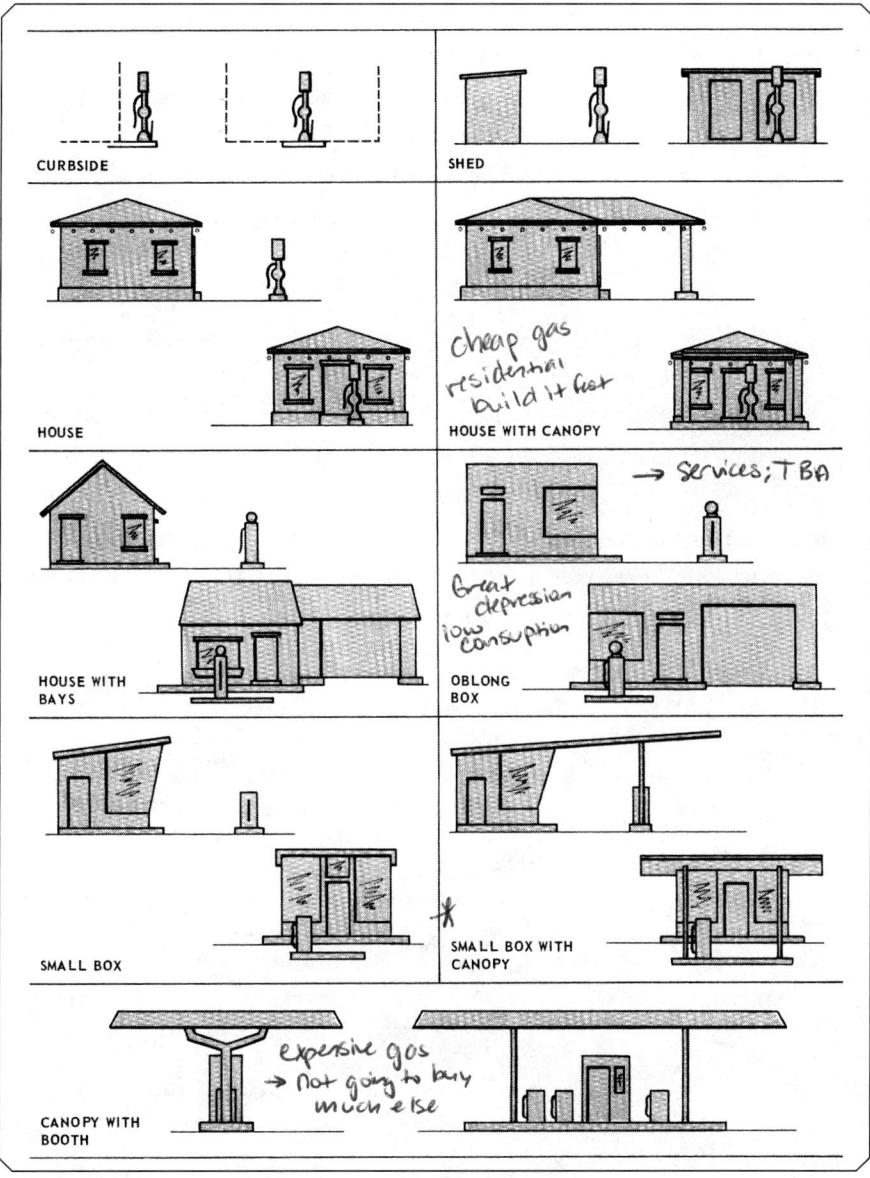

Figure 3.8. Gasoline station building types predominant in the United States, 1910–90. From Jakle and Sculle, *The Gas Station in America* (1994), 134. Courtesy of Johns Hopkins University Press, Baltimore.

consumption down, corporations embraced enhanced car servicing (lubricating, light engine repair, and washing) and the sale of so-called TBA (tires, batteries, and accessories) products (figs. 1.8 and 3.10). The "canopy and booth" station reflected the rapid increase in the price of gasoline following the Arab oil embargo of 1973, when "big pumpers" that were corporate-owned or owned by wholesale jobbers came to the fore (fig. 3.11). Everything gave way to today's convenience store, where the large canopy, more often than not, remains as an important signature of place.

Automobile servicing changed drastically when car engines were computerized. Gas station mechanics could no longer handle the engines' complexity. Car service was reduced mainly to lubricating and washing. The computerization of the gas pumps, of course, brought self-service to gasoline retailing, precipitating further change in how gas stations were staffed. In the 1990s Environmental Protection Agency requirements imposed expensive retrofitting of underground storage tanks, which resulted in the closure of most of the nation's older gas stations. The traditional gas station became a roadside relic.

Looking to the Future

Although Americans often assume that change mostly brings progress, it can also bring regression and decline. Along many older commercial strip vintage gas stations do not stand alone. One encounters old motels, many converted to

Figure 3.9. A "house with canopy" gas station, Constantine, Michigan, 1978.

rentals by the week or the month, attracting not only transients who are less affluent than the guests had been, but often the unsavory as well—drug dealers and prostitutes among others. Or the structures just stand abandoned (figs. 3.12 and 3.13). Increasingly, vintage shopping centers are used only marginally or are abandoned altogether (fig. 3.14). Underutilization, disinvestment, vacancy, and

Figure 3.10. An "oblong box" gas station, Champaign, Illinois, 1976. This gas station design dominated gasoline retailing from the mid-1930s through the 1960s.

Figure 3.11. A "canopy with booth" gas station, Chicago, Illinois, 1992. As "big pumpers" they cut gasoline prices through larger scale of operation, all other activities and product lines being eliminated.

Figure 3.12. Vintage Motel 66 on former Route 66, Tulsa, Oklahoma, 1985.

dereliction outline a process of change all too apparent on many an older commercial strip, especially those bypassed by new highways or simply located in areas of poverty.[68]

Age, of course, takes its toll. Strips like everything else mature, often in clear stages from youth to old age. Today many vintage strips are undergoing rebirth, especially as a part of neighborhood gentrification in central cities. Concern with "first generation" or "secondhand" strips, as Timothy Davis called them, has grown rapidly in recent years. Buildings take on new functions (a gas station converted to a coffee shop, for example), but often they are also given a new look, restyled in one or another version of academic postmodernism—a fashion trend that owes much, according to Davis, to memories of roadside architecture, especially the funky stuff early on that was displaced by the "austere facades of mass-market modernism."[69]

Strips were bound to change. Edmund Faltermayer foresaw some of what was coming, although he substantially misjudged what the nation's response would be. In *Redoing America*, he wrote: "Sooner or later the existing commercial strips will have to be done over, and some of the worst stretches will have to be ripped out completely." His reasoning was quite pragmatic. The worse strips run through suburbia's valuable front yard, he said, where much of the nation's future population growth would be concentrated. With planning, he thought,

Figure 3.13. Abandoned motel property on U.S. 19, Perry, Florida, 2004.

strips could be "turned to advantage." Optimistically, he predicted, "Some of the land now consumed by hamburger stands and scattered used-car lots can be more intensively developed with apartment houses, shopping centers, and office buildings, or simply cleared and planted with grass and trees to supplement the meager parklands in the newer suburbs."[70]

In areas of growth, commercial strips change constantly, much of it only cosmetic—buildings, for example, are given new signs or simple facade upgrades. But buildings are also replaced with frequency—so much so that locals who regularly frequent a given roadside may have trouble remembering what was once there. The United States remains in an era of rapid redevelopment, especially in the suburbs around major cities. Redevelopment forms along major corridors of movement—along the vital "arteries of commerce" that tend mainly to be commercial strips. Interestingly planning, as Faltermayer termed it, imposed few rules in most local jurisdictions—strip zoning being concerned mainly with issues of auto access (the locating of driveways) and off-street parking (the dedicating of space for the cars of customers and employees). Parking is a major zoning issue, and the ubiquitous parking lot is perhaps the most important common denominator of strips everywhere.

Where zoning restrictions have been abolished, or where they were never imposed, strip evolution has produced some striking results. Houston, Texas,

Figure 3.14. Vacant shopping center, Inwood Avenue, Dallas, Texas, 1989.

the nation's fourth largest city, has never had zoning, relying mostly on property deed restrictions to control or stabilize land use. Implicit restrictions lapse legally after set periods, thus giving property owners the flexibility of eventually rehabilitating or replacing buildings on their properties. Some extraordinary commercial strips are found in the city today, so diverse as to be exciting to the eye. What strikes most visitors and residents alike is the surprising juxtaposition of such things as gas stations, fast-food restaurants, and used-car lots, all often overloaded with advertising signs, with elegant office and apartment towers that are often surrounded by elegant landscaping (fig. 3.15).

In Las Vegas, "The Strip" of Venturi's, Scott Brown's, and Izenour's sleuthing no longer exists. It has been largely replaced by an extravaganza of huge casino/hotel complexes, which are self-contained minicities in themselves. The rhythm of the strip remains, however, with the new casinos, like their predecessors, distributed up and down the thoroughfare at regular intervals. They are now huge complexes with truly impressive hotel towers. Also, rather than using mainly desert themes as previously (the Sands, the Desert Inn, and so on), the new complexes mimic the world's greatest tourist attractions—Paris, Venice, or, as pictured here, New York City's Manhattan (fig. 3.16). Nonetheless "The Strip" in Las Vegas no longer reads the same, in part because so many of the small, auto-

Figure 3.15. Westheimer Road near Post Oaks Center, Houston, Texas, 1996.

oriented businesses along the street (the gas stations, the fast food restaurants, the wedding chapels, and the like) are gone. Additionally the new casinos open differently to the street, as many now have pedestrian-friendly courtyards. Largely missing, at least out front, are the large porte-cocheres and their nearby parking lots. Las Vegas Boulevard has become more pedestrian-oriented as the hoards of visitors regularly seen strolling its sidewalks fully attest (fig. 3.17). The larger-than-ever electric signs of the strip and those along Fremont Street in the city's old downtown continue to create a light extravaganza at night, but now they are joined by the hotel towers, most of them outlined in neon or otherwise sheathed in light (fig. 3.18).

Strip development in Las Vegas has seemingly produced not just a whole new kind of casino architecture, but indeed a whole new kind of city—what the architect Alan Hess has called a "strip city." "It may be just as well that most professional planners left strips alone as they grew," Hess mused. "Freed from the strictures of architectural theory and high-art taste, strips could often respond to the economic energy, commercial forces, and cultural inspiration at play in mid-century America." Rather than developing methodically, Las Vegas's Strip grew "by experiment, mistakes, wild visions, pragmatic solutions, and chaotic collage." It did become a kind of "collective art" as thousands of independent decisions

Figure 3.16. Approach to the New York, New York Casino, Las Vegas Boulevard, Las Vegas, Nevada, 2002.

"by clients, architects, sign artists, government officials, and marketing mystics (divining the taste of the people) accumulated over the decades."[71] The Las Vegas Strip may or may not have become an ideal urban model, Hess concluded. But it was well worth considering as such as the nation continued to grope toward new definitions of what cities ought to be. Las Vegas was, he said, an honest outgrowth of automobility—a half-century of "car culture and its remodeling of the city."[72]

Roadside America has always been about attracting the eye, particularly the eye of the motorist. Roadside architecture is all about buildings and signs combined to attract visually in "speed reading." But what makes it work? Las Vegas is all about entertainment, of course. "The Strip" is not about convenience so much as entertainment. But then, entertainment is what all of Roadside America as been at least partially about. The fiction writer Peter S. Beagle penned in 1965 a novelette, *I See By My Outfit,* that follows its hero across country on a motorbike. In Las Vegas the adventurer marveled at the Strip, not yet the grand extravaganza of today, but a place that was amazing enough. The "magnificently tasteless facades floated by, shivering like mirages of cuckoo clocks and wedding cakes, of gingerbread houses and funeral homes and Howard Johnson's." What

Figure 3.17. Las Vegas Boulevard, Las Vegas, Nevada, 2002.

he saw was at once fully expected but yet very much surprising. His travel guide established that eminent entertainers displayed their talents in the casino nightclubs. "Yes, I know about this part of town," he said. "I have been to so many movies, seen so many night-club acts televised, memorized and chanted so much show-business mythology, that I could probably draw a map of the Strip without mislaying too many colorful casinos."[73]

The geographer Kent McDonald pursued a similar track, tying the ordinary commercial roadside firmly into the context of television entertainment, which he saw as increasingly dominating the nation's view of itself in the 1980s. The commercial strip was entering a period in which the nation's "latest love"—television—had begun to mediate the typical American's experience of environment. "Nowadays," he wrote, "as much as we like to drive, we like to watch. And through the 'windshield' of our television screens we derive much of our information about the world." Especially important, of course, were the commercials. Kent McDonald was writing at a time when McDonald's—the fast food chain—was television's largest advertiser. "We experience McDonald's, Wendy's, and Exxon, both out on the road and in the transient images of television," he wrote, "and the mutual dependency of the road and television has changed our architecture. The Strip has become the Television Road."⁷⁴ What he insinuated, of course, is place-product packaging, the reconfiguring of roadside architecture well within overall corporate marketing initiatives, including advertising through mass media—originally in newspapers and magazines as well as through outdoor advertising, and then on radio, but more recently on television and websites.

Was the world viewed through television screens actually being grafted onto the motorist's view of the road? Roadside entrepreneurs had realized early on that success depended first on adapting sales pitches to the reduced field of vision imposed by car windshields. They instinctively knew that drivers could process only a limited amount of information as they sped by. The pedestrian's freedom—"the ability to stop and turn easily to backtrack, and, most important, to linger and look"—was lost when he or she "grew wheels," McDonald said.⁷⁵ One could not just stand leisurely in front of a display window and browse any more.

Symbolic heraldry had come to the fore, and that symbolization in turn had been extended to entire buildings—buildings as symbols in and of themselves. The next logical step, perhaps, was to use television advertising to add the details—or at least to allow motorists, as potential customers, to remember details conducive to their stopping and their buying. In the 1980s actual signage on many roadside businesses was reduced to little more than logos. Signs displayed little information about the actual products and services available. But then no additional information was actually needed since it had all been communicated already—transmitted previously by television. The information necessary for deciding where to stop for food or buy gas had already been provided. One only had to identify the place. "The overt message is only half the story," McDonald wrote. "The subtlety of the staging, lighting, costumes, and music in the television commercials conveys messages just as important as the overt ones." These indirect messages were the video equivalents of architectural appliqué. It was of course all illusion. "When we enter a McDonald's outlet, we do not really expect to see a marching band, corn-fed teenagers behind the counter, or nine-foot clowns. Still, when we are out driving and we see the golden arches, it is difficult to stifle those images that flicker again in our mind's eye."⁷⁶

* * *

What American roadsides will become, and just how they will figure in American life in the future, is anybody's guess. As long as cars remain central to getting around, however, commercial strips will certainly remain of vital importance and central to how we organize physical environment, especially in urban places. Just what role various media will play in sustaining such centrality remains to be seen. Television's computer graphics might well push Roadside America back into an age of fantastical or whimsical delights, making the pre–World War II era of kitsch seem merely flaky in comparison. On the other hand, another era of modernistic standardization might be launched, if only in reaction to today's postmodernism and its quirkiness.

What impact will interactive computer graphics have on Roadside America? Already the on-line selecting and ordering of consumer goods by computer and then having them delivered directly to one's door by truck looms large. Will this mean that less retailing will be roadside-oriented? Will it mean that only selected services and selected convenience goods (food and other perishables, perhaps) will be offered there? Our guess is that the nation's commercial strips will remain important as engines of consumption, but not as they are now constituted. Probably they will be less fully retail-oriented and thus open to a wider variety of land uses, including residential uses. They will probably be built to higher building densities, with mass transit likely playing an enhanced role in their development, especially should gasoline prices soar. Roadside architecture will certainly continue to evolve, driven by new stylistic fads and fashions if nothing else.

As change continues apace, vintage Roadside America will prove vulnerable. Gone will be much of what we see and use today, making it all the more vital that we think seriously about protecting at least selected aspects of today's, if not yesterday's, roadsides. Roadside America has for several generations now constituted an important kind of container for everyday life. Without physical evidence surviving through the years, future Americans may find it difficult to understand that history. They may not remember their roadside "roots" as a society. For historic preservationists, especially those concerned with protecting the "recent past," Roadside America should loom as something worthy of careful consideration. So also it should loom large for those who collect and interpret the material culture of the past in museums, especially outdoor museums where the culture of past built environments can, if so desired, be interpreted at the scale of landscape and place.

Figure 3.18. The Golden Gate Casino and Hotel, Fremont Avenue, Las Vegas, Nevada, 2002.

CHAPTER FOUR
PRESERVING ROADS AND ROADSIDES

*N*owhere was twentieth-century modernism embraced quite as fully as in the United States, at least as evidenced along the roadside. Nowhere were so many cars manufactured and so many roads built or rebuilt. And nowhere else in the world were towns and cities so substantially reinvented, as they were essentially turned inside-out in reorientation to those roads. Only in America did roadside selling evolve so quickly and was the commercial strip fully accepted as a way of organizing space. In no other part of the world was such change deemed so progressive. Only in the United States, perhaps, was change itself so unquestioned, especially as wholly new kinds of auto-oriented landscapes and places came to the fore. Not until well after World War II, when modernism's acceptance seemed complete, did traditional landscapes and places rooted in the pre-automobile era become valued. The historic preservation movement in the United States originated as people recognized the need to save buildings of extraordinary merit.

Most historic preservationists seriously questioned unfettered automobility. When the nation's suburbs boomed out along new highways and as old neighborhoods in towns and cities declined, many of them were disrupted by new freeways, and the flight of affluent Americans accelerated, especially white Americans. In large city centers federally funded urban renewal programs wrought the wholesale destruction of traditional landscapes and places, and much valuable historic architecture was placed in jeopardy. Parking became the largest land use in the central business districts of large cities, with most becoming little more than skyscrapers in parking-lot surrounds. Even monuments of obvious heritage value were unsafe. In all of this, the automobile was made out to be the villain.

In recent decades, when preservationists began to move beyond saving individual structures to whole landscapes (or historic districts), Roadside America was not what came to mind (fig. 4.1). If the automobile was running roughshod over old landscapes and places, then even those built environments that were directly automobile-generated seemed to many preservationists to be villainous themselves. Additionally Roadside America was notoriously changeful. Little survived there long enough to be very old, let alone historically significant. Changefulness was intrinsic (fig. 4.2). As we have argued, flexibility, through flimsiness of construction, for example, or the placing of buildings on big lots with room for expansion, was implicit in most roadside architecture. Constant facade renovation and changed signage also typified the landscape. Roadside America has always been about future "becomingness." Accordingly "forgetfulness" has been all too easy.

Nonetheless automobility, although not alone as a technological force for modernization, was perhaps the major instrument of environmental or geographic change in twentieth-century America. So it continues in the twenty-first century. And understanding requires degrees of preservation—preservation of

Figure 4.1. Historic preservationists preferred to idealize humankind and nature in harmony so that human inventions such as the automobile would gain welcome admission. The back of this postcard from the early twentieth century rhapsodizes about the sightseeing bus at Lookout Mountain, Tennessee: "There is hardly a spot on any road reaching the city that does not afford a scene of beauty."

aspects of built environment that are reflective of automobility's coming to the fore. Architecture, considered alone, may not be enough. Landscapes and places ought to be front and center, especially built environments that were fully organized in the past through automobile-oriented convenience. In other words vintage Roadside America ought to be the main focus. Is this possible? What role might historic preservations play?

Historic Preservation's Expanding Objectives

No matter what the subject of their efforts, almost all those who have worked for preservation over the years have sought the maintenance of a hallowed sense of place in their hometown, city, state, or region. It is no overstatement to say that historic preservation is a civic faith.

Historic preservation in the United States has routinely been dated from 1850, although the inclination to save buildings and commemorate a battlefield can be traced back to the late eighteenth century.[1] The start is marked at 1850 because in that year the Hasbrouck House in Newburgh, New York, Washington's headquarters in the final two years of the Revolution, was the first success.

Figure 4.2. Hot 'n Now, Kalamazoo, Michigan, 2009. The double drive-through for hamburger chains is representative of the brevity of individual styles and even companies along the roadside. Hot 'n Now and the double drive-through survived only twenty years.

Preservation in previous cases failed for want of funds or support despite the historic significance of the structures involved.[2] In explaining why the state of New York was asked to invest in the preservation of the Hasbrouck House, the governor of the state said, "how much more will the flame of patriotism burn in our bosoms when we tread the ground where was shed the blood of our fathers, or when we move among the scenes where were conceived and consummated their noble achievements."[3] Preservationists customarily employ a moralistic vocabulary, imparting a transcendence or religious quality to their work. "The majority of those who joined the movement saw it as a crusade," in the words of one preservation historian.[4]

Over the years it has also been characteristic of historic preservation that individuals have coalesced into groups such as "the friends of" some particular building, site, or monument to work for a wider public recognition of its significance and these groups have mobilized support at critical intervals without any intention of forming wider affiliations. Goals have been satisfied often with organizations sufficient just for those aims and without the need for long-standing bodies and great clout. Commentators generally observe that private work has characterized preservation from its earliest days, whereas government involvement has emerged comparatively recently. Until the passage of the National Historic Preservation Act in 1966, power remained in the exercise of individual missions and not in state much less federal authority. Historic preservation has been for most of its life what can be labeled a grass-roots movement.[5] This imparts an often-inefficient structure to preservation in the United States but one very open to the perceived public benefit. This may, however, test the bounds of credulity in a quite power-conscious era.

For slightly more than half a century after 1853, the Mount Vernon Ladies Association of the Union set the founding paradigm for historic preservation in the United States. Worth underscoring here is the contribution of women in the public work of preservation; women have been important from the outset and have remained so. The prevailing paradigm included these principles: (1) sites of significance had associative value, that is, places where important people lived or worked and/or events occurred; (2) military and/or political people were of paramount importance; and (3) preservation was achieved through private, not governmental, initiatives.[6] The swell of patriotic organizations at the nineteenth century's end was possible in part because of the talent of the female manager and assistants trained in the Mount Vernon Association in Virginia and its national network.[7]

By the early twentieth century, the sources feeding the preservation movement proliferated. In addition to the patriotic theme and its associative significance, there was the significance of aesthetic value.[8] William Sumner Appleton took one of the first steps in 1910, when he formed the Society for the Preservation of New England Antiquities. Appleton's interests ranged from buildings of architectural merit to places that were of lesser merit themselves but suitable as settings for historic furnishings.[9]

Meanwhile, inside New York City, the American Scenic and Historic Preservation Society, as its bifurcated name indicates, attached meaning to the look of things as well as their remembered history. It aimed at an appreciation of not only buildings but urban parks, battlefields, and natural areas antedating the city's rapid growth in the industrial era and consolidation in 1898. Although this farsighted attention to what would later be called "cultural landscapes" achieved some victories, there was a lack of regulations such as those later concerned with landscapes.[10]

These aesthetic movements about landscapes may appear as natural antecedents to road and roadside preservation in the late twentieth century, but in fact they stood apart from that later work and were not referred to by later-day preservationists of the automobile age or by intellectuals of a like mind. The early twentieth century's aesthetic preservation capitalized on broad popular appeal yet it remained didactic, a preachment to do right. In contrast road and roadside preservation nearly a full century later welled up from challenges to the established aesthetic canon. It was populist in origins, an expression of democratic faith.

In the last half of the twentieth century, preservation changed from an activity of a comparative few "to a passion shared by large numbers of ordinary Americans."[11] Formation of the National Trust for Historic Preservation in 1949 gave historic preservation in the United States a privately based national presence with federal sanction. The trust administered a group of nationally important buildings, and in 1956 the holder of a doctorate in classical studies became its first president.[12] The trust's sentiment remained initially disposed in favor of places from elite culture. Its intellectual moorings, however, eventually would be reoriented toward a more inclusive definition of what was suitable to save. To a considerable degree, the work of the Department of the Interior in the late

1930s to identify places of significance had spurred the trust's founding and passed on the charge to look at "the historical landscape rather than a few isolated sites," according to historic preservation's first historian.[13] Shortly after the trust's founding, it established the Committee on Standards and Survey, whose expanded definition of what constituted a historic site would influence the work of the National Register.[14]

Historic preservation had accomplished much by the mid–twentieth century. Yet, as is inherent in a growing and more widely creditable movement, more change was in the offing. Elitism undergirded the newer preservation about architecture as it had originated the movement in the celebration of patriotic sites.[15] The latter formed a sizable share of the sites preservationists had saved from destruction or decay but emphasis rested with the oeuvre of great architects, the celebration of their affluent clients, and their display in fashionable and monumental sites or buildings. Where landscapes were included, they were carefully designed ones, not utilitarian ensembles of vernacular origins. Such landscapes were hardly ubiquitous, and their rarity made them valuable in the estimation of fine arts arbiters. As a consequence, the most influential of early historic preservation pedagogues, James Marston Fitch, couched his directives in the terms of fine art and artifacts, subtitling his primer "curatorial management."[16] History often occupied a secondary status because its places were not universally acknowledged by architects concerned with architectural significance, and historians were often of local stature without academic standing. The local interests were seldom esteemed among academicians.[17] Local history was judged to be the pursuit of dilettantes, or so academicians considered them. History among local students was attributable to influential individuals and events. History is process, and by the mid-twentieth century social-class relationships remained largely outside the scope of determining which places deserved historic preservation. Not until the "New Social History" in the 1970s would academicians commonly take up topics that led them into local history.[18]

The entrée to road and roadside resources in the pantheon of sites that had been "ennobled" as worthy of historic preservation came with the National Historic Preservation Act of 1966. The Special Committee on Historic Preservation, under the auspices of the United States Conference of Mayors and with a Ford Foundation grant, convened in 1965 to look into how the federal government's urban renewal and interstate construction's radical change of the American landscape could make a safe harbor for historic buildings. "Lady Bird" Johnson, the First Lady at the time, had a general concern with environmental control, or beautification, in the 1960s that mirrored the younger converts' amazement at the extent of ruined or razed resources of acknowledged pedigree. She was upset that almost half of the twelve thousand structures listed in the Historic American Buildings Survey had been razed. The wanton destruction, she believed, could not be stopped soon enough, and she concluded in prophetic words, in keeping with preservation's consistently moralistic fervor that "prompt action" was required.[19]

The Special Committee on Historic Preservation concluded with a set of recommendations. They called for (1) a comprehensive federal policy to guide other federal programs; (2) an advisory council on historic preservation to achieve action between the relevant government agencies, the states, the local governments, and groups in the general public; (3) "a greatly expanded National Register program to inventory and catalogue" places nationwide as well as offer federal assistance and public information from the inventory; (4) federal financial assistance for federal acquisition and expansion of urban renewal to non-cash contributions for such acquisition; (5) federal financial assistance to expand state and local preservation programs; and (6) financial aid for and through the National Trust.[20] The National Historic Preservation Act of 1966, which embodied these recommendations, triggered a "frenzy of activity" that made "the years leading up to its passage seem tranquil by comparison."[21] The 1970s witnessed an unprecedented commitment to the identification and understanding of resources as an essential preliminary step to their protection.[22]

The authors can attest to their own awakened beliefs in this productive whirlwind within their home state of Illinois. It was in their collaborative work for the Illinois Historic Structures Survey that they innocently came upon the Greek Revival gas station mentioned at the start of this book. Keith A. Sculle was completing the survey in twenty-six Illinois counties to help fulfill a small part of the third point, above, in the Special Committee's recommendations. Between 1974 and 1976 John A. Jakle, drawn to the preservation calling, also held a seat on one of the first Illinois Historic Sites Advisory Councils created to increase the state's National Register listings, also to fulfill its obligations under the third point listed above. In this realm of newly identified resources and their official public certification, the discovery of road and roadside resources occurred.

The authors' participation in one state is simply a single narrative like many others set off nationwide. In North Carolina a surveyor receptive to industrial archaeology—a newly founded field in the preservation renaissance of the 1970s—and the staff of the State Historic Preservation Office (SHPO) provided documentation for and then guided the designation of the first gasoline station to be individually listed in the National Register of Historic Places.[23] This was the Quality Oil Company's now renowned "sea shell" gasoline station in Winston-Salem, North Carolina.[24] Three years later a member of the New York SHPO long persuaded of technology's power over social change and an active preservationist, later the State Historic Preservation Officer, effected the second gasoline station's way into the National Register of Historic Places.[25] This was the Pure Oil Company's "English cottage" in Saratoga Springs, New York, saved in 1978 from an urban-renewal project made weary of inadvertently razing any historic resources since the Special Committee's final recommendations.

Concurrent with attention to previously ignored or unthinkable structures, preservation experienced a movement-wide renaissance. Academic courses, degrees in preservation design, and careers in preservation, plus the work of the National Trust and the National Register, gave new life to the movement. Its philosophical underpinnings were also aggressively reexamined.[26] Optimism and excitement characterized preservation in the 1970s.

Landscape, as the concept necessary for the preservation of road and roadside resources in situ, has still barely entered the consciousness and vocabulary of most preservationists. Not until the awareness of cultural landscapes as part of preservation's ferment in the late 1970s and 1980s did preservationists conceive of landscapes as something in addition to the material culture inherent in the spaces under consideration. Landscapes were gardens or grounds adjoining mansions that had been conceived, set up, and curated. Or they were natural areas of concern to environmentalists. Commenting on the need for a new preservation strategy beginning in the 1990s, an attorney and zoning commissioner noted that "because preservation concerns have broadened ... it makes good pragmatic sense to forge new alliances with environmental groups of virtually every type."[27] The inclusion of historic districts in the National Register of Historic Places, at first in defense against urban renewal projects, considerably advanced public awareness that buildings or sites alone were insufficient to preserve resources to the fullest. The ever-expanding definition of preservation-worthy resources moved to "cultural landscapes" by the late 1970s.[28] The National Park Services' education series, "Preservation Briefs," utilized the term *cultural landscapes* for a broad readership. There were four varieties. One of the four categories, the "historic vernacular landscape," might seem by its name to include the road's and the roadside's places, but the examples given avoided the road and roadside: "rural villages, industrial complexes, and agricultural landscapes."[29] Even a recently published intellectually progressive anthology on cultural landscapes brushed past the automobile culture's suburbia with only a mere mention of commercial strips and shopping malls and no in-depth treatment.[30]

Enactment of the Native American Grave Protection and Repatriation Act of 1990 (NAGPRA) finally took the step of recognizing the value of sites and objects not within the hegemonic elites' value system, although this is not to say that Native Americans were advocating for the admission of the road's and roadside's commercial and industrial values.[31] Notwithstanding the very different, even opposed value system between Native American concerns and those of road and roadside aficionados, NAGPRA can be credited with finding a place for what had been previously ignored or, in the case of road and roadside, for resources seen as enemies of preservation itself. A liberalizing reform helped make a respectable niche for otherwise dubious resources in a diversified society.

Geographers understand "landscape" in the more nuanced way akin to Native Americans than the earlier definers who thought in terms of a completely objectified and monocultural sense. Geographers attend to the material remains on or above ground at a particular site but also the various associations they stimulate in different individuals or groups. The commercial strip, for example, can be desired as a constellation of various buildings and sites evolved from the consumer culture and technology, but it means different things to different people. Although they were fixed in the past and alterable only on the condition of newfound evidence such as archaeological items or personal correspondence, these meanings are constantly elaborated and redefined in the present.[32] Landscape at its fullest means something more than architecture, and landscapes are holistic entities, being both cognitive and material.[33] It is because of landscape's very mutability that its preservation deserves serious attention, especially in the case of the road and roadside where meaning still unfolds.

Advocates for Road and/or Roadside Preservation

What difficulties did road and/or roadside preservation face? Who has concerned themselves with the challenges to date, whether they involved architecture or ensembles of architecture and place in fully defined landscapes? What has this advocacy accomplished? Road and roadside preservation faced challenges as no other resources had for the very reason that their central meaning was at odds with the goodness that preservation had held heretofore. Because of the acceleration of change in the nationwide economy and resultant erosion of the local sense of place throughout the nation from the late nineteenth century forward, preservation satisfied the yearning for memory and local identity. The project of building the institutions, and conceiving a shared past to which Americans were so firmly committed throughout the nineteenth century, produced the dialectical reaction of saving whatever was perceived to have local meaning. Sites and rituals of local significance multiplied simultaneously from the nineteenth throughout the early twentieth century.[34]

Accommodating the automobile was something preservationists could not ignore once the automobile age dawned. Where were cars to go—moving cars, but also parked ones? This was especially so of historic preservation activity across a sizable area—a historic district, for example, encompassing an entire urban neighborhood. An early case in point was Old Salem in Winston-Salem, North Carolina, the section of that city settled beginning in the 1760s by members of the Moravian Church. Close to downtown on the city's near south side, a considerable number of late-eighteenth- and early-nineteenth-century buildings clustered there, many of them arrayed along Main Street, which had by the 1920s become one of the city's main traffic arteries, U.S. 52. In succeeding decades gas stations and other road-oriented businesses had intruded, and many of the area's houses were converted to rented apartments. In 1950 Old Salem Inc. was organized to buy, rehabilitate, and resell properties for purposes of neighborhood upgrading, retaining ownership of some buildings for museum purposes.[35]

Cars were a fact of life. Automobility would have to be managed if the neighborhood's historical ambience was to be fully enhanced. A bypass road was built to carry through-traffic around the area. Local traffic was not prohibited, and parked cars continued to line Main Street and its cross streets. However, street surfaces were repaved to look old, as if surfaced by vintage macadam. Standard traffic signs were removed and replaced by small, highly flexible, rubberized signs placed unobtrusively in the streets themselves. Brought back to life through gentrification, this was an extraordinary place, and the automobile had been held partially in check in the process (fig. 4.3). Along Main Street today is a sign that first adorned a tinsmith shop in the 1850s. It is perhaps the oldest roadside sign extant in the United States (fig. 4.4).

The nation's early historic preservation set a barrier against roadside buildings. In Charleston, South Carolina, one of the birthplaces of preservation of extensive sections of a city, the automobile and its landscape accessories indeed were defined as the enemy—as the destroyer of grand, old buildings.[36] In the 1920s Standard Oil of New Jersey began to buy properties in Charleston at highly visible corners where main thoroughfares intersected. Eighteenth- and nineteenth-century mansion houses sitting on large corner lots were especially vulnerable. Their demolition for lowly gas stations clearly disrupted the traditional city's fabric, an action spawning preservation sentiment in its wake. So vocal did opponents become that Standard Oil quickly turned to designing their stations with "colonial" references in order to blend them into residential neighborhoods; many of the stations were veneered in brick salvaged from the very houses demolished to accommodate them.

Figure 4.3. Main Street, Old Salem, Winston-Salem, North Carolina, 1973. The towers of downtown show in the distance. In the foreground a traffic sign is embedded in the street and surfaced to look like vintage pavement. Historic architecture has been restored, but also a historic landscape or place, one well rooted in the pre-automobile past, which most historic preservation has emphasized in the United States to date.

Figure 4.4. The Old Coffee Pot, Main Street in Old Salem, Winston-Salem, North Carolina, 2005.

One gas station, which opened in the 1930s but is pictured here in the 1970s, still stands along Charleston's Meeting Street (fig. 4.5). The Historic Charleston Foundation has rehabilitated it for its Architecture Interpretation Center. Inside it is given almost exclusively to celebrating Charleston's surviving eighteenth- and nineteenth-century houses (fig. 4.6). Only a small display focuses memory on the fact that the center was originally a gas station and that once there were many just like it built in the city—gas stations trying desperately to be fit in. Their memory today is cherished no so much through respectable historical interpretation so much as through popular nostalgia (fig. 4.7).

The road and roadside ran directly counter to historic preservation's redemptive work. Those twin agents of economic change seemed to accelerate the process like no other before them. Their ubiquity was plainly evident to anyone paying attention to their invasive expansion and they seemed to assert an imperial domination. Older buildings were razed in order to construct the new infra-

Figure 4.5. Esso Standard gasoline station, Meeting Street, Charleston, South Carolina, 1977.

structure, and unoccupied space was gobbled up too. More cars to satisfy popular demand meant more highways and more services to feed and lodge the travelers and care for their vehicles. And the growth seemed unstoppable, out of control, and ugly. When corporate services surpassed those of small ownership, a bland sameness spread across the margins of the road, and, of course, with federal standards ascendant, roads looked alike everywhere—especially those that were part of the Interstate system. The local no longer meant a different appearance from place to place; it meant only a different location for the same place everywhere.

Several national public organizations have worked at raising awareness and in the process built an institutional structure for the judicious contemplation and preservation of road and roadside resources. Regardless of its opposition to highway construction as a destructive force and the commercial strip's constant encroachment into previously underdeveloped space, the National Trust for Historic Preservation pushed ahead on educational grounds. Most prominent early in these accomplishments was the presentation by the administrator of the trust's prestigious home and grounds of Daniel Chester French, Chesterwood, to the trust's annual meeting in 1975 on the subject of gasoline station architecture.[37]

Figure 4.6. Interior, Historic Charleston Foundation's Architectural Interpretation Center, 1996. Charleston's pre-automobile era architecture is emphasized along with the former gas station, itself little recognized as having architectural value.

The trust's *Preservation News* and *Preservation* have carried relevant news and magazine articles, respectively.[38]

In 1991, on the twenty-fifth anniversary of the National Historic Preservation Act of 1966, the National Trust convened a broadly based conference of amateur and professional preservationists, academicians, government officials, and laymen to think in broad terms of where preservation had come from and where it should go in the future. Long-range collaborative planning had come to the preservation movement. Many of the presenters whose papers were published in *Past Meets Future* raised important philosophical points; among them was Richard Longstreth with his work on the architecture of the recent past addressed to "removing taste from decisions," thereby pushing wider the door already ajar for a fuller reception of the roadside vernacular. He called on "professional judgment" to establish a building's historical significance, not its approval among people of taste; for "tastes vary; tastes change." As if historical significance rendered by professionals was not subject to change, Longstreth, however questionable in his own assumption, implicitly spoke well of road and roadside resources.[39] He la-

Figure 4.7. Bay Street construction site, Charleston, South Carolina, 2000. Contractors for a new high-rise building remember the former gas station that the new construction has replaced.

mented the ordinary roadside buildings that went unchampioned by students of architecture, such as the last outdoor custard stand in Fairfax County, Virginia.[40] He also challenged one of the cardinal principles of faith in the National Register, one that worked against roadside resources: a building less than fifty years old had to be of exceptional significance to be designated in the National Register.[41]

As preservation intellectuals assumed prominent leadership roles and longer-range planning gradually became characteristic of practitioners, roadside preservation also earned increased respect. Concurrent with the trust in the early 1990s, the National Park Service furthered validation of roadside resources through its publications. In *CRM* in 1993, an issue dedicated to "cultural resources from the recent past," the theme of the recent past's significance became a mantra, and an architectural historian with the National Register of Historic Places wrote about roadside preservation of individual buildings. "Disappearing Ducks and Other Recent Relics," the title of the contribution, disclosed a valid case for such preservation, yet one limited to architectural understanding, as can be understood from the use of the term *ducks,* as mentioned in Venturi's, Brown's, and Izenour's *Learning from Las Vegas*.[42] Repeating the theme of preserving the recent past, a well-attended and cosponsored conference resulted in 1995 in a publication that included an entire section on roadside gasoline stations, drive-in restaurants, and tourist courts.[43] *CRM* in 1996 featured a section entitled "The Automobile Landscape" with articles on individual parts, hardly the entire landscape: the Lincoln Highway, an early drive-in chain, the preservation of one gasoline station, and the loss of another.[44] An author in a previous section made extensive use of restaurants from the McDonald's, Wendy's, and White Castle chains to address the difficulties in dealing with the recent past.[45] Five years later, in 2000, conferees once again reprised the recent past theme but with an even greater sense of urgency about the identification, comprehension, and preservation.[46] Presentations on supermarkets in New Jersey and tiki-style restaurants and bars broadened the roadside inventory for preservationists.[47] Even parking garages—the most terrible of scourges in urban and suburban domains to most preservationists' way of thinking—gained a chapter in the resulting publication.[48] Had the exploratory phase of roadside resources reached an end as the devotees of various styles and building types gained admission among preservationists?

If respect for buildings of roadside commerce had been achieved among some individuals, it is not surprising that the ranks of preservationists, so greatly expanded over the century, now encompassed a heterogeneous assemblage of crusaders. It would be unrealistic to expect that roadside buildings would gain universal acceptance given the fact that different groups select and sustain their own memory of the past in every nation.[49] Not everyone had put aside their elitist persuasions. At the 2000 installment of the *Preserving the Recent Past* conference, nine years after Longstreth confirmed the doubts many held about resources unless they were of high style, he reported in print the "murmuring in the halls of preservation" about the post–World War II suburbs because they were so numerous and so big.[50] Two presenters at the same conference asked pointedly how those treasuring the "unique, rare, and unusual" could warm to "that which is ubiquitous, uniform, and composed of interchangeable parts." Many "early gas stations, drive-in movies, space-age style coffee shops, and the first generation of Las Vegas casinos" had been lost simply because of the rapid rate of change on the landscape in recent decades. Preservationists working within their own communities still needed to overcome their distaste for the voluminous and commonplace and to survey and inventory such buildings.[51] It can reasonably be inferred that the resources of the automobile age lay among these still-fugitive categories.

Before the National Park Service and only a short time after the National Trust began their clarion calls with well-publicized national effects, a small private organization of devotees and professionals, the Society for Commercial Archeology (SCA), focused their attention exclusively on the study and heightened public awareness about road and roadside resources. Its interests were understandably part of an aroused general awareness about the built environment in the late 1970s. "Archaeology" hardly sounds like a means for understanding a living society, but the SCA's founders wanted to emphasize their interest in material culture, a realm for which archaeology was better known at the time. The modifier *commercial* helped distinguish the founders' intent from that of the Society for Industrial Archeology (SIA), founded only a few years earlier. Chester Liebs, who had been active in the SIA, gave great impetus to founding the SCA and in so doing helped confer the modifier distinguishing the SCA from its sister organization. While the SCA declared interest in the artifacts, structures, signs, and symbols of the commercial process, it has narrowed in practice to structures and often those of symbolic value that look like other things. Venturi's ducks and decorated sheds have drawn more attention in the society's publications than any other of the four subcategories of originally declared interest.[52] Highways, the other half of the commercial culture that automobility generated, have been the focus of a comparatively few members; again, architecture reigns among these preservationists despite their off-beat interests.[53] The mission of educating the public to the importance of these sites for the very reason that they are ephemeral also survives as a traditional goal with this untraditional society. Preserving the road and roadside is still a point to be made.

Road and roadside studies can be traced to many inspired individuals as outlined previously. In the early twentieth century a series of publications about the National Road was authored in the belief that the new age of bicycle and automobile travel would renew life and commerce along the road.[54] But in the late twentieth century it was Route 66's decommissioning that stimulated, perhaps more than any other event, vast popular interest and sound scholarship.[55] Rising interest in this fabled highway later engendered a second scholarly monograph, which concentrates exclusively on the highway's cultural aspects.[56] Stretches of former Route 66 are preserved today at the bridge crossing of the Meramec River west of St. Louis, Missouri, where a state park has been established to celebrate the old highway (figs. 4.8 and 4.9).[57]

Compared to nostalgic and analytical narratives of a single road, however, one body of work that stands out is that of Daniel Paul Marriott, who fathered an overarching study of automotive highways as historical entities and ones deserving preservation. With the same mission-driven urgency that characterized the first preservationists of the roadside, Marriott alerted his audience.[58] Perhaps it was the comparative difficulty of retaining their historic features at the same time as compliance with contemporary federal standards that delayed attention to road preservation as opposed to roadside preservation. Roads, after all, were required to meet regularly upgraded safety standards that rendered historic features dangerously obsolete; roadside features changed as a matter of competitive commercial advantage.[59] Unquestionably the road itself, often not as noticed as the resources alongside it, entered preservationists' list of concerns later. In

Figure 4.8. Meramec River bridge deck, former U.S. 66, Times Beach, Missouri, 2003.

1998, under the auspices of the National Trust for Historic Preservation, Marriott published a primer for identifying historic roads and working with their constituents and administrators for harmonious and productive preservation. That same year he also initiated with the trust a biennial series of meetings called the Historic Roads Conference, but recently he has carried forward without the trust. International topics about roads were included; so too were various amenities associated with roads.[60]

Two federal programs with great potential for the automotive road, coupled to its automotive resources, are the National Trails System and the National Scenic Byways. The former began in 1968 and the latter in 1991. The former has come to include mostly roads that were significant before the arrival of the automotive highway, but it does include the Blue Ridge Parkway.[61] The latter is a federally administered program dependent on the voluntary participation of local communities.[62] A few are significant because of their association with automotive traffic, for example, the Arroyo Seco Parkway, an early freeway still fully integrated into the Los Angeles freeway system, and the George Washington Memorial Parkway, a surviving example of 1930s parkway enthusiasm embraced by the National Park Service. Neither, lacking as they do roadside commerce, remind us of what became prevalent as Roadside America (figs. 4.10 and 4.11).

Figure 4.9. Meramec River bridge supports, former U.S. 66, Times Beach, Missouri, 2003.

Figure 4.10. Arroyo Seco, Los Angeles, California, 1968. Limited-access right-of-way precludes roadside development.

Begun in 1999 and extended for another ten years in 2009, the Route 66 Corridor Preservation Program—among those promoted by the federal government but also involved with local initiatives—is the most promising of the programs with roadside potential. In cooperation with municipal, state, and private organizations a significant number of buildings and neon signs have been preserved. The intellectual horizon has occupied the program too; historic contexts and more than thirty National Register nominations were researched and written and oral history workshops conducted. Native American were included in this wide-reaching preservation effort.[63]

These achievements helped open eyes to the frontier of road and roadside preservation. Preservationists have wrongly, yet fondly, adopted the phrase "coming of age" to characterize the status of resources finally deserving inclusion among those already hallowed; it implies that the resources' final acceptance is unquestioned. Many preservationists, however, are still slow or seem unwilling at all to be persuaded of the roadside's merits for historic landmark status. In fact advocacy is never done.[64] In the wake of the aesthetic and intellectual cutting edge that advanced the preservation agenda for road and roadside preservation since the 1960s, many artists, authors, and photographers have entertained, in-

Figure 4.11. George Washington Parkway, south of Alexandria, Virginia, 1968. Here the immediate roadside, although accessible by car, includes landscapes as park.

formed, and thereby recruited a vast popular audience. The *Route 66 Magazine*, begun in the winter of 1993–94, and the *Route 66 Pulse* newspaper, begun in 2006, have provided many opportunities for them. The two publications have faith in interest acquired through travel on the road to augment intellectual reflections, along with the embrace of the popular media of videos and DVDs on various aspects of the highway to complement many published works.[65] Route 66 remains the most prominent of the venues for the preservation of automobility's vestiges, but it is not alone.

The public has discovered and even joyfully affirmed Road and Roadside America. What will it take to convince professional preservation administrators and managers that a setting is needed for thinking about those places and landscapes in perpetuity? When will those resources truly come of age?

Important Cases of Roadside Preservation

Formally organized meetings and publications by organizations are not the only measure and mode of the roads' and roadsides' increased understanding among preservationists. Their work remains very much a grass roots activity wherein unaffiliated individuals pursue preservation objectives without thinking of them

Figure 4.12. H. P. Sears Service Station Number Two, Rome, NY, 2007.

as such but rather as labors of love. In their remembering, they are members of a vast assemblage that is "mostly local, particular, and highly personal" whatever the objects of their passion, roads and roadsides included.[66] In fairness it must be admitted that some of this road and roadside preservation with a personal purpose may have been inspired by formal preservation organizations or otherwise influenced by them, but there is often no proof of this. Having the same moralistic drive as the self-conscious preservationists, these spontaneous founders and managers are no less ardent stewards than those of the established order schooled at conferences and read in the published preservation catechisms. Not elusive but presently only known by random identifications while on vacations or other work, these spontaneous personal road- and roadside-preservation projects, to

Figure 4.13. Vintage pump at H. P. Sears Service Station Number Two, Rome, New York, 2007.

distinguish them from the formal, are difficult to catalog. There are too many of them, and yet their popularity demands a place in the record. Their presence is fragmented, lacking the advantage of a national institution to publicize them, rather like local theater groups and small museums. Future scholarship should take on the exhaustive work of a survey before attempting a definitive analysis of the myriad cases. The authors' acquaintance with these spontaneous and personal preservation projects permits the following provisional assessment.

Perhaps the most common of these spontaneous personal roadside preservation projects are gasoline stations that are treated almost like shrines in terms of setting and interpretation. At Rome, New York, the H. P. Sears George Street Service Station, built in 1929, was fully restored in 2006 (figs. 4.12 and 4.13). At

Figure 4.14. Phillips 66 gas station, Creston, Iowa, 2001.

the edge of Creston, Iowa, on U.S. 34, one finds an early cottage-style Phillips 66 station dating from 1928 (figs. 4.14 and 4.15). It was from Creston that Frank Phillips left for Bartlesville, Oklahoma, hoping to cash in on the oil boom there. His company prospers today as Conoco-Phillips. People fond of motoring and the car culture, sometimes members of a family whose forerunners managed a gasoline station, gain ownership of a particular station no longer in service, repair its weathered and used architectural shell, and leave it out of service except to memorialize the building and stimulate memory. Numerous too are the stations adaptively reused but still with obvious architectural features from their original function. At the west edge of Mansfield, Ohio's downtown, travelers pass a Texaco station converted from the corporation's "city style" to a law office (fig. 4.16).[67]

The individuals who labor to keep their stations, as much as is practical, in service like they once were are rarer. Terry Kinsinger proudly offered full service including gasoline pumping and repairs in a Sohio station built in Piqua, Ohio, in 1959. The station was rebranded under the BP logo when British Petroleum took over Standard Oil of Ohio in the 1990s. Never having discarded the station's old signage (and indeed nearly everything else used over the years of operation), Terry Kinsinger reverted to the station's Sohio "look" when he lost his BP con-

Figure 4.15. Vintage pump and hanging sign at Phillips 66 gas station, Creston, Iowa, 2001.

tact (figs. 4.17, 4.18, and 4.19). Townspeople were charmed by Kinsinger's genuine congeniality and good service and remained loyal customers. He hoped to interest the local historical society in maintaining the building when he retired.[68]

Mike Kertok of Norman, Oklahoma, has added to his architectural practice by designing four adaptively reused Phillips 66 "cottage style" stations. These remain unmistakably gasoline stations in their origins, given their small size and distinctively pitched roofs above the entrance to their offices. Kertok has painstakingly worked in the Phillips company archives to learn about their original locations in hopes of adding to this small niche in his practice, and he calculates that sixty to seventy buildings might await his specialty. Alert to this possibility,

Figure 4.16. George Merschdorf's former gas station, Mansfield, Ohio, 2006. The building housed a law office at the time of this photograph.

the first four buildings' owners approached Kertok. Their reasons varied from having a "preservation bug," to family forerunners in the retail oil trade (see fig. 5.22, next chapter), to the conviction of a local historical society that a station would make a good visitor center (fig. 4.20). Here preservation genuinely arose from small private interests and has inspired the possibility of a profitable source of architectural income.[69]

What uses might be made of latter-day resources such as the Phillips post–World War II design with its extensive glazing and huge swept-wing canopy? Is there a limit to their appeal even in the current era of "green" preservation, making the old domestic-style station not only an artifact of petroleum's mark on history but a preservation-era favorite as well? Is quaintness a tap root and yet a limit to more widely embraced gasoline-station resources?

Diners have won the most passionate long-lived following of the three paramount roadside services, and it is little wonder that in an age of fond retrospection their appeal should be sustained. Their small interiors, commonplace cuisine, storied personal service, and family kitchen and table setting combine for a very unassuming and nurturing sense of place. Perhaps because they are vital to life, as they provide food, after all, people also associate diners intimately with

Figure 4.17. Terry Kinsinger's former BP station, Piqua, Ohio, 2005.

Figure 4.18. Interior of Kinsinger's gas station, Piqua, Ohio, 2005.

Figure 4.19. Terry Kinsinger in vintage gas station attendant's uniform, Piqua, Ohio, 2005.

key points in their life. One aficionado who wrote and illustrated a column on diners for the Society for Commercial Archeology's publications for nineteen years recalled how he first became interested in diners when he was six years old and how he had continued this interest throughout his life.[70] An architectural historian and preservationist documented the history of Landrum's Diner in Reno, Nevada, and noted that the state's governor avowed after it closed: "It is part of Americana and I hope they will keep it forever."[71] Could such a front-ranking political-office holder do more to bond himself in the public memory as a man of the people than by praising to the highest a place of everyman's fare?

Figure 4.20. Mike Sager, a developer of historic properties in Tulsa, Oklahoma's Greenwood District, engaged Kertok's talents for this former Phillips station (left) and garage (right). Courtesy of Mike Kertok, restoration architect.

Todd Bucher and his wife, Nina, involved in the pursuit of a restored diner for a remote location in northern Wisconsin, confirm the strong currents of humanity that make diners something even more meaningful than a source of physical sustenance offered in eye-catching architecture. The Buchers appreciate a diner's evocations as more than a marketing tool wielded for profit. In addition Todd Bucher's education in anthropology and sociology has enabled him to touch briefly, on the diner's Web site, on these human dimensions by detailing the decisions that led to the Buchers' diner being created.[72] A Delta Store preceded incorporation of the town by one year, in 1923. The store was the town's center, comprising a general store, bar, restaurant, post office, ice house, gas station, and railroad station. "What strikes you about a diner is the 'story' that is inevitably woven into its fabric." It was more important to extend the life of a diner no longer functional elsewhere by relocating it and putting it into use according to new building codes because the creation offered "depth." Here is a place that evokes the spiritual (fig. 4.21).[73]

Of the three paramount roadside services—gas, food, and lodging—the latter has most often faced the greatest likelihood of obsolescence. People like the greatest possible comfort for themselves, and motels house people for considerable

Figure 4.21. Delta Diner, Delta, Wisconsin. Owner Todd Bucher explained that he commissioned Rick Maki's drawing above to familiarize local people with the look "of a traditional East Coast diner in Delta . . . on the site of the historic and sociologically important Delta Store" (email to Keith Sculle, Mar. 4, 2009). Diners unquestionably have powerful place-making sway. Courtesy of Todd Bucher/Rick Maki.

lengths of time, whereas gas stations and restaurants provide comparatively brief acquaintance. Some owners of older motels have been able lately to draw lodgers for a night or more by blending some concessions to contemporary convenience while playing on the yearnings of those who want something of a historical experience—the retro market. These are not derelict hotels on the margins of social respectability but indeed are quite the opposite: places modernized to a degree yet convincingly older in appearance.

These stimulate the imagination. One lives in them, if only briefly, trying to experience what earlier lodgers might have experienced as one's night passes to morning: the grasp at history through a material-culture setting.[74] The yearning for transcendence, something other than an analytical understanding of history, makes this nostalgia a spiritual quest. Roadside nostalgia tempts the time travelers' belief in a community of like-minded souls cruising the road in search of a pleasant past, unhurried, where time and the lodgers' cars stands still, their essence—mobility—denied. The current vernacular dubs them "retro."

Figure 4.22. Lincoln Motor Court, Tulls Hill, Pennsylvania, 2001. A view of the units on the west side of the U-layout, which contributed significantly to the lodging's historical ambiance.

The Lincoln Motor Court, astride the Lincoln Highway at Tulls Hill, Pennsylvania, enables one to peer over a long time into the time travelers' transcendent quest. Built in 1944, the Lincoln Motor Court was off the beaten path by the 1970s. Lodgers tended to stay in places close to the Pennsylvania Turnpike.[75] The next phase began with Bob and Debbie Altizer, a couple who fled the hectic pace of life in Washington, D.C., for a quiet life in the Pennsylvania mountains where they bought the motel in 1983. Ten years later, nostalgic yearnings and boosterism amid the nationwide culture of leisure gave birth to a new Lincoln Highway Association. A historian and photographer engrossed in his work on a travel guide of the highway in Pennsylvania and an eager proponent for combining heritage tourism and road and roadside preservation counseled the Altizers on the possibility of reviving their business by appealing to travelers seeking to re-enact a trip on the Lincoln Highway. Advertising its historical qualities made the retro business profitable, and other entrepreneurs near the Altizers also successfully adopted the strategy (fig. 4.22).[76] This heritage phenomenon had already taken a firm hold on the revived Route 66 in the Southwest. The market of "good ol' days" has expanded nationally to the point where the subtitle of a book, *A State-By-State Tour Guide To Nostalgic Stopovers,* promises a national niche for the time traveler from coast to coast.[77]

Widely shared memory forms the foundation of all successful preservation, road and roadside alike. Roadside resources, however, face a dilemma peculiar to them; for if the passing traffic remains sufficient, newer business prospects threaten the older ones. Thus roadside past confronts roadside future beside a constantly reinvented road. One well-documented case illustrates the complexity of this peculiar irony, namely, Coral Court in suburban St. Louis. To date it is one of Roadside America's most renowned and lamented lost causes.

Coral Court, located beside Route 66 in Marlborough, Missouri, was built in the Streamline Moderne style beginning in 1941. The complex of units on 8.5 acres expanded from a main office with ten cabins, each with two rooms, to twenty-three cabins of forty-six rooms in 1948, and finally three two-story buildings with eight rooms were added in 1953.[78] Lore was added to the architectural elegance to make Coral Court a storied and memorable lodging. Coral Court, it was claimed, had been started for the convenience of long-distance truck drivers; a room there could be rented for as short a time as four hours. It soon built a contrary reputation for couples to rendezvous untroubled by surveillance, a privacy that was attributed to the access to the garage, which was not in open view. In addition to these common liaisons, in 1953 a man was apprehended at the motel after he had spent the evening with three or possibly more ladies of the night after he had kidnapped, held for ransom, and murdered the six-year-old son of a well-known merchant. Of the six-million-dollar-ransom he took, only half was left at the time of his arrest. Rumor had it that the missing treasure had been hidden in the hollow-block walls of the motel. The missing money was never found.[79] By the 1970s and 1980s, high school students added to the motel's titillating reputation by making it a destination of their own short stays.[80]

An aesthetic stature came to balance Coral Court's shady reputation. In 1983 the St. Louis Department of Parks and Recreation acknowledged the lodging.[81] That same body's architectural historian and an active preservationist in his own right, Esley Hamilton, gave further respectability to Coral Court in its final days, describing its physical features in elegant prose (figs. 4.23 and 4.24).[82]

Coral Court's secured place in community memory was enough to help boost the interest in its physical preservation. Following the owner's death in 1984, his

Figure 4.23. Coral Court, Marlborough, Missouri, 1994. Esley Hamilton pointed out the distinguished details of this landmark, such as the curvilinear entrance carried through the massing on the motel units seen on the left mid-ground.

wife tried to keep it in business, but it gradually deteriorated. Strip-mall developers prepared to raze the lodging and build their new business beside the busy highway. A rising cry to save Coral Court, along with the strip-mall developers' inability to buy sufficient adjacent land for their project, left the motel in limbo for eight years. In 1989 Esley Hamilton's class in historic preservation succeeded in placing Coral Court in the National Register of Historic Places. Later the Coral Court Preservation Society produced a brochure showing the development options of adaptive reuse for at least part of the property.[83]

Time took a toll on the idle motel and eventually forced its sale for less than what could have been had from the market. While it was on the market, souvenir hunters plundered the site, especially the empty cabins, and the owner gladly sold it for about one-third of the asking price. Village officials paid lip service to the building's beauty but eagerly condemned the site and rezoned it for residential development.[84] Coral Court's opponents surely saw its preservation as foolishly troublesome, but it remained a hallowed part of the public memory. Even the demolition crew hired to end the motel's life stirred community memories anew by posting this sign: "IT'S CHECKOUT TIME AT THE CORAL COURT—NO MORE ONE NIGHT STANDS."[85]

In 1995 the decrepit motel was razed, and work began on single-family residences but not before the National Museum of Transportation in St. Louis was granted permission to salvage two buildings from the complex.[86] An artist and photographer brought additional celebrity status to the lost site with her book billed as a "scrapbook of memories, first-person narratives, trivia questions—the true story behind the notorious no-tell motel in St. Louis."[87] Thirteen years later it was recalled among several of St. Louis's "demolished buildings that have left an unfillable gap" in the city's "collective memory."[88] For some the storied life and slow demise of Coral Court registers it as a martyr of the fabled Route 66 if not of Roadside America itself.

In retrospect it appears that an array of roadside businesses, each in an architectural form taken to symbolize the whole category, had enthusiastic fans. If cottage- and Art Deco–style gasoline stations were popular, so too were diners of the prefabricated metal variety, and not the store-front cafes on Main Street without styled pretense, as were Mom-and-Pop operated motels in a "retro" motif, and not the corporate chains and larger buildings of an earlier vintage. Individual car collectors, who were potential collaborators, in some places included the buildings that historically serviced their cars. As a result the professional and public organizations were not short-sighted in their ambitions for roadside preservation. They stood abreast with knowledgeable amateurs in all but embracing a place type replicating the roadside in toto.[89]

The Challenges in General

The fact that the roadside's buildings were new compared to those preservationists traditionally address required advocates to coin the cry to "preserve the recent past." Such were buildings not yet relics, but still in profitable use, and they were dismissed because most preservationists and unpersuaded members of the general public remembered when they were built.[90] So too the problem of

Figure 4.24. Coral Court, Marlborough, Missouri, 1994. Two of the infamous garage doors on units on the left and the backside of a unit on the right.

rapid obsolescence and the disappearance of certain roadside types, most prominently the drive-in movie theater, was troublesome for preservationists of the roadside.[91] The younger generation, which had grown up with them from childhood, often appreciated them intuitively, and yet still those roadside buildings fell short of that period when scholars would take them into account as of a "historic age." Instead of the scholarly reserve against younger people's inclination toward an intuitive acceptance, the substitution of time as a continuum has been suggested, thus allowing whatever themes can be identified to come forward as significant and their material embodiments to be selected for preservation rather than after a few linger only as remains.[92] Fear not abundant examples from which to pick while they are yet abundant. Neither fear sheer numbers for their own sake. Disarming traditional preservationists' principles helped open the way to preserving the vernacular, which already had gained creditability of late among certain arbiters of good taste and in certain scholarly disciplines. Yet an elitist trope consistently ran through architectural history, which had disproportionate power in the preservation community. Although the National Register of Historic Places had encouraged landscape surveys to search out the significant buildings, the fifty-year prohibition against younger buildings, except in the case of exceptional significance, hobbled the opposite thrust toward wide representation at the foundation of most preservation programs nationwide.[93]

Beyond individual buildings selected for distinction--still most often architectural distinction--no group of roadside preservationists has called for work at the landscape scale wherein an entire commercial strip will be the objective. Historic districts themselves have been comparatively late objects of historic preservationists. Limited types of buildings have gained acceptance, notably those of the triune roadside services--gas, food, and lodging. Signs too, but most especially spectacular neon examples, have broken through the long-standing resistance to the roadside's gaudiness and gained some ardent followers. Gains have doubtlessly been made, for sure, but more could be done to reach a more comprehensive understanding of the roadside as a functioning ensemble and not just its spectacular parts. A latent resistance, even among younger preservationists, may yet rise up when the great physical extent of the commercial strip is addressed; for surely some owners will decline inclusion of their property. Future preservation may be more in the direction of guided community self-interest than toward what intellectual leaders would like a community to accept.[94] Preservation's future may be more about locations of satisfactory living where the history is already a vital aspect of shared community values rather than an intellectual lesson to be taught. Roadside preservationists have pressing work at hand.

★ ★ ★

A larger sense of place awaited future roadside preservationists. Perhaps serious critics so long rebuked the roadside as a place of shameful profiteering without social conscience as reflected in no or poor aesthetic sensibilities that the thought of a preserved or replicated roadside setting remained preposterous, if not laughable. To many the roadside was too unstructured, too inauthentic, to rank with historic and architectural sites as worthy of commitment to an enduring public guardianship. How could stewards pass these places to future generations in good conscience as building blocks of a better future? Historic preservation's stirrings as a moral mission, a work of saving civilization's most meaningful past accomplishments, bedeviled road and roadside preservation for traditionalists. Those who may have been receptive of these resources faced practical impediments. Perhaps funding the work and accommodating traffic laws boded such difficulty with an acreage so large that no one took up the prospect. Commercial strips were not petite parcels. Still, there lingered too the possibility that so many had grown up with the commercial strip that it was unimaginable as venerable heritage. It was not something that came down in time to them; in a way, they came up with it.

What could those preservationists do who were less hobbled by philosophical considerations and prepared to come to grips with matters of implementation? Should they preserve only relic buildings in situ? Or should they preserve them in ensembles? And, if the latter could be addressed, was rebuilding, replication, or both the way to proceed in capturing and preserving the buildings, activities, and equally important sprawling open space, thus enabling that otherwise elusive sense of the roadside's place? Might the outdoor museum provide a viable template for preservation at the landscape scale?

CHAPTER FIVE
HISTORICAL MUSEUMS AND ROADSIDE AMERICA

Modernism's penchant for discard was nowhere more evident than along America's highways. If early Roadside America little lent itself to the actions of preservationists, then what about the collector's instincts? And, better still, the instincts of the museum curator? Remnants of the past traditionally accumulated in the nation's antique shops, to be sold to enthusiasts personally enamored of one or another aspect of historicity. Historical relics were likewise collected in museums to be publicly celebrated, not just for the lessons they might teach about the past, but also for their rarity as curiosities. From the gathering and display of things that could be held in the hand, the collector's instinct as a force for conservation steadily evolved in scale—from that of the large machine (automobiles and trucks included), to the scale of the building (from log cabins to gasoline stations, for example), to the scale of the built environment (such as a roadside). To date, however, outdoor museums in the United States rarely celebrate landscapes of automobility. As architectural ensembles they celebrate almost exclusively pre-automobile themes—for example, frontier pioneering, traditional family farming, or life as lived along the Main Streets of small-town America. Indeed, outdoor museums in the United States are often rationalized as a means of remembering life here before automobility; the coming of the motorcar and motor truck is rendered symbolic of the very coming of modernism itself. When and where will the auto age with its roadside landscapes enter the world of the American outdoor museum?

Museum Preconceptions in the United States

American museums originated in the Victorian ethos of consistently progressive societal improvement, with life collectively getting ever better and with the calm assurance that the past was knowable, a dimension understood by means of objective analysis in archived documents. With such a positive spirit, it is perhaps understandable that museums have celebrated the grand American accomplishment in its many forms. Throughout the twentieth century, accumulated doubts withered the faith in progress and eventually a belief not only in a single knowable past, recoverable for everyone, but a yen for entertainment. Public education endured as the museum's mission, to be sure, but each visitor's understanding of self continually became more important. In this radical flux, a roadside museum came to have a greater likelihood of appearing. It did not seem so for many years. In fact the very traits of mobility and the value of ceaseless novelty were at essential odds with how museums habitually portrayed the past.

Beginning with the Renaissance's assumptions, museums in the Western world, the United States included, labored with them until well into the twentieth century. The very word of origin, *musaeum,* derived partly from the word *muses,* predicated the belief that studied experts wisely collected and arranged displays for an unknowing public who would be uplifted in a learning experience. The studios wherein early collectors gathered their holdings and theaters wherein the surprising discoveries of the early modern age were on display made the museum that combined these functions into an enclosed space implying completeness. Museums were places where the entirety of ever-growing knowledge through collections was rendered complete. Europe's encounter with new forms of life in the New World during the 1500s and 1600s further ensured the role of the museum. Men almost exclusively dominated in the collecting and creation of museums, and the process became one of self-promotion, transferred from private interests into public benefaction. That museums manifest a constructed narrative of the past is inherent. Under these terms the first public museum was founded in Bologna, Italy, in the early eighteenth century; this was the *Instituto della Scienze* in 1714.[1] Defined, contained, patriarchal and didactic, the museum came to America narrowly circumscribed in meaning.

Museums took hold there beginning in the late eighteenth century; the first public one, the Charleston Museum, in Charleston, South Carolina, antedated the nation's founding by three years.[2] The long duration of museums in the United

States notwithstanding, the precise definition of terms and widely shared self-conscious participation in a tradition went lacking until comparatively recently. In the 1970s William Alderson and Shirley Low, two museums practitioners seeking to raise the intellectual bar, decried the absence of general principles governing historic site interpretation.[3] With deep interest as a young site manager of the Old State Capitol in Springfield, Illinois, one of this book's authors, Keith A. Sculle, felt securely guided in his work by Alderson's and Low's *Interpretation of Historic Sites*. They speculated on the very classification of sites, pointing out the inadequacy of the prevailing vocabulary dominated by a vernacular and uncommitted to professionalized terminology. In these fluid conditions, some practitioners referred to what interpreters did as work in a *historic house museum*. This, Alderson and Low rightly observed, took no account of places other than houses such as battlefields or restored villages.[4] It is worth considering the kinds of museums that would likely influence the planners and staff of one conceived for Roadside America with professional stature and public utility.

The most common form of history museum in the United States indeed has been the house museum. These were usually single structures, some with outlying buildings and grounds, although others had been razed but with some individual rooms saved and moved off site into other museums and made into showpieces, such as period rooms. House museums varied considerably from one to another.[5] Their curators were usually local antiquarians, untrained as museum professionals, and, despite a keenly felt sense of mission and readiness to serve the public, museum staffs remained largely volunteers, and their enterprise was commonly underfunded. The first reliable account places the number of house museums nationwide at about five hundred in the 1930s.[6] Too little has been written of the history and philosophy of house museums as a type compared to their role in public education and numbers. Thus a brief mention of the Abraham Lincoln Home in Springfield, Illinois, allows a compensatory opportunity for a degree of instructive generalizations via a meticulously documented example (fig. 5.1).

In 1861, after the departure of the Lincoln family for Abraham's presidential administration in Washington, D.C., a succession of private families lived in the home. Perhaps naturally, they ran it like a personal holding. The occupants who rented the home the longest from the family following his assassination contributed to the public mourning by draping the home on the day of the assassination.

Figure 5.1. Postcard view of the Lincoln Home on South Eighth Street, Springfield, Illinois, circa 1910. In this view Lincoln's residence is fully divorced from its surroundings, a typical means of visually emphasizing a building as an object in the landscape rather than as part of a landscape or surrounding built environment. As house museums tended to stand apart from contemporary settings, so also did interior displays serve to isolate life in a contemporary temporal frame—with the past sacralized accordingly.

They also welcomed the curious into the house thereafter, but they gave no formal tours.[7] Physical changes were made to the house to rid it of dilapidated elements and to accommodate the need for more space.[8]

Osborn Oldroyd was the most colorful of the occupants who treated it like his own. A Union veteran of the Civil War, Oldroyd moved his collection of Lincoln memorabilia, which he had displayed in a nearby home for several years, into the Lincoln Home when he rented it from the deceased president's son and in 1883 moved in. Oldroyd lived on the second floor and maintained his "Lincoln Collection" on the first floor. He launched the enterprise amid much fanfare, including a formal opening on the night of April 14, 1884, the nineteenth anniversary of the president's death, while crowds of curious onlookers waited in the neighborhood to gain access.[9] Authorities disagree as to whether he charged admission or instead accepted voluntary contributions thereafter.[10] But, to support himself, he definitely sold souvenirs, such as wood and brick fragments salvaged from repairs made on the house.[11] He played to the appetite for authenticity, noting he had made only necessary changes and retained intact the wallpaper the Lincolns had hung in two rooms.[12]

A shrine, as indeed it was called, had been established, complete with pilgrims on tour to a significant place in a venerated figure's life and their chance to hold and own a physical fragment of that place. People perceived the properties of a house museum to include what can be explained as a talismanic power to transport visitors in time. President-elect William Howard Taft evoked something of the craving to relive the past by literally touching physical remains of it when he stopped in Springfield on the fiftieth anniversary of Lincoln's departure for the presidency and stated to his guide at the house: "I wish to walk upon the floors that Lincoln trod."[13] His may also have been a politically symbolic act to associate himself with a deified predecessor. Might the ordinary visitor beholding the artifacts, not themselves symbolic figures, have hopes that these too could perform good services for society as did Lincoln, whose reliance on those artifacts proved his mortality?[14]

Public responsibility for the shrine shifted from the private in 1887, when the house's owner, Robert Todd Lincoln accepted the state of Illinois's appointment of a board under the governor and several elected cabinet officers and signed a deed stating that "said Homestead shall be forever kept in good repair and free of access to the public."[15] Oldroyd had used whatever political influence he had to engineer this shift, but his motive was more likely the desire to live free of rent in a public building while he managed it for the new owner than to ensure its perpetual survival.[16] For his part Robert Todd Lincoln, the last surviving Lincoln, was glad to be free of the responsibility for the house.[17] Tired of Oldroyd's having given the home the look of an "antique shop," as Lincoln's son called it, Robert Todd Lincoln was also eager to expel Oldroyd and took the chance in 1893, when a governor took office who was of a different political party than the one that had chaired the shift from a private to a public responsibility six years before. Oldroyd emptied the home of his collection when he was removed by the new governor but moved it to Washington, D. C., where he took occupancy in another Lincoln shrine, the house where the president died after being shot at nearby Ford's Theater.[18]

Between the late nineteenth century and 1972, when the National Park Service gained ownership from the state of Illinois, management of the home was far less dramatic than it had been. Its managers were not professionally trained, to be sure. Rather they were quietly capable overseers but in fairness no professional training for such work was available anywhere in the nation during those early years of the twentieth century; people learned on the job. Repairs were made to keep the structure weather tight and respectable in appearance. The death of the elm Lincoln is claimed to have planted and its removal in 1905 marked a decline in integrity. The house, however, survived an attempted arson in 1908 during the infamous Springfield race riot. In 1950 Governor Adlai Stevenson, a Lincoln admirer, lent a willing ear when the home's custodian spoke up for the necessity of various changes to improve its physical condition and to alter its physical arrangement to enable a historically accurate presentation. A comprehensive plan, the first in the home's existence, was to be based on an archaeological investigation by well-regarded professionals. The custodian moved out too; henceforth none occupied the home. The backyard woodshed, privy, and carriage house were reconstructed in keeping with the best evidence, and in 1955 the second floor was opened for regular visitation for the first time. Paint, decorative detail, and gutters with downspouts were the principle parts of the house that were restored according to the most carefully researched sources available.[19] Thus dawned an administrative practice based on a desire to restore the home to the way it actually was during its most significant period, the Lincoln family residency. The duties were discharged in the fullest and most sincere sense of responsibility for the public into perpetuity.

Landscape concurrently held the attention of the home's governing boards, managers, and the public. Tim Townsend, one of the National Park Service's best-informed staff members of the home at the time of this writing, summarized the variations in landscape concerns over the two-thirds of a century before the National Park Service took ownership. All the proposals for management aimed at the appropriate: "What changed over time was what was considered to be appropriate . . . [and] until the late 1950s it was felt that the best treatment was to remove all of the surrounding distractions," or other residential buildings making up the domestic neighborhood. In this way the Lincoln home would be "the centerpiece of a landscaped setting." Thereafter, and through the present, a commitment was made to retain the Lincoln home "in an historic context that would reflect the residential character of the neighborhood."[20] Respect for larger swaths of real estate, in keeping with an awareness of historic districts since the new preservation under the National Historic Preservation Act of 1966, discussed earlier, became the principle of landscape management, even if this did not always involve restoration. For example, a grand vision in keeping with the Beaux Arts classicism of the City Beautiful approach in 1921 contained plans for a multiblock park to include a national memorial for soldiers of World War I and a designed landscape with a road to the Lincoln Tomb on Springfield's north side and the reconstructed New Salem Park nearly twenty miles north.[21]

The Lincoln Home was located some four blocks southeast of the heart of Springfield's downtown, on South Eighth Street, where after 1900 newer houses had come to replace older ones, save, of course, for the Lincoln Home. Although the immediate neighborhood retained its essential residential character, it did not retain its nineteenth-century historical integrity. When, in the 1920s, nearby South Ninth Street was selected to carry the newly designated U.S. 66 highway north-south through the city, the proprietors of the Lincoln Home found themselves in a zone of rapid urban transition, especially as Springfield's central business district continued to expand ever outward. From the 1950s South Ninth Street had become a commercial strip lined with businesses including numerous gas stations, several drive-in restaurants, and several motels (fig. 5.2). Over the years numerous tourist information stands operated there, complete with billboards and other signs to divert visitors attracted to Springfield's several Lincoln sites, including most especially the nearby Lincoln Home. On South Eighth Street itself, houses close to the Lincoln Home were converted into gift shops and/or demolished for commercial buildings that housed Lincoln-oriented private museum displays (fig. 5.3). Parked cars lined Eighth Street at all hours (fig. 5.4). By the end of the 1960s, numerous houses in the neighborhood had been removed for off-street parking. One block north on South Eighth Street the city of Springfield had begun clearing land for a new civic center, using federal urban-renewal money. The automobile's impact was pervasive as was the penchant for modernism. The new civic center that evolved in the 1970s carries few if any allusions to the past, not even the important Lincoln association so close at hand. By the 1990s the commercial strip along South Ninth Street was well into decline as traffic on Route 66 had been diverted to a bypass on the city's far east side several decades earlier. South Ninth Street today carries Business Route I-55 and a new Historic Route 66 designation.

In the 1960s the Illinois state historian inspired a series of moves to put the entire Lincoln neighborhood back to something of its appearance when the

Figure 5.2. South Ninth Street immediately east of the Lincoln Home, Springfield, Illinois, in 1971, remained an active commercial corridor. Lined with telephone poles and automobile-convenient businesses whose ample space to pull over and park exemplified modernity, it offered a jarring contrast with the sedate Eighth Street of mid-Victorian vintage in front of the Lincoln Home. Courtesy of the Lincoln Library, Springfield, Illinois, Sangamon Valley Collection.

Lincolns lived there. Intervening physical changes had no acceptable role in this concept, which found significance for one period only. The accumulated changes since the premier occupants enshrined the home by their presence were insignificant; historical time stood still. Landscape, in these terms, did not embrace evolution. At this interval, however, the city's aforementioned landscape of modernity and its concomitant automobility encroached. Route 66 had passed the site from the highway's inception until its rerouting through Springfield, and the continued designation of the city's arterial Third Street had ensured that traffic was welcomed to the city in close proximity. But by 1960 a three-story motel of concrete block within eyeshot of the Lincoln shrine loomed, a TraveLodge, and this was not the customary "Devil in Paradise" gas station. This change threatened the 1960s project for an authentic landscape surrounding the home. The city's newly created Historic Site Commission carried its work for a historic district forward, although commercial development on Third Street, including the TraveLodge motel, was allowed to develop adjacent to the historically correct landscape.[22] Under the National Park Service's administration work was assiduously carried out to make the surrounding neighborhood look like the place to which the Lincoln family would feel at home, even if they were to arrive by car. The vast majority of visitors to Springfield's Lincoln sites today arrive by private automobile or tour bus.

Figure 5.3. Mr. Lincoln's neighbor, "Books, Gifts, and Autographs," South Eighth Street, Springfield, Illinois, 1971. Limited land use control through zoning before World War II led to a steady commercialization of Springfield's Eighth Street on either side of Lincoln's former residence.

Tourism and the pervasive appetite for entertainment had come to reign. These may both be traced from big urban centers at the end of the nineteenth century. Fairs and exhibitions were laced through American life long before the century's end; small towns and big cities had their share. In 1893, however, the Chicago Columbian Exposition introduced a size, duration, architectural grandeur, and multiplicity of displays that made any of the foregoing fairs seem nothing like antecedents to the fair in Chicago. It built on a tradition of deviance; for, while the Chicago Columbian Exposition reinforced the prevailing values of the time, it offered a much bigger stage on which fairgoers could take the experience on their own terms. To a considerable degree, it wrested the meaning of the displays from their designers' intentions. Fairgoers played on the grounds, casually interacting with other people at the displays, midway, Ferris wheel, and refreshment stands. They did as they pleased. Here germinated a democratized theater. The fair in Chicago provided pastoral alternatives to urban congestion but also urbane and cosmopolitan settings for those of isolated small-town and rural settings. Geographic boundaries were breached at the Chicago fair; the appeal reached broadly. Film's and radio's appeal surpassed that of the numerous fairs succeeding the 1893 event in Chicago, but the penchant for grandiose outdoor settings inviting casual strolling mixed with educational opportunities had been molded in public thinking.[23] The automobile's very definition to help

Figure 5.4. Lincoln home, Springfield, Illinois, early 1960s. The divided ambiance of right now and back then is clear in this view. Illinois's prominent secretary of state Charles F. Carpentier greets a party disembarking a bus and streaming down the sidewalk lined with parked vehicles, then to enter the Lincoln Home, which stands in its historic setting at the far right. Courtesy of the State Journal Register and Lincoln Library, Springfield, Illinois, Sangamon Valley Collection.

drivers and their passengers reach destinations of their choice on their schedule also spurred the taste for self-definition. Museums would not fail to see this. Within a century museums openly acknowledged that, except in very general terms, visitor responses could not be programmed by the selection of objects and their particular arrangement.[24]

Automobile-Convenient History

The automobile was itself a principle factor in the early-twentieth- century proliferation of U.S. museums. Although the automobile was invented abroad, it was the rapid mass consumption of cars in the United States that marked the nation's automobility worldwide.[25] By 1927, the last year Ford manufactured the Model T, which had made the automobile so popular in America, 1 in 5.3 Americans owned an automobile, roughly four times more than in the other leading industrial nations.[26] Leisure travel became common, and museums offered both educational and entertainment opportunities along the way to travelers and income to entre-

Figure 5.5. Eskimo Museum and Gift Shop, Fairbanks, Alaska, circa 1980. Many roadside museums hewed to the pre-automobile age. This one, peculiar to Alaska's frontier, jointly featured Eskimo artifacts and a gift shop on the Richardson Highway. By 2008 the prestigious collection, named for Maxine and Jesse Whitney, was moved far south to a museum at Prince William Sound Community College in Valdez, Alaska.

preneurs.[27] This numerical prominence and consequent tendency toward "roadside attractions" unfairly predisposes elitists against a venue many have found enjoyable (fig. 5.5).[28]

Unquestionably, though, many roadside entrepreneurs were driven by commercial opportunism rather than reverence or interest in history (fig. 5.6). As the traveling public in the twentieth century began to include the middle class more and more, as opposed to travelers in the nineteenth century, who had been more likely to be upper class and thus fewer in numbers, the appeal of the commonplace in many museums became an understandable if not calculated strategy. Auto travel guides soon included directions and brief descriptions of historical destinations, both museums and sites. The widely distributed state-based guides in the Federal Writers' Project of the 1930s, despite the Great Depression, expanded access by automobile to historical destinations. The concomitant trend of more automobiles and more museums as intervening opportunities to lure tourists grew even greater. Museum-like exhibits and even small theme parks of regional orientation were pitched along the nation's highways (fig. 5.7). By the early 1970s there were more than 120 examples of the outdoor museum, the type most likely to be visited.[29]

Outdoor Museums

Some format of the outdoor museum lends itself most effectively to Roadside America. An emphasis on the roadside's aerial diffusion and its location of various structures and spaces can help illuminate how we manipulate nature, or the landscape, for our purposes. Outdoor museums, however, originated far away in time and location from Roadside America, making them an honored strategy, but one with its advantages and disadvantages. Although in 1881 King Oscar II of Norway began the interest in outdoor museums with only a few buildings on a site near Oslo, Artur Hazelius is commonly attributed to be the outdoor museum type's true founder. In 1891, near Stockholm, he opened Skansen, a depiction of a preindustrial Swedish village made of numerous buildings collected from throughout the nation (fig. 5.8).

Figure 5.6. Advertising postcard for the Sod House Museum near Moorcroft, Wyoming, circa 1935. The caption declares: "The Sod House Museum is a replica of the sod house in which 90 percent of central West population lived in the [18]60s. House is plastered with gumbo, sand and wood ashes. Floor is flagstone, roof is log. Standard Gas, Souvenirs, Lunches, Soft Drinks Served. Free Camp Ground and Trailer Parking. Don't Miss It. None Like It in the U.S."

Figure 5.7. Advertising postcard for the Longhorn Ranch, Moriarity, New Mexico, circa 1935. The card was captioned "New Mexico Museum of the Old West. A Revival of the Old West Amid a Setting of Modern Convenience on Highway 66. Restaurant—Curios—Indian Trading Post . . . From the Land of Enchantment."

Figure 5.8. Norsk Folk Museum, Oslo, Norway, 2006. Tucked among seventeenth-, eighteenth-, and nineteenth-century folk structures in this museum for which Skansen was the prototype, a twentieth-century gasoline station boldly shows its face. It is a vernacular (if not a folk) form exported from the United States as the Standard Oil Company of New Jersey marketed its ESSO brand across northern Europe. The gasoline station quickly became an important symbol of the common place both in Europe and in America.

The proliferating European examples were unlike the American examples because the former focused more on architecture than lifeways.[30] In the United States, the first living-history museum, where history was reenacted, can be traced back to 1909, at the John Ward House, a house museum in Salem, Massachusetts. However, the grandest and most influential example is at Williamsburg, which from its inception in 1926 has combined living history in an outdoor museum.[31]

Colonial Williamsburg is anchored for approximately one mile along the Duke of Gloucester Street and includes 173 surrounding acres (figs. 5.9 and 5.10). In the early 1990s these included more than one hundred gardens and greens, eighty-eight original buildings, another fifty major buildings and many smaller structures.[32] About three dozen of these buildings were open to the public.[33] Aspects of its accuracy are surely open to doubt. The capitol that burned in 1747 was reconstructed rather than choosing one of the earlier colonial period structures, although that is what Williamsburg is intended to represent. And there is no end of criticism for the underrepresentation of the African Americans who were much of the literal backbone of the city's economy and for the avoidance of many unpleasant daily aspects of slavery.[34] About seven hundred buildings that

Figure 5.9. Duke of Gloucester Street, Williamsburg, Virginia, 1964. Helping to maintain a sense of the past, as well as making it safe to walk through Historic Williamsburg, motor traffic has long been curtailed along Williamsburg's main thoroughfare during morning and afternoon hours.

Figure 5.10. Entrance to Historic Williamsburg on the south, 1990. Lack of motorized traffic has in itself come to symbolize the past in the nation's outdoor historical museums, although use of vintage automobiles and trucks in recent decades has somewhat changed the equation of history with animal, water, and steam power exclusively.

occupied the area subsequent to the period of interpretation were razed for this imagined landscape, and a railroad was rerouted.[35] These changes represent concessions to tourists' sensibilities in order attract more visitors to the landscape. A lack of total coherence with a particular period of the colonial era, nonetheless, does not discredit the quality of staff-conducted research and pedagogic concern for interpreter training.[36] Yet it is not for an education in analytical and critical history that people flock to Williamsburg. It is for a particular image: "a fairytale community of neat houses, cheerful residents, fine craftsmanship, and wholesome, unambiguous values."[37]

Consistent with the irony that outdoor museums and their lure of a simpler life often led to patronage by individuals of great wealth in the industrial era, Henry Ford founded Greenfield Village (fig. 5.11). This outdoor museum in Dearborn,

Figure 5.11. Greenfield Village, Dearborn, Michigan, 1938. Henry Ford separated his conception of history so stunningly from the present in his outdoor museum that he did not embrace early automobility in his outdoor museum. This postcard view illustrates the horse-drawn vehicles he revered, not the horse-powered transportation he helped perfect. Courtesy of Lake County Discovery Museum/Curt Teich Postcard Archives.

Michigan, is the largest of its type in the United States. It was dedicated to his belief that if the objects of common Americans' labor were preserved from the preindustrial era, an essence of national greatness would be forever available for reference and edification. Ford had collected items such as steam engines and farm machinery since the early twentieth century and brought them to the Edison Institute, named for another of the industrial age's self-made entrepreneurs and inventors, Thomas Edison. These items were somehow to impart a "true picture of the development of the country." He enlisted no help from academicians or their published work. Although contemporaneous in their creation of the earliest outdoor museums, Ford and Rockefeller appear not to have interacted regarding their creations. Renamed Greenfield Village and dedicated in 1933, Ford's establishment comprised a group of buildings from off-site locations to meet his idiosyncratic needs--a courthouse, post office, farmhouse, and railroad station, but Cotswold cottages from England and Edison's laboratory buildings from New Jersey, as well.[38] He retained a huge collection of vintage automobiles, not on the grounds, but displayed inside an adjacent building (fig. 5.12). Simultaneous with Greenfield Village's opening, Ford continued to treat the automobile

Historical Museums and Roadside America

Figure 5.12. Henry Ford Museum, Dearborn, Michigan, circa 1970. This automobile museum was very traditional in its manner of presentation although it included the evolution from very early models to a prototype of "tomorrow's car" and all three of the major means of propulsion: steam, electric, and gasoline. From the Collections of The Henry Ford; and courtesy of Lake County Discovery Museum/Curt Teich Postcard Archives.

as a thing apart in a world's fair of technological progress (fig. 5.13). The building that housed it was redesigned as the Rotunda and moved onto the company's grounds for its fiftieth anniversary in 1953.

Rockefeller's and, to a lesser extent, Ford's initiatives soon set in motion the founding of other outdoor museums. Some started piecemeal, not from a grandiose scheme full blown at inception; for example, the pharmaceutical mogul Eli Lilly started with the restoration of the William and Elizabeth Connor House in the early 1930s, and, by the 1960s, his project came to include numerous buildings in the Connor Prairie assemblage. More swiftly, a New York City resident and heir to the Singer sewing-machine estate who was attracted to the upstate New York summer resorts in the Cooperstown area encouraged the state's historical association, which held a collection of paintings and sculpture in the fine arts genre, as was typical at the time, to relocate its headquarters from Ticonderoga. Several academic historians, mavericks for their interest in museums, helped guide the project at Cooperstown by encouraging the addition of farm and domestic tools. In 1944 its acquisitions grew further to include buildings brought to the site where the Farmers' Museum took shape. In the 1930s the

Figure 5.13. Ford Exposition, Century of Progress Fair, Chicago, 1933–34. "Ford's Drama of Transportation" in the fair showed a collection of his cars in this postcard art in a cathedral-like setting, as if the automobile was blessed with heaven's approval.

state of Illinois reconstructed buildings alongside an original building to contrive Lincoln's New Salem State Park. On the other hand, in Massachusetts, Old Sturbridge Village, another setting comprising buildings that had been reconstructed or moved onto the site, took full shape—sited around a village green with a church at its head—before it opened in 1946. More outdoor museums were founded in the 1950s and the 1960s. And now an illustrious assemblage includes Historic Deerfield in Massachusetts; Mystic Seaport in Connecticut; New Salem in Illinois; Old Salem in North Carolina; Old World in Wisconsin; Plimoth Plantation in Massachusetts; Shelburne Museum in Vermont; and Stuhr Museum of the Prairie Pioneer in Nebraska.[39]

The best-known outdoor museums and many of purely local renown share a common programmatic value. Pastoral landscapes have the advantages of open space as opposed to the dense city, and yet the conveniences of urban life combine to give the best of both worlds: these features reign at outdoor museums. Thomas Schlereth, one of the first academic historians to respect the educational potential of museums, has called on their managers to include the unpleasant, the inconvenient, and the ugly aspects of past life, not just the harmony and the beauty. We are not the only ones to concur. Not to dismiss the rigorously analyti-

Figure 5.14. Miner Grant's General Store interior, Old Sturbridge Village, Sturbridge, Massachusetts, circa 1950. According to this postcard's text printed on the reverse, the general store offered a sensory panoply along with some of its mind-triggering souvenirs for sale: "Oldtime sights, smells, flavors and geniality. . . . A few old-fashioned items are sold over the counter. Other exhibits include glass and glass-making tools, a potter's wheel and pottery, copper and brass, dress-making and millinery."

cal and continually researched programs open to new conclusions at many of the outdoor museums, most of them still portray small-town or farm life before the advent of industrialization. And they do so substantially in ways that are endearing—a romanticized if not a sanitized past. For example, Old Sturbridge Village has emphasized its crafts (fig. 5.14), and, at mid-continent, in Nebraska, Harold Warp's Pioneer Village near Minden has beckoned with a pioneering theme: "The Story of America and How It Began" (fig. 5.15).[40]

Consistent with the outdoor museums' becalming effects are the demonstrations of their craft-based economy. James Marston Fitch, who was concerned foremost with historic preservation as necessary to save prototypical artifacts, divined an essence of the craft-demonstration strategy: "The success of the working historical farm with the American public stems from a basic pedagogical principle: demonstrations of process—even when they do not permit participation—are a most effective means of imprinting them on the minds of the spectators."[41]

It was for urban dwellers, specifically industrial employees, that, he implied, demonstrations of the manual arts were aimed.[42] Two exemplars of the new

Figure 5.15. Pioneer Village, Minden, Nebraska, 1996. This site boasts twenty-eight buildings on twenty acres but has appended sundry items including Currier and Ives prints, a Pony Express Station, antique tractors, and the world's oldest Buick.

social history in the 1980s, Eric Gable and Richard Handler, judiciously took to task the premier outdoor museum, Colonial Williamsburg. After a careful two-year study of the program and interviews, of both staff and visitors, they concluded it was impossible to expect interpreters, however bright and well trained, to educate the public about complex historical issues.[43] The tendency lingered from earlier eras at the site to give the public what it wanted. Another museum scholar adjusted this claim somewhat, noting it was traditional visitors—not the general public—who came expecting a reassuring repetition about the high principles of the good old days.[44] For the Farmers' Museum in Cooperstown, the Web site extends the familiar invitation to celebrate: "Rediscover the innocent beauty, the intricate wisdom and the enduring charm of our rural past."[45] It is this tendency to celebrate, rather than critically investigate the past, that will limit the educational capacity of any museum except perhaps one of Roadside America; for that place still has its eager detractors.

The most restrictive and pejorative meaning of *museum* in common parlance is a consequence of the museum stereotype: a musty display of strange

Figure 5.16. Main Museum, South Barracks, Fort Ticonderoga, New York, 1940. The Pell family adhered to the prevailing standards of museum exhibit design in the early twentieth century as part of their memorable private restoration of Fort Ticonderoga. A handwritten note dates this display of cabinets and curios to be in use at least to 1948. Courtesy of Lake County Discovery Museum/Curt Teich Postcard Archives.

artifacts removed from their original context and labeled for identity in specialized jargon for the general public's edification. Much of this is attributable to an early museum paradigm known as a cabinet of curiosities. Gary Kulik described these traits in his treatment of the early Smithsonian Institution: "dull, dark, and lifeless . . . mausoleums of the old."[46] Taxonomy, or the principles of natural science, had informed such exhibits since the late nineteenth century. Implicit in their design was the Victorian assumption that civilization's progress could be traced and undeniably confirmed by the procession of artifacts from simple to complex and their increasingly greater utility. Lamps and spinning machines stood with Washington's tea set, Kulik pointed out.[47] At Cooperstown's Farmers' Museum, for example, blacksmith tools, carpenter's tools, and spinning and weaving implements initially made up separate sections on the first floor.[48] At Fort Ticonderoga, soldier mannequins stand at attention to protect display cases dedicated to relevant categories of historical objects (fig. 5.16).

Roads and Roadside Museums as Futuristic Displays

Museums have always sparked visitors' imaginations in one or another way. But those featuring automobility have seldom sparked grand visions in keeping with automobility's actual effects on the landscape. Although the antithesis of museums' usual concentration on the past, the General Motors Highway and Horizons Exhibit at the New York World's Fair for its two seasons in 1939 and 1940 represented the magnitude of automobility's potential at the time (fig. 5.17). Limited-access highways were at the center. Instead of the comparatively small and congested highways of the immediate pre–World War II era, the celebrated industrial designer Norman Bel Geddes conceived seven-lane highways flowing in one direction and four-level streets and bridge approaches in city scenes. Traffic coursed at speeds of fifty, seventy-five, or one hundred miles per hour on the highways "engineered for easy grades and for curves that require no reduction in speed," the *American City, a* planner's trade publication, quoted from the display in 1939. Lighting and ramped-loop access to crossing highways made for effortless and safe passage through a landscape cleared of "outmoded business sections and undesirable slums" in a "1960" city of "abundant sunshine, fresh air, fine green parkways, recreational and civic centers—all the result of thoughtful planning and design."[49] Visitors to the museum exhibit of idealized future automobility rode above it, enhancing the impression that nothing unfortunate was possible in this fully controlled contrivance. Public awe and cultural vanity stimulated a remarkable attendance record. "Crowds far bigger and more thrilled than have ever been attracted by any other exhibition of city and regional planning" queued daily to take the ride, the *American City* reported a month after it opened.[50] On many a day, ten thousand people waited for two hours to get in, and, by the time it closed after the last season, ten million had visited it.[51] Other features at the fair centered on the automobile, but none left so great a memory as the brief fifteen-minute ride into the future.[52]

Roads and Roadsides as Historic Display

Roads present a resource both attractive and staggering for those who would establish a museum of Roadside America. Although the totality would include the roadway that was an important determinant of a particular roadside, the roads' own conditions and those of the places along them were so voluminous and varied that some preservationists are discouraged from attempting the preservation of a road and its roadside in a museum.[53]

Figure 5.17. Spectators peer onto "Democracity," a city of the future covering 8 million acres with seventy towns, and boasting a population of 1.5 million. "General Motors," *Architectural Forum* 70 (June 1939): 401.

An installment in Pennsylvania illustrates how at least one untrained group came up with a unique answer that their deep interests compelled. Given the respected work of miniatures and dioramas in museums, it is a wonder that other museums have not followed Laurence and Paul Gieringer's example in Shartlesville, Pennsylvania, where they eventually built "Roadside America." They started as excited young boys in 1903 from a simple landscape perspective—the god's eye perspective—peering down from above, in their case, from Mt. Penn in Reading, Pennsylvania, and asking why not "make little houses the way they appear from here?" At present "The World's Greatest Indoor Miniature Village," as advertised by the later generations of the Gieringer family, encompasses more than four thousand square feet of a hand-crafted landscape of buildings that "is much more than just an 'attraction,' . . . It is more of a Shrine where one may find in the replicas of life's yesterday--a renewed faith in this country of our's [*sic*] and that makes the passage across time that much easier and happier." The message classifies the museum as traditional nostalgia, but its means are significant

Figure 5.18. Roadside America, Hamburg, Pennsylvania, vicinity, circa 1940. The revered small-town landscape at this site highlights Henry Ford's First Shop but also shows horse-drawn wagons and a trolley card. Courtesy of Roadside America, Shartlesville, Pennsylvania.

departures. First, it is innovative in its model of a budding automotive landscape. It is largely a model of a pedestrian landscape in the railroad age but there, prominently situated, is Henry Ford's first shop pointing to the incipient automobility (fig. 5.18). It is also a miniaturized model landscape with potential for the roadside.[54]

More commonly log cabins have drawn enthusiasts to large-scale outdoor landscape museums. The log cabin's powerful stimuli yet relatively simple construction are the reasons. Epitomizing America's revered pioneer age, our capacity to make do with what nature provides, and a belief in one family, one house, these full-scale individual log cabins and also collections are easy to find throughout the mid-continent (fig. 5.19). As the opening stage of the narrative about America's conquest of a rude landscape, log cabins are akin to the many restored gas stations breaking through the wilderness of poor mobility.

Still, the possibility of a large-scale outdoors roadside museum has been investigated. These investigations blend museums with preservation. Two different potentials exist for how Roadside America might be represented. First, there is historic preservation as a planning strategy that attends to the future development of existing and still-viable economic places, albeit with concern for their physical integrity from a period. Second, there can be museums whose strategy seizes hold of a particular past period without the intent that the museums turn a profit.

In 2000 the National Park Service undertook a study of the Lincoln Highway along its 3,380-mile transcontinental length. For a federally designated admission into the nation's park service, the resources along it had to meet four criteria. Two were satisfied: to be an outstanding example of its type, a road, and to provide the opportunity for public enjoyment or scientific study. Two were not satisfied: to exhibit exceptional significance in natural or cultural themes of national heritage and to maintain a high degree of physical integrity. In 2003, failing to find the resources of exceptional significance required for designation as National Historic Landmarks and noting large stretches that were void except for one or two features "to remind today's travelers of its history," the National Park Service team of evaluators assembled for the task was unable to recommend inclusion in the federal system. Given the highway's limited but not altogether insignificant stature, the evaluators advised that either a new not-for-profit organization be

Figure 5.19. The Lincoln Group, Century of Progress Fair, Chicago, 1933. Half of the replicas walled inside the group were log structures depicting stages in the ascension to greatness of Abraham Lincoln, also known as the "Rail splitter" for his skill with hewing logs. Here both iconic man and material multiply the importance of this museum behind stockade walls. The absence of a historic landscape surrounding the tight assemblage building by building--rendering it an "architectural zoo"—illustrates the designers' concern with symbolism over objective history. Courtesy of Lake County Discovery Museum/Curt Teich Postcard Archives.

established or that the extant Lincoln Highway Association be adapted for the work.[55] In effect the National Park Service was unprepared to assume responsibility for a museum, but it welcomed historic preservation, as we defined it above.

Absent an overarching federal authority, the Lincoln Highway's fortunes as a museum have been, since the inception of the preservation movement, in the hands of individuals and locally based initiatives. In 1992 fifty-seven people founded the not-for-profit Lincoln Highway Association in Ogden, Iowa.[56] It has been interested in scholarly studies as well as shared news about relevant current events, rendering its quarterly publication, the *Lincoln Highway Forum*, of considerable value for information as well as for stabilizing the organizational structure. Projects sprang up along the route. Four years after the association was founded, for example, people in the hamlet of Clarks, Nebraska (population 370 in 1990) collaborated, and high school students painted a mural of the highway through Clarks on the side of a brick building at the main downtown intersection. Residents with memories of the highway when it was still named the Lincoln Highway prepared their stories of it for the local newspaper. This form of shared memory has also grown common for Route 66. In 1992 supporters also greeted cars passing through Clarks on their way to the association's national convention.[57] The entire length of the highway in Pennsylvania was declared a state heritage corridor in 1995.[58] It unleashed funds for various projects along the route that would be of interest to travelers, aficionados, and businesspeople alike. At the intersection of Routes 30 and 29 in Westmoreland County, plans were laid for the "Lincoln Highway Experience attraction," an indoor museum exhibit that had been waiting for several years. At the Lincoln Heritage Corridor's headquarters in Ligonier, Pennsylvania, a gift shop also sold souvenirs to passersby.[59] Public encouragement and private management may be the most common future means of maintaining a museum along the road, but it is not the only one. In Story County, Iowa, at Niland corner, where the Lincoln Highway and the Jefferson Highway crossed before they were numbered 30 and 65, respectively, after 1926, the county's Lincoln Highway corridor study identified a complex common to early auto travelers. It was the Niland family's business, which comprised a gasoline station, a café, tourist cabins, an outdoor restroom-shower building for those at the cabins, a motel, and an apartment building. The Nilands donated the collection to the Colo Development Corporation, which is planning for its preservation as one of the best sites like it, not only in Iowa, but perhaps even the nation.[60] Restoration neared completion within two years, and the city of Colo hoped to earn maintenance funds by operation of the café and apartments (see fig. 6.10, next chapter).[61]

The national Lincoln Highway Association's own viability grew by 2007 to the point of opening a new national office in South Bend, Indiana, and delegating the previous one, in Franklin Grove, Illinois, to the national organization's tourism headquarters. National membership numbered about one thousand. Celebration, rather than critical analysis, typical of outdoor museums, remained the relative priority of the association's new director: "Highways embody our love of cars and the freedom to go where we want, and the Lincoln Highway continues to be a place where you can do just that."[62]

Individual buildings or an assemblage of a few at individual locations, federal resource surveys, and encouragement of private enterprise, indoor museums of traditional exhibit design, and the pleasure of the open road are all potential subjects of impartial study. Route 66, its acclaim greater than that of the Lincoln Highway, has followed the same pattern for a museum landscape. It took but five years after Route 66 was decommissioned from the federal highway system before public acclaim and lobbying caused the U.S. Congress in 1990 to enact legislation for a resource study to determine the corridor's significance and preservation options mentioned earlier. The four-year study concluded that services should remain locally managed while the federal authority could offer traditional advice and could guide preservation of buildings according to the secretary of the interior's Standards for Historic Preservation. In keeping with Congress's enabling legislation, overall management devolved to local authorities. Michael Romero Taylor and Kaisa Barthuli, respectively program director and deputy program director of the National Park Service Route 66 Corridor Preservation Program, advised that the local management strategy was best because local initiative had given rise to Route 66's life and later its resurrection.[63] Here historic preservation was articulated, and not a museum strategy. Through 2007 about one million dollars in grants was given to sixty-eight preservation and research projects.[64] In the private sector, by mid-2003, Hampton Hotels paid a half million dollars for SAVE-A-LANDMARK signs along Route 66.[65]

Historic preservation and museum strategies remained compatible. In New Mexico, the state's not-for-profit heritage preservation alliance, for example, promoted preservation of Route 66 signs it determined were "historic" after applicants contacted the alliance (fig. 5.20). Examples illustrated in its brochure for recognizing and saving historic signs included a few that were no longer in use by companies but also many that were. Tracing concern along Route 66 for saving its past in some fashion reveals that Barstow, California; Pontiac, Illinois; and Lebanon-Laclede County, Missouri, housed examples of the numerous traditional museums for Route 66. Illinois invited bicyclists along its Route 66 Trail to raise awareness. Cuba, Missouri, painted twelve murals along the route in its town, fostering an historic preservation sensibility (figs. 5.21 and 5.22). Elk City, Oklahoma, maintained the National Route 66 Museum Complex, albeit it was one depicting a Victorian house, a Stars and Stripes room, a Farm and Ranch Museum, and an interactive ride in a 1959 Cadillac; this reflected a concern for a past Route 66 but one liberally blended with several pasts other than that of Route 66.[66]

Other kinds of transportation offer a wide gamut of formats with attendant experiences for visitors. Railroad museums range from stationery displays of locomotives (steam, diesel, and electric), to rolling stock amid other objects in a park, to those where trains are ridden or their locomotives are even driven by visitors. Some are situated on retired rights-of-way or locations not in service before. Passenger depots are the ancillary railroad structures most often on site. The subcategory of rail services for which the intercity landscape is prime is the trolley. Steamtown National Historic Site administered by the National Park Service on forty acres in downtown Scranton, Pennsylvania, occupies the former rail yards of the Delaware, Lackawanna, and Western Railroad. Railroad educational programs for younger children are offered, and the site is dedicated to the technology of steam railroads in their heyday, between 1850 and 1950 (fig. 5.23). Mystic Seaport at Mystic, Connecticut, is the premier U.S. museum for the maritime industry, and it covers forty acres and includes a nineteenth-century village and working shipyard. Four of its ships are individually designated National Historic Landmarks. Aviation museums are no less diverse, but none of the transportation types are represented in facilities so obviously relevant to automobile transportation as are automobile museums. Petroliana, for example, occupies no major museum exclusive of other automobile-related artifacts.

Automobile museums, as much as museums for other transportation types, often display their objects in static, taxonomic order. Given the mass consumption, this is not unfathomable, considering the tendency for many people to have

Figure 5.20. The New Mexico Heritage Preservation Alliance's brochure on sign preservation along Route 66. It briefly informs of the various sign-mounting styles and neon signs, and it draws parallels with highway signs elsewhere as well as enlisting volunteer help. Courtesy of the New Mexico Heritage Preservation Alliance.

Figure 5.21. Restored (1932) Phillips 66 Gasoline Station, Cuba, Missouri, 2009. Lynn Wallis, owner of a gasoline wholesale and retail business, had this station on former Route 66, restored. Her family operated it in the 1960s and 1970s.

owned a favorite car. Men raised in the early twentieth century were the first to grow fond of automobiles from that period, preserve them, and raise questions of how to preserve them.[67]

Among academicians the one most concerned with the manner in which technology is treated in museums is the social and cultural historian Joseph Corn. He has identified four styles: internalist, celebratory, social historical, and cultural historical. The internalist dominates automobile museums because, Corn maintained, they do not have the funds to explore other options, and often men who have spent their lives working with or around automobiles staff this sort of facility. Here interpretation predominates, rather than accumulations of performance statistics and motoring potential that would diminish the artifacts' brilliant achievements. Unfortunately this sort of operation also enables a traditional belief in male ascendancy and continued power. The celebratory praises the technical accomplishments of individuals, nations, or cultures. Critical analysis, most often the domain of academicians, addresses in the social historical vein the implications of automotive or other technologies between groups and

Figure 5.22. Gasoline station murals, Cuba, Missouri, 2009. Depicting the area's early automobile period became the local Viva Cuba Club's intent with its mural program begun in 2001. The station now sports a set of murals suggestive of the town's roadside landscapes of some seventy years ago. The project's popularity has induced several property owners to restore roadside buildings, the start, perhaps, of a roadside museum.

in the cultural historical vein the interplay between the values that made the hardware acceptable. Corn found the latter two styles were seldom practiced.[68]

The Auburn Cord Dusenberg factory, administration building, and showroom in Auburn, Indiana, a National Historic Landmark of recent designation (2005), well represents the internalist style and a bit of the cultural historical. A showroom as museum gallery is rooted in the suave allure of prestige vehicles and the quaint charm of marques not mass produced by a giant corporation. A recent and brief introduction to the museum in the National Park Service's *Common Ground* elaborates on the glamorous theme. "In the 1920s and 30s, Auburns, Cords, and Dusenbergs Represented [sic] car manufacturing's apogee of style and engineering."[69] Models are displayed in taxonomic order, perhaps best suited to objects d'art. In Dayton, Ohio, Bob Signom II found a suitable location for his long-standing private collection of Packards, Packard Company artifacts, and historical memorabilia, namely, the former building of Citizens Motorcar Company, a Packard dealership (fig. 5.24). Signom acquired the building in 1991 and restored the interior. Known in popular parlance as "America's Packard

Figure 5.23. Steamtown National Historic Site, Scranton, Pennsylvania, 1997, giving a view of a steam and diesel locomotives in the railroad yard.

Museum," it includes the showroom, service department, and pavilion. Henry Bourne Joy, a prominent founder of the Lincoln Highway Association in 1913, and Packard president, owned several of the Packards on display, making them highlights in the showroom-displayed collection (fig. 5.25).[70]

In Springfield, Illinois, a former Ford dealership has been adapted for use by several banking operations, and a former Chevrolet dealership next door has been restored for other reuses.[71] Such facilities could be recategorized as museums, or showplaces of historic preservation, should historic autos replace the current businesses.

In Murdo, South Dakota, two generations of the Geisler family have founded and maintained a museum more fully akin to the sort of representation of Roadside America that could be actualized in other locales. A. J. "Dick" Geisler, a native of New Ulm, Minnesota, had moved to California, where he married and started a family. But a John Deere and Chevrolet dealership at the junction of U.S. 16 and 83 in Murdo, South Dakota, sparked his interest, and he moved there and acquired the property. With his new possession located at a busy intersection, the wily Geisler appreciated how fascinated were travelers after he parked an old car outside his new gasoline station by the dealership. He and his sons be-

Figure 5.24. Packard Museum, Dayton, Ohio, 1987. Signom's building is proudly advertised to be the only restored Packard dealership used exclusively for a Packard museum.

came car collectors, and, following their father's death, the boys managed what had become the Pioneer Auto Museum. Now, just off the intersection of I-90 and U.S. 83, the museum comprises ten acres onto which forty-two buildings were moved and accompany the autos, trucks, a motor home, and tractors Dave Geisler has acquired. Dave took pains to acquire a wood-frame filling station from nearby Vivian and restored its manual gasoline pumps, billboard, and restrooms for exhibit at his outdoor museum.[72] Rocks, gems, fossils, jukeboxes, and "turn-of-the century" clothing on display break up the automobile setting, but the awareness of a landscape of broader appeal than just to auto buffs certainly distinguishes the Geislers' work. It opens possibilities for similar collectors (figs. 5.26 and 5.27).

In step with professional museum standards and with the consultation of social historians of the automobile, "The Automobile in American Life" exhibit at the Henry Ford Museum and Greenfield Village since 1987 has won praise for its innovation. Inclusion of roadside artifacts—such as flashing neon advertisements for a McDonald's restaurant, drive-in theater, diner, tourist cabin, Holiday Inn room, and gasoline station—help contextualize the exhibit and help explain the automobile (fig. 5.28). It has been widely praised for emphasizing the meaning

Figure 5.25. Packard Museum, Dayton, Ohio, 1989, showing one of Henry Bourne Joy's personal Packards. He drove this one himself on the Lincoln Highway.

of the automobile as extended from the artifact itself on display in myriad rows throughout the museums galleries (see fig. 5.12), but it does nothing to grasp the kinetic dimension of motion down a highway lined with specialized services for automobilists.[73]

Smaller museums, measured by professional respect and/or popular publicity, serve interests or social groups often overlooked or suppressed in the culture of the standard way of belief.[74] As the number of such museums, especially those along the roadside, grows, they deserve serious study not only of their subjects but for suggesting how the roadside itself might be remembered. Roadside America's often improvisational nature may be its own best milieu for seeking to construct a museum of Roadside America.

* * *

Collector-founders, seminal patrons, curators, and exhibit designers have overtly shaped museums in various ways for centuries and, relatively recently, also visitors, by their invited interaction. An overview of these accomplishments is not easily achieved; no one specializing in museum studies has attempted it to our

Figure 5.26. Pioneer Auto and Antique Town, Murdo, South Dakota, circa 2005. The foreground in this aerial view of the site reveals something of a historic Main Street setting, albeit with contemporary automobiles, a truck, and a van. Courtesy of Pioneer Auto and Antique Town.

knowledge. Until recently, academically inclined scholars were not even partners in the manifold responsibilities of guiding museum theory and the means of representation.

Long after the museum's inception, it was nonetheless a specific type of place. Where discoveries in all their startling novelty set observers to integrating them into a received body of knowledge, museums were welcome contrivances. The New World had long necessitated this as did the Renaissance's recovery of ancient knowledge. The consequences were a nervous taxonomic display strategy. How did this or that artifact or natural object relate to others? Knowledge was a means of control, and representation of the things from which knowledge followed; for the museum was after all a scientifically guided inclusive enterprise and produced a kind of confinement. Also, to museum visitors, knowledge on display was information they were intended to learn, certainly not question or even extend to wider applications through their life experiences or insights.

When pride in modern accomplishment became a self-conscious faith in advancement over the past, museums were assigned another new role. They were a primary place for celebrating the achievements of the better life. This could encompass military museums where the victory of technologically advanced peoples celebrated the conquest of native peoples and their presumed savage lifestyle. It could include museums of technology where the hardware of the triumphant was displayed for public approbation. Where leaders of various movements or key events once dwelled, there, house museums had cause to exist.

By the early twentieth century some of these preconditions for museums were out of sync with popular values. Outdoor museums came primarily to embrace nostalgic recollections of ways and objects lost in the unsettling aspects of industrialization. Moguls of this fundamentally new way of life were themselves key founders of museums looking to the past for comfort and cultural reassurance that civilization had not gone astray albeit to greater comfort and widely shared affluence.

How then could the automobile's profound impact on American life find a place of honor? Why would any museum celebrate the principle artifact and technology of this revolution? It would only if it dwelled on the automobile's materialism in the manner of its physical beauty and staggering numbers. No role was yet feasible in places with limited budgets for big machines that needed to

Figure 5.27. Pioneer Auto and Antique Town, Murdo, South Dakota, circa 2005. To underscore the age of architectural and automobile artifacts, antique cars from the collection are occasionally parked on the street in the town shown on the aerial view. Courtesy of Pioneer Auto and Antique Town.

move along costly highways or streets to capture an essence of automobility. By the twentieth century's close, cars and trucks had little representation in museum planning except as part of static exhibits. Was the concept of the material object controlled by elites––an old museum strategy––still at odds with fully represented automobility? Automobility was unquestionably something that millions of nameless individuals had brought to fruition in redefining the U.S. landscape. Motorists and their passengers needed gas, food, lodging, auto repairs, and other services located where they were convenient for the consumers and not necessarily for roadside entrepreneurs. Museums were also preconditioned to respect what was enduring and physically substantial. Automobility on the landscape was predicated by the very antithesis, the cheap and the ephemeral.

Arbiters of tastefulness in the landscape and later on environmentalists added explicitly to the negative side of the ledger about automobility's impact. If consumer convenience concomitantly meant suburban sprawl, along with the frenetic abandonment of older shopping malls and strips for newer ones, then the costs outweighed the advantages to a capitalist economy driven by ever greater

Figure 5.28. Sign from Douglas, Michigan, Drive-In Movie Theater displayed at the Henry Ford Museum at Dearborn, Michigan, 1988. The Henry Ford Museum now emphasizes the history of the automobile and the automobile's impact on life in America, a mission quite apart from its founder's wish to preserve the history of the pre-automobile era. History was "bunk," Henry Ford was reported to have said. What he meant was that written history is bunk. What he appreciated was vintage material culture displayed so that Americans would be more appreciative of how life was once lived.

expansion and seemingly ceaseless novelty for its own sake. Carbon emissions were tangible threats with lethal consequences, not just eyesores like the roadside. Why display, much less celebrate, unchained automobility? The very representation of a phenomenon that is still ubiquitous also violates the illusion of a bygone past that museums used to lure the curious.

Evidence of changed museum preconditions glimmered, however. Some professional and amateur-staffed automobile museums were not the only settings to break with honored traditions. No longer did the "Great Man" theory of history hold exclusive sway so that widely honored figures such as Abraham Lincoln were expected to have a house museum. Nor were single structures alone deemed up to the task of embodying the various new kinds of significance. Lincoln's Home too was but one building in a coveted neighborhood landscape. Putting a landscape back to a specific time, as if a snapshot of time, was no longer insisted on. Landscapes could embody change over time.

An exciting new era might dawn, and it is worth considering how automobility's full meaning might be achieved in a museum of Roadside America. Celebration seems less important when exploration becomes the goal.

CHAPTER SIX
EXPERIENCING THE PAST AS LANDSCAPE AND PLACE

Can Roadside America's rapid and ever-changeful evolution be remembered more accurately?[1] How might a very fluid past, and yet one most significant in the American experience, be better assigned historical meaning and thus better sustained in public memory? Material culture is an essential key. The concern here is with whole landscapes—built environments experienced at scales broader than that of mere architecture. Building ensembles have in the relatively recent past characterized places organized around automobile convenience, especially along the margins of streets and highways.

But roadside landscapes and places have proven most impermanent, a feature, it could be said, that has been preprogrammed. Especially early on, Roadside America was quite changeable, being, for the most part, highly experimental given the uncertainties of success. In the early days of motoring, the automobile by no means enjoyed a certain future. Auto-oriented landscapes and places in the United States very much evolved through trial and error. And yet understanding that process, irrespective of the general lack of durable built environment that has resulted, remains important to comprehending how automobility in the United States ultimately triumphed.

It appears that the historic preservationist's approach to remembering early Roadside America has but limited application when it comes to matters of landscape. Preserving significant buildings that are relics from the past, especially in situ, remains important. Such activity potentially contributes much to contemporary environmental diversity, giving today's landscapes a sense of time depth, and this heightens our understanding of the past. Additionally it adds visual interest to contemporary scenes. It represents good stewardship whereby architectural resources of the past are recycled toward future use. But the fact remains that such activity, as important as it is, mainly heightens how we experience contemporary places by sustaining elements of pastness that would otherwise be missing. Only in a limited way does it encourage experiencing landscapes or places in ways fully reminiscent of past circumstances. To bring the past—or at least some version of the past—more fully alive, the historic preservationist's penchant to conserve would seem to require adding something of the museum curator's penchant to simulate or replicate. If early roadside landscapes are largely gone, then perhaps they ought to be reconstituted in some sense, if only on a limited basis. It is that thinking that has brought us to consider the outdoor museum as a means of celebrating early Roadside America.

What would such a museum contain? As important a question as that may be, it is not the purpose here to detail the kinds of buildings and other artifacts that an outdoor museum of Roadside America might contain, as interesting a speculative exercise as that might be. It is certainly not intended to suggest just how a museum ought to be laid out—how period landscapes ought to be simulated as history-based places. Nonetheless the appendix does offer a checklist that outlines the museum elements that future planners might consider in replicating Roadside America as an outdoor-museum display.

Why a Museum?

There are some eight thousand museums in the United States.[2] Do we really need another one? Yes, because what is lacking is a museum—particularly an outdoor museum—that fully explores the automobile's impact on the American experience, especially its impact on and through built environment. A museum is needed that effectively interprets early-twentieth-century landscapes and places that were specifically auto-oriented and auto-convenient, or, in other words, a museum that considers frontally the rise of Roadside America. As we have argued, nothing has affected American landscape more dramatically than use of motor vehicles. The nation's geography has been substantially reorganized around the use of motorcars and trucks—what first emerged along the nation's highways but now dominates life nearly everywhere. Yes, there are car museums. Many old gas stations have been restored. There are old stretches of highway that have been preserved as well. But will such venues suffice to communicate fully the important historical and geographic lessons fully implicit in the roadside's rise to prominence?

Perhaps the nation's numerous car museums point the way, especially those that have added aspects of vintage Roadside America to their displays of vintage automobiles. In the Studebaker National Museum in South Bend, Indiana (containing the former Studebaker Corporation's collection of historic vehicles dating back to the 1890s), a vintage gas pump and the figure of a gas station attendant stands among the cars being displayed (fig. 6.1). At the Antique Car Museum of Iowa at Coralville, just outside Iowa City, curators have gone a step further, mocking up a vintage gasoline station as a centerpiece for display

Figure 6.1. Vintage gasoline pump, Studebaker National Museum, South Bend, Indiana, 2009.

(fig. 6.2). Although such exhibitions offer mere genuflection to landscape and place, they are a start. Of course, what would be preferable is not vintage cars contextualized by selected aspects of vintage roadside so much as vintage roadside contextualized by vintage cars.

It is the outdoor museum that offers real opportunity. As for outdoor museums as a genre, there are today many re-created "villages" located across the breadth of the United States, as previously discussed. Most of them, as mentioned, are oriented to celebrating America's pioneer past and/or agrarianism, including the valorizing of today's less frequently encountered family farm. Some museum villages celebrate the small-town America of the past and its romanticized Main Streets. In some of these museum villages, it is not just the horse-and-buggy days that are remembered, but also the early days of motoring, with a gas pump or two displayed in front of a general store or even an old gas station in sight. But there is no outdoor museum specifically focused on interpreting early automobility. There is no museum dedicated to remembering early roadside culture, material or otherwise.[3]

Roadside America does not just have an interesting history, but a most significant history. It lessons are not trivial. They invite serious attention well

Figure 6.2. Vintage gasoline station re-creation, Antique Car Museum of Iowa, Coralville, Iowa, 2009.

beyond a quest for kitsch and nostalgic embrace and well beyond, it might be argued, traditional forms of historical documentation—social and architectural histories, for example. Roadside America also invites serious attention beyond the embrace of popular culture, be it in music, film or literature. For Americans there are lessons to be learned through directed kinds of firsthand experiencing—by confronting things more or less as they were once experienced by our predecessors. In other words, how are Americans going to remember the history of automobility? It is unlikely that reading books, viewing photographs, viewing films, listening to stories, or even searching contemporary roadsides for architectural and other relics could fully suffice.[4] But if we are to experience past landscapes and roadside places explicitly, then re-creations are needed.[5] Again, that is what suggests to us the importance of the museum—the "museumscape" if you will—where things can be encountered at scales at or approaching those of lived-in landscapes and places.

Landscape and Place

In 1991 Edward T. McMahon, formerly the executive director of Scenic America, published an article circulated in various newspapers that was entitled "Let's Save the Landscapes, Not Just the Landmarks." "It is one thing to save a structure; it is quite another to save a place," he wrote. "While we've been saving landmarks, we've been losing our landscape." He was not particularly a champion of landscapes and places that are roadside-oriented. Indeed he, like most preservationists at the time (and even today), saw automobility more as a threat to historic landscapes and places than as a creator of them. "Today, a person suddenly dropped along a road outside almost any American city would not know where he was, because it all tends to look the same." At Gettysburg, he intoned, the visitor encounters car dealers, wax museums, fast-food restaurants and tract housing ringing the battlefield." Major approach roads, in other words, were lined with billboards and dreary strip development.[6] The automobile, especially at Gettysburg, appeared to be the enemy of preservation. Yet, for the better part of century, visitors had come to Gettysburg primarily by car. Was there not something from that automobile-relationship worth appreciating—something worth preserving?

In the 1970s the geographer Peirce F. Lewis speculated as to why the historic preservation movement in the United States appeared truncated. It was not just

Roadside America that was unappreciated in a historic sense. Public apathy reflected a kind of blindness to built environment in general. But landscapes, especially those with strong evidence of the past well rooted in them, could foster a fuller and more sophisticated historical sensibility, he said.[7] Seeing some things from the past at the scale of landscape might even be essential—that is, built environment represented either through on-site preservation and/or museum re-creation. Then visitors could have the pleasure of physically moving around a place reminiscent of the past, thus experiencing not only textures of the past, that is, the surface look and feel of things, but also past proxemics, or the spacing of things. This would lead to a fuller appreciation of history—specifically of how places once functioned. It is important to allow personal experiencing of the past to accrue at an actual geographic scale of life. Such experiencing might, among other benefits, provide modern Americans with alternative views as to how the future might be more successfully configured—"alternatives," Lewis added interestingly, "to the plastic homogeneity of endless suburbs."[8]

There are at least two points Lewis makes in his essay. First, many persuasive voices advocate knowing the past in landscapes or places configured as they existed in the past—enabling a knowledge of the past through personal encounter with material culture at the landscape scale. Second, he also seemed to say, just as McMahon had, the past one might prefer to know was not necessarily one that encompassed the full effect of the automobile. But what of those important landscapes of transition whereby automobiles gained acceptance in traditional places—to produce, eventually, those "endless suburbs"? Of those overly homogeneous, "look-alike" commercial strips?

Again automobility's neglect as a historical force reflects in part a penchant to cherish the past in terms of highly selective, yet very powerful myths, especially as regards types of places thought fundamental to formation of the American experience—for example, wilderness and nature, the frontier, the family farm, Main Street America, and so on. It also reflects a tendency to celebrate famous and historically significant people and events, such as Robert E. Lee or Civil War battles. Americans tend to prefer the heroic to the commonplace when thinking about history. They favor the historic over the historical, and they tend to overlook significance in commonplaces, such as the nation's evolving roadsides. And many, if not most, commentators on the American scene, both past and present, have tended to follow suit.

Perhaps familiarity does breed contempt, especially when dated things are contrasted with the better things that had been anticipated. The architect Robert Venturi thought such thinking was especially dismissive of the vernacular in U.S. architecture. Whereas the frontier log cabin might be valorized for its presumed folk implications, if not the presumed heroism of American pioneering, the same was difficult to say about the equally significant buildings of, for example, Roadside America. Whereas elite buildings designed by gifted architects for affluent clients, both public and private, were easily appreciated, commonplace gas stations, motels, and the like were not. There was an "American snobbery" concerning the nation's commercial and industrial architecture, he noted. It was too common. And yet vernacular architecture could be as significant as great architecture in its aesthetic as well as its historical, technical, and contextual dimensions. "All the world admires the vitality and validity of our iconographic roadside architecture—except snooty Americans in the land of the free," he wrote. "Some day architects will derive inspiration from the American commercial vernacular . . . and some day billboards, as well as advertising, will grace the walls of craft museums, hanging next to hand-quilted bedspreads."[9]

It was essential, John B. Jackson argued, to understand the contemporary scene in terms of what had come before. People needed to know how things got to be, not just in terms of what had been accepted and retained from the past, but also in terms of what had been rejected. Thus Americans needed to understand the commercial strip, for example, not merely as a "degenerate version of the traditional landscape," but as something important in its own right. People needed to see its history not just "as a long, drawn-out backsliding, the abandonment of old values, old techniques, old institutions," but also as something fully rationalized on its own merits given emergent new technologies and new circumstances.[10] To comprehend a landscape, one started with a piece of land and then turned to the buildings thereon. But the road or the highway was also important, Jackson claimed, as "the more powerful force for the destruction or creation of landscapes." The automobile, of course, was the reason. At first the automobile had "introduced the notion of exploration" and brought "abstract joys of relatively effortless fast motion." But the road soon began to change the landscape itself, he noted. "The road or street or highway became the armature, the framework of landscape." And not only was speed introduced, but also accelerated impermanence.[11] Personal convenience also became a factor, as a sense of individualized mobility made motoring and the landscapes and places it fostered fully seductive.[12]

To appreciate how automobility affected life in the United States, we need to keep at least some of the material culture of early motoring close at hand.[13] Old cars and trucks certainly should be included, and also pieces of old roads and old roadside buildings, such as restored gasoline stations, which have become in recent decades a competitor to the log cabin as fodder for historical imagination. And things preserved in contexts simulating past landscapes and places are necessary to tell the fuller story.

Interpreting Geographic Change

Interpreting the automobile's impact on life in the United States at the landscape scale is what a museum of the American roadside would readily enable. Outdoor history museums involve simulation, and they need not require that all things actually be objects of survival, and certainly not objects of survival in situ. As "museumscapes" they are most often constituted out of parts taken variously from other places, and gaps are often filled by things that have been newly built to seem old. History museums re-create as well as preserve as they offer displays for firsthand experiencing. Outdoor history museums are three-dimensional displays. The best of them are accurately presented at the geographic scale of life as actually once lived. They enable visitors to have firsthand experiences with places that are no longer extant.[14]

Museums are perhaps the most familiar means of showcasing artifacts from the past. Worth considering is the outdoor museum as a genre and its potential for interpreting the history of American automobility, especially its impact on landscape. It is helpful to contrast the outdoor museum with the historic district and the historic or heritage corridor, as the two other venues are also capable of amplifying comprehension of the past in landscape terms. Outdoor museums, as we have seen, contain old buildings, many of which may be authentically historic, but which nonetheless are usually moved in from other locations. Often buildings are arrayed in some kind of idealized configuration (often called a "village"), but seldom, unfortunately, in ways that reflect an understanding of actual landscapes or kinds of landscape. Accordingly, outdoor museums as a genre in the United States have often been likened to zoos, where animals rather than buildings are displayed totally out of their natural or original context.[15] Too often the disciplinary orientations of historians and architectural historians have been at play rather than the orientations of historical and cultural geographers.

Only a few outdoor museums in the United States have attempted to create displays at the actual scale of landscape. Instead most compress geographic space. Compressing space by crowding buildings reduces costs, including the expense of buying real estate for museum development, but this also reduces the expense of day-to-day upkeep and supervision once a museum is established. Further, it reduces visitor effort or inconvenience in accessing the individual displays that are arrayed. However, compressed sites distort basic spatial relationships once prevalent in actual historical places. They provide incorrect cues regarding past human spatiality, especially as regards human proxemics. Thus in most outdoor museums spaces between buildings are inaccurately portrayed. The relationships between public and private spaces are especially misrepresented.

Such is not the case at Old World Wisconsin near Eagle, Wisconsin, an expansive outdoor museum created to showcase Wisconsin's rural ethnic heritage (fig. 6.3). Houses and barns (and indeed whole farmsteads) have been moved to the site thus to represent German, Danish, Norwegian, Finnish, and

Figure 6.3. Old World Wisconsin near Eagle, Wisconsin, 1982. The view looks across fields toward what once was the farmstead of the Koepel family, German immigrants of the 1850s. It is not just preserved buildings that we see here, but a "museumscape" historically accurate in the spatial relations of buildings to the road, buildings to the fields, and buildings to one another.

other ethnic groups in the nineteenth century. Located in what was previously a forest preserve of over thousand acres in extent, the reconstituted farmsteads are accurately spaced, surrounded by cultivated fields and pastures, and connected by roads, as they actually would have been. Thus the accuracy encompasses not just the careful architectural restoration, but the landscape re-creation as well. Visitors, if they choose, can move from farmstead to farmstead on foot, but most choose to ride on buses or trams provided for their convenience, as the total display is spread out along several miles of road. Even relic fence lines have even been imported and set up along rights-of-way. Many fields are tended using traditional tools, and the crops that are planted are those that were common during the mid- to late 1800s. Horsepower, of course, is emphasized.

However, might the museum's era of interpretation be extended? Might it be made to reflect rural life in Wisconsin into the early decades into the twentieth century? If so, vintage automobiles and trucks—and especially early tractors and other farm equipment—might easily be introduced, and thus the museum could be enabled to emphasize not just a traditional pre-automobile world, but a world of important transition whereby rural Wisconsin acceded to modern life. Refocus on rural modernization might make the museum more relevant to visitors who come today largely from urban backgrounds, with most being removed from farm life by at least several generations. The coming of the automobile would be an important story, including subtexts such as the coming of free rural mail delivery and consolidated schools, for example. History could thus be interpreted less as a static condition—something fully past—and more as a process of change that continues yet today.

In contrast, preservationists, rather than museum curators, have championed the historic district, as we have seen. Historic districts are areas designated for their relic architectural resources. But they involve not just buildings per se, but buildings as arrayed along streets or around public squares or other open spaces in ways that are often distinctive vis-à-vis contemporary subdividing proclivities. Indeed the spaces between buildings are often considered as important as the buildings themselves. Architectural codes and other zoning restrictions frequently dictate what property owners can and can not do with their properties, the idea being to stabilize physical change in thwarting untoward development that might diminish an area's historical ambience. "History," in other words, is made into a device for managing unwanted geographic change.[16] Historic districts involve architectural ensembles that have survived largely in situ, although where gaps exist old buildings might be moved in or new buildings built as sympathetic fill-ins. Historic districts enjoy a kind of historical authenticity. They are landscapes designated and variously managed not just for historical significance (as material evidence of the past), but for their physical integrity (as the past incarnate).

Old Salem in Winston-Salem, North Carolina is an example of a particular variety of historic district worth noting. There was a recognized need to protect an inner-city neighborhood from increased car and truck traffic—the main highway south out of downtown ran through the area—as well as from the continued intrusion by light-industrial, wholesaling, and other commercial activities because the area had not been adequately zoned and from the continued deterioration of its housing stock as slumlords had come to the fore. Thus a not-for-profit foundation was created for the purposes of property rehabilitation and resale in fostering gentrification, but also for the protection of selected buildings as museum displays. Although a bypass road dampened traffic on the area's streets, cars and trucks were not prohibited. Parked cars line the district's streets at all times (see fig. 4.3). Although clearly rooted in the past, Old Salem is very much a contemporary scene.

Even more effective in controlling the automobile are the curators at Shelbrooke Village at Shelbrooke, Nova Scotia (fig. 6.4). Here the idea was not

Figure 6.4. Sherbrooke Village, Sherbrooke, Nova Scotia, 1985. Closed off as an outdoor museum during the day, this section of the village is not a museum re-creation so much as a venture in historic preservation, and its buildings are preserved on their original sites. Buildings not containing museum exhibits are indeed lived-in, with the historic district remaining an integral part of the town.

just to create a historic district where a local population would remain in residence, but, as at Old Salem, to create museum displays in a host of buildings spread throughout the area.. The purpose of the venture was to create a visitor industry capable of energizing a faltering town economy, with the town being located in an area of declining agriculture and far distant from the employment opportunities of a city. At Shelbrooke part of an actual village is cordoned off as an outdoor museum during the day, and perhaps half of the area's nineteenth-century buildings are open to visitors as museums venues. Only after evening hours are cars and trucks freely permitted, and residents are exempted during the day. Thus Shelbrooke combines museum and historic district impulses.

Think of what might be accomplished in such a place, but with old motorcars and trucks allowed and their presence tied in with added museum interpretation of early automobile implication. That this sort of thing has not happened here, or rarely elsewhere, suggests that outdoor museum curators, like preservationists, may have their biases. Through the twentieth century, museum curators in both the United States and Canada looked to the pre-automobile era—especially its pastoral or farm-oriented aspects—as something lost or soon to be lost. North America, it was argued, was rooted historically in the frontier, or pioneering and family-farm traditions. Preserving the vestiges of this life was of primary importance. That kind of thinking, as mentioned earlier, was what drove Henry Ford, as a collector of old things, to emphasize the pre-automobile past at Greenfield Village, despite his significance as a purveyor of modern automobility.

Most outdoor museums, whether in the United States or in Canada, do not focus on the coming of the automobile or on its consequences. Rather they largely reject the automobile in valorizing life as it was before the automobile. One exception, also in Canada, is the Heritage Park at Calgary, Alberta, created in the 1960s (figs. 6.5 and 6.6). Located there is a reconstituted town, and its parts are displayed rather accurately on a grid of streets very much at the scale of real life. The display is intended to interpret life in Alberta before the rise of modern Calgary (Canada's Houston), a city built on the discovery of petroleum and very much a metropolis that is largely auto-oriented today despite an elaborate mass-transit system. The museum, however, does include a few anachronisms—a replica of an eighteenth-century Hudson Bay Company fur-trading post, for example. Nonetheless visitors can walk the streets as if in a time warp, and the more discerning of them ignore, at least for a moment, the evidence of fur trading.

Think what might be accomplished with even greater emphasis placed on automobility. Significant additions might be made—for example, a livery stable converted to an auto-repair garage, an automobile storage garage with vintage cars on display, a hotel parking garage with even more cars, several early gas stations, an early tourist court, and so on. Such additions would enable museum curators to illustrate better the social and economic changes wrought a century or so ago by modernization in small towns across the whole of North America.

The historic or heritage corridor is a relatively recent but important preservation concept. In the United States, highways such as the Lincoln Highway across Iowa and historic Route 66 from Illinois to California have enjoyed interpretative programs of this sort.[17] The heritage corridor (today most preservationists seem to prefer the term *heritage*) represents an embrace of traditional historic preservation philosophy, highly valuing as it does the conservation and rehabilitation of structures in situ. But those buildings, arrayed

Figure 6.5. Postcard view of Heritage Park, Calgary, Alberta, circa 1970. Calgary, a modern metropolis of more than one million residents, sustains this outdoor museum in a south-side municipal park to remind residents and visitors alike how life was for Albertans early in the twentieth century. Courtesy of Heritage Park Historical Village.

Figure 6.6. Street scene, Heritage Park, Calgary, Alberta, 1978. The museum sustains a collection of iconic buildings. Depicted here is a small-town hotel, a grain elevator, and, on the right, a livery stable, all authentic buildings moved in from distant sites. The geographic scale of the typical early-twentieth-century Prairie Province town has been used.

individually along a route, also enjoy integrated interpretation. Visitors are sent from one to another. Corridor programs encourage visitors to travel from site to site in order to obtain an overall picture adding up to more than its parts. But, again, by offering a sense of time-depth spread geographically along a path of movement, heritage corridors say more about contemporary landscape than historic landscape. They assert only weakly how built environment in the past once fit together and how, of course, it once functioned. They say relatively little about how places were once experienced. They do, however, facilitate contrasting the past with the present. And they facilitate visitors coming in their own cars—thus to commune with travel in the past through travel today. The automobile is clearly made frontal. But the emphasis remains *today* rather than *yesterday*.

It should be emphasized that heritage corridors need not link only individual buildings. They can also link sections of restored landscape, embracing, for example, building ensembles in original roadside orientations. At Shamrock, Texas, along Route 66, preservationists have fostered a stunning restoration of a late-1930s vintage gasoline station (fig. 6.7). The building today serves as a visitor center for the town. Clearly it stands an important roadside landmark, a major architectural anchor for Route 66 interpretation across the Texas panhandle.

Figure 6.7. Restored gasoline station, former Route 66, Shamrock, Texas, 2003. An important landmark, the building has been carefully rehabilitated to serve as a visitor information center. Its size, along with its distinctive Art Deco styling, makes it an important anchor on the Route 66 Corridor east of Amarillo.

However, only two blocks to the south, off former Route 66 and one block east of the town's Main Street, sits a cluster of buildings residual from the earliest days of motoring in Texas. At a single intersection there are two early gasoline stations (one restored by the local historical society), an even older service garage of the kind that predated gas stations, and an early auto-era hotel (figs. 6.8 and 6.9). On one nearby lot a house stands, a structure potentially ideal as a reconstituted tourist home should museum curators in the future want to showcase such a facility. Numerous lots in proximity that now stand vacant invite various kinds of useful architectural additions, buildings brought in from other locations or perhaps constructed from scratch following historical templates—an auto dealership, a tourist court, or a drive-in restaurant, for example. How readily outdoor-museum initiatives and historic- or heritage-corridor initiatives might be made to complement such an effort.

Outside Colo, Iowa, an ensemble of roadside buildings survives, restored to their 1950s appearance and function (fig. 6.10). This building cluster personifies the nascent commercial strips that evolved along highways peripheral to small towns. In 1923, at the intersection of U.S. 30 (the former Lincoln Highway) and U.S. 65 (the former Jefferson Highway), the Reed family opened a gas station to

Figure 6.8. North Madden Street, Shamrock, Texas, 2008. Located several blocks south of Route 66 and one block east of Main Street, a cluster of early roadside relics includes two vintage gas stations dating from the early 1930s, a hotel from the 1920s, and an automobile repair and storage garage from the 1910s. They are not located on Route 66, but instead augment the town's downtown, which was originally oriented to the railroad.

be joined several years later by relatives, the Nyland family, and their roadside cafe. In the late 1940s the Nylands added a motel. Closed in 1997, the complex sat vacant until a local group formed—the Reed/Nyland Corner Committee—to plan restoration. Promotional literature for the site proudly states today that it is "the most intact 'one stop' site on the Lincoln Highway in Iowa and possibly the entire United States."[18]

Initial Questions to Ask and Answer

Each sort of interpretation—the outdoor museum, the historic district (especially with museum venues), and the historic or heritage corridor (linking museums)—has its pros and cons. Each involves a consideration of different conservation and interpretation options. Combining the better attributes of each ought to be vigorously pursued—with the outdoor museum, of course, as the key concept. Additionally our living in a computer age ought to be considered. How might museums, whether or not they are lodged in historic districts and/or arrayed along historic or heritage corridors, be amplified through digital display?

In the outdoor museum, the simulated past can be created and then managed effectively as a period display at the scale of landscape. Certain questions are

Figure 6.9. North Madden St., Shamrock, Texas, 2003. Motorists were required in many towns along early Route 66 to leave the new highway and seek gas, food, and lodging in or near traditional Main Street business districts. Indeed the history of Roadside America is fully rooted in such locations.

implicit, such as what kinds of buildings and other structures ought to be installed (see the appendix); how they should be arranged to replicate authentic settlement morphology; what kinds of experiences and, more important, what memories might visitors be expected to form (or re-form), and take away; how visitors might be encouraged to explore, and for what purposes; and how change over time should be treated. In regard to social change, one might also consider how issues of gender, race, ethnicity, age, and income should be treated. In regard to economic change, questions abound: What role did big corporations play? How did small-business operators fit in, especially mom-and-pop outfits? Particularly important, what were the consumer satisfactions (and dissatisfactions) that Roadside America accrued?

Certainly the historic district, specifically one partially turned to museum use, represents an important option. A speculative National Museum of the American Roadside could be a lived-in place. In other words, it might be a contemporary place that functions selectively in everyday ways, but with significant history-museum implications. Are there existing landscapes appropriate to such development, and, if so, where? In Dayton, Ohio, as previously discussed, stands Citizen's Auto (the National Packard Museum) in a former Packard dealership

Figure 6.10. Reed/Nyland Corner, east of Colo, Iowa, 2009. Here the classic trilogy of roadside services—gas, food, and lodging—are remembered in two restored buildings (a gas station and a motel) and a roadside cafe that has been substantially rebuilt.

building (see figs. 5.24 and 5.25). Other buildings that formerly housed other auto dealers as well as repair garages are located nearby. Thus in recent years the city of Dayton has designated the area "The Motor Car District." What once was the city's "automobile row" is now celebrated. When such locations exist, how ought they best be developed? Contemporary functioning could be mainly commercial, as in the past, and there is the question of whether visitor-oriented retail operations should be encouraged. It stands to reason that they might. If so, what kinds of goods and services ought to be emphasized? A reconstituted roadside could be turned to selling souvenirs—perhaps, souvenirs oriented to car history. But to what extent could such places also be residential, that is, actually lived in?

The historic or heritage corridor deserves careful consideration also, perhaps because it may be in the long run the only form of actual road and roadside preservation economically feasible. After all, who is to pay for an outdoor museum, or even a historic district's partial development as a museum? In Canada federal and provincial governments have been forthcoming in supporting outdoor museum creation, but not so in the United States, where private interests have tended to dominate, largely through philanthropy. But there is a limit to such private funding. A nation can support only so many history museums. And in recent years museum attendance, and thus sustaining entrance fees, have been in decline nationwide. Is it really wise to consider creating something totally from scratch? The heritage corridor, however, is already there. It does not have to be created so much as simply reinterpreted. Sections of road and roadside features that can be considered relics already exist. They may require renovation and alteration as visitor attractions, but they do not need to be inserted on a contrived "game board" of visitation expensively generated anew at the scale of landscape.

With corridor interpretations, however, contextual historicity is an issue largely ignored. The contemporary scene, whatever it might be, stands fully acceptable. Again questions arise, such as which relics would deserve the preservationist's or the museum curator's attention and whether, for a given corridor, a program of triage should be devised to determine what gets interpreted and what does not and on the basis of what criteria, with an eye to overall balance. Someone must ensure that a sampling of potentially significant things survives and just which periods are to be emphasized as well as the transitions from one period to the next. Perhaps several "museumscapes," constituted at various scales and with various topical and temporal emphases, ought to be arrayed along established heritage corridors.

The cost element in museum, district, and/or corridor development brings us to still another option—the virtual outdoor museum. We live in a digital age, and children in the last twenty years have grown up with computer screens looming before them as second nature. Increasingly across the United States we see museum advocates (many of them frustrated in their attempts to launch actual museums) resigned to abandoning real time and real space for electronic simulations thereof. Their intent is to play with virtual realities. In proposing a museum of folklife focused on the material culture of nineteenth-century rural southern Indiana, the folklorists John H. McDowell and Trevor J. Blank saw both pros and cons to such a venture. "Granted," they wrote, "a digital display is not the same as a physical facility, and scrolling is hardly the same as strolling. But then again, the medium of digital display offers possibilities for interlinking resources that cannot be accomplished as efficiently in the actual physical world." What they had in mind is allowing "visitors" to access and wander electronically through a visual display backed up by educational materials (such as model school lesson plans and multimedia games) and a blog or chat room to facilitate the discussion thereof. Their "museum" would consist essentially of a pictomap on a computer screen with "stations" for a visitor to click on—a covered bridge, barns and houses of various styles—especially log buildings—and a cemetery, but also sites that emphasize woodworking tools and furniture making. The "visitor" would click and explore.[19] Of course, such technology could also be used to amplify actual "on-the-ground" displays, aiding historical interpretation in an outdoor museum, at a site in a historic district, or at a stop along a heritage corridor. Even more intriguing is the idea that visitors to a virtual museum, once donning eye goggles or a helmet, might move a digitized space of visual simulations as if bodily walking or even motoring in an actual place.

Such speculation, of course, begs the questions of how visitors might move through the real space of an actual outdoor museum display. They could move by car, perhaps their own car, or by museum vehicles (vintage autos and trucks) or by bus. To what extent would visitors be expected to walk? At least one theme park in the United States has offered visitors the opportunity to ride in vintage cars around a track simulating a vintage highway (fig. 6.11). In a museum, how would visitors be encouraged to do more than merely come, look, and go and to

Figure 6.11. Postcard advertisement, Chaparral Antique Car Exhibit, Six Flags Over Texas, Arlington, Texas, circa 1960. Visitors were offered rides in "horseless carriages" in order to relive the Roaring Twenties, resulting in a historically inaccurate conflation of two very different periods in American history. In many theme parks, however, what is historically accurate counts less than what is historically plausible. Courtesy of Six Flags Over Texas.

what extent would they be encouraged to participate? They might experience the past as a kind of customer—buying gas, having their cars serviced, buying food, and even renting overnight accommodations.

Authenticity and Detail in Outdoor Museum Display

Any museum whose test for success is crowds of interested, if not excited, visitors runs the risk of a abandoning the critical capacity that is essential to an educational agency. Roadside America is a topic well suited not only to museum development, but to theme-park development as well—something we would hope to see avoided. Theme parks are commercial enterprises designed for profit—venues intended primarily to entertain, although educational objectives also may be emphasized in their promotion. Accordingly exhibits in theme parks are built around historical persons, events or activities, and/or architecture, but need not necessarily be historically accurate in terms of what they display nor historically correct in terms of what they suggest. Theme parks include large amusement complexes such as Six Flags over Texas (fig. 6.11). Closely related, however, are small venues, especially those that from the very beginning of the auto age were a part of evolving Roadside America. Witness the Dogpatch Reptile Garden and Hillbilly Farm at Lake Ozark, Missouri (fig. 6.12). Here entrepreneurs suggested a kind of game with which most visitors, one suspects, readily engaged. Fantasy had entered. Everyone knew that an authentic historical view, or authentic regional view for that matter, was hardly at hand. But it was fun.

All the past cannot be conflated in one place to depict real history, which is perhaps the central problem with most history-based theme parks. Of course, the same applies to interpreting the past in history museums also, and, for that matter, in historic districts and along heritage corridors. Choices need to be made. Which era or eras are to be represented? How is each separately, or when taken together, to be treated programmatically? Alden Hopkins at Williamsburg in the 1940s designed decorative gardens for various historic properties that dated from different periods, but through a single "historic" garden style.[20] Thus even highly regarded professionals can succumb to the temptation to apply a universal motif in the face of historical diversity. Alone those motifs do not make for a theme park, but they demonstrate how even the best designers can succumb to an urge for inner satisfaction (be it quest for aesthetic solution, personal acclaim, or some other reason) thus to erase the distinctions of past times.

Figure 6.12. Postcard advertisement, Dogpatch Reptile Garden and Hillbilly Farm, Lake Ozark, Missouri, circa 1960. Like most commercial roadside history venues, here is a tourist attraction largely built on fantasy. Visitors are invited to play games of pretend regarding history and place. Courtesy of Lake County Discovery Museum/Curt Teich Postcard Archives.

For museum curators Roadside America, as a theme, may readily foster the creation of a timeless sense of place or foster conceptions of place that conflate very different eras of the past. No one can confidently say what belongs where or when, given that Roadside America has proved so changeful. It is difficult to discern specific eras in understanding roadside history, so constantly fluid has Roadside America been. Ordinary Americans may not have much of a problem with mixing things up from different past eras, given their tendency to consider the past to be just that—past. It is easy to lump past events together. History looms as a convenient category into which things no longer current may be bundled. There will likely be aroused an inherent tension between professional and public standards in the dialogue about change and changelessness at roadside-oriented museums, but this tension can be addressed in ways equitably and mutually beneficial.

Central to any historical presentation is the identification of origins, the treatment of when something began. People will want to know who created it and why, and how long it lasted. It is necessary to anchor things in time, ideally through a sense of cause and effect. In the matter of Roadside America, where the whole comprises multiple elements and where all elements are in constant flux, historical understanding needs to be carefully time-centered. The Pueblo Court at Amarillo, Texas, pictured here in the 1930s, had evolved over some fifteen years and would continue to change (fig. 6.13). Should museum curators choose to reconstitute it today, what date—what era—ought they choose to represent? Perhaps it might be the date of its opening, the time of its greatest popularity, the time of its greatest profitability, the period of its maximum physical development, or even the date of its closure. Or a museum curator might best assign the period for which maximum documentation survives, thus to allow for enhanced accuracy in restoration. Multiple dates could be selected and represented through different portions of the exhibit. The latter would allow for interpretation of change over time. Different sections of a museum might emphasize the material culture of different decades (see the appendix).

Actual buildings may survive that are fully reflective of a past date or era, but, if they are of some vintage, it is more likely that they will display evidence of significant modification over time. Ought that modification be the thing emphasized? Given the volatility of the roadside, ought volatility be what curators focus upon? That seemingly argues for museumscapes that deliberately range

Figure 6.13. Pueblo Court, Amarillo, Texas, circa 1950. Hardly a set piece created at one time, the Pueblo Court evolved incrementally over more than a decade. The advertising signs often changed. In the years immediately after World War II, the large state-of-the art neon sign was quite noticeable. Courtesy of Lake County Discovery Museum/Curt Teich Postcard Archives.

over one or more periods, even indiscriminately juxtaposing things of different eras together. If change is not made implicit in a single building, then it can be suggested through building juxtaposition. Or perhaps the juxtaposition of different era landscapes may hold the solution, with each landscape representing accumulated change over time in its assemblage of structures and artifacts. Visitors would move between these museumscapes, and each landscape would range over a period. Thus together they could illustrate the wide sweep of overall change that has affected Roadside America. The problem then becomes how to relate each display, how to enable the visitor to transition from one to another.

Questions of authenticity are especially important when totally new construction is inserted into a museum complex. What is wholly original, what is partially reconstructed, and what is wholly a replica should be recognized. Perhaps each kind of thing would be carefully labeled and interpreted differently, or at least with different emphases. The museum curator should take care that something inserted as newly constructed accurately represents the past, but it is possible that an entire set piece mixing old and new could be presented as universally authentic, as neither authenticity nor accuracy may be the museum curator's most important concern. Certainly visitors to a historic site ought to feel that they are reliably guided. As time travelers into the past, they do not want to be misled. But they also want to be fully interested, if not excited, by what they find. Kenneth Hudson, in his review of leading history museums worldwide, concluded that it is the museum curator's purpose to encourage museum patrons "to feel involved in history," that is, to identify themselves with aspects of the past that are personally significant. It may not be so much that a thing that is encountered is thought to be true or real so much as it is thought to be plausible, at least in terms of the visitor's own past experiences. However, reliance on authentic objects (on materials that are actually relics from the past) offers the greatest personal payoff, he concluded. Original objects, he said, have a power to engage people that relics, irrespective of how iconic they might be, do not.[21]

Structures of various kinds dominate our conceptualization of places, but landscapes do not consist solely of structures. Old structures do not themselves suggest historicity.[22] Also important are the spaces between structures and their sizes, configurations, furnishings, and, most important, the uses to which they are put and the people that engage in activities there—how they are dressed and how they generally behave. Things deemed "natural"—slope, drainage, and vegetation, for example—and even the surfaces which museum visitors walk and stand on, especially the pavements, are likewise important. The question arises of whether these things need to be fully authentic to sustain accurate historical interpretation.

Coauthor Keith A. Sculle, in his career at the state of Illinois's Historic Preservation Agency, administered for a short time the historical program at Lincoln's New Salem State Park near Petersburg, Illinois. New Salem, begun as a village display in the 1920s, was one of the nation's earliest outdoor history museums. Only two original buildings, both much modified, survived on the site when museum development began. Therefore the bulk of the village was almost totally fabricated anew. It comprised newly constructed buildings intended to simulate what once had been (fig. 6.14). Unfortunately, at the time there was very little documentation as to what actually had once typified frontier buildings in Illinois. And no documentation as to what New Salem had once been like. Nor was archaeological expertise readily available to help the site developers. Buildings were erected patterned on highly generalized notions of what New

Figure 6.14. Lincoln's New Salem State Park, Petersburg, Illinois, 1969. Animal power is clearly on display here at one of the nation's earliest museum "villages" created at the start of the auto era. Curators, in approximating what New Salem had once been, adopted a generic log-cabin motif—only a rough approximation of what once had actually characterized frontier Illinois.

Salem's log architecture had been and how they had been arrayed. A landscape was created that simulated the past only crudely. Although the site is authentic, for the most part the buildings and their positioning are not. Additionally the grounds have been substantially hard-surfaced to facilitate visitor access and museum maintenance. They were landscaped like a park, which, of course, was exactly what the site became. And yet New Salem immediately began to attract visitors, as it continues to attract them today. Contrivances aside, it remains an important pilgrimage place for Americans to pay homage to the nation's martyred Civil War president.

Lincoln's New Salem claims to represent things as they actually were. And most visitors no doubt readily buy into the assertion. The anthropologist Edward M. Bruner, unlike Kenneth Hudson, holds that tourists are satisfied if a site is merely "credible and convincing." They do not require, nor are they necessarily aware of, professional standards. Tourists at New Salem and other such places thus become active collaborators in what Bruner terms "constructed authenticity."[23] It is perhaps more seriously undertaken but no less involves the same kind of game-playing orientation encouraged by the silliest of snake farms and hillbilly roadside attractions. Evidence exists that tourists will even accept known fakes as no less authentic than originals, especially in displays that feature both.[24]

Even more troubling, at least for those who would seek only landscapes unhampered by restoration or accept only reluctantly exhaustively documented reconstructions, is the fact that people from different social backgrounds, and especially from different societies, tend to define authenticity differently. Whose sense of authenticity is to count?[25] Most museum curators undoubtedly attempt do their best. When setting up museum exhibits, they seek degrees of authenticity suitable to visitor expectations. When visitor expectations change, and certainly when society dictates a different take on what is and what is not authentic, most museum curators will seek to redo exhibits or at least will interpret them differently. Indeed the recasting of historical meaning has accelerated in recent years, led by ever-changing fads and fashions in historical scholarship. Historical reassessments along Marxist, feminist, and other ideological lines of thought have become legion. To what extent should museums assign the values (social, economic, political or otherwise) that were predominant in the past as opposed to those fashionable and faddish in the present day? Presumably they should assign both.

Artifacts in museums very much help serve to ground our thinking. Thought centers on the thing, its origins, its uses over time, and its larger social implications as changed over time. Artifacts, including landscapes as artifact ensembles, anchor confrontation with the past, largely restricting flights of fancy as to what can or should be surmised. The solid object remains the reference point for past assessment. Visitors readily take interest in museum artifacts as sources of information. For some, future inquiry may be suggested. For at least a few, their own artifact collecting may be encouraged. And then there is the sheer aesthetic enjoyment of encountering old things, especially things that carry a strong patina of time-worn use.[26] Some academic historians, recognizing their profession's current tendency to reinterpret the past in faddish ideological terms, have come to value material culture's anchoring influences highly. The questions invited are basic, including how the thing originated, who originated it, how and why it has changed, what it meant in the past, and what it ought to mean to us today. Perhaps it is in answering the last question that currently fashionable ideologies should prominently figure.

Historians, especially "public historians" working in museums, have become self-conscious in their use of artifacts as a source for historical knowing. In particular they have focused on how artifacts "work" on museum visitors and thus on how museums can more effectively communicate with visitors.[27] Disputed authenticity offers opportunity. It can have educational value to the extent that curators welcome its discussion, setting forth for museum visitors alternative points of view and even alternative conclusions about what it is they see. Such disputes are useful in sketching out the untoward aspects of life as once lived. A thing is a thing. But the question remains who benefited from its making and its use, and who failed to benefit. Understanding the past should not be restricted to generating warm feelings.[28] Learning from a museum visit, however, probably does need to remain somewhat pleasant. Perhaps untoward stories need to have satisfactory endings or at least point toward satisfactory outcomes in order to help a museum to attract visitation.

Not completely divorced from authenticity is the matter of detail. Perhaps it has more to do with accuracy. In a museum of Roadside America, even the smallest and less significant things should be carefully displayed, such as curb indentations, parking lot stripes, and manhole covers. Street surfaces could be of the period, or they could be calculated mainly to present-day expediency.

Just how specific such a museum should be in simulating of a past actuality and whether all the negative aspects of Roadside America would be included would have to be decided. Among the less pleasing aspects are the noise, the dirt, and the safety hazards of motoring and the auto graveyard, along with power poles and power lines and, for that matter, billboards—what many Americans considered in the past, and still consider today, to be forms of landscape desecration. The roadside could be seen to sprawl with abundant wasted space or with weathered and neglected buildings displayed, seen as a thing in decline. Should roadside dereliction have a place? Vacant buildings, after all, have always been part of changing roadside scenes (fig. 6.15).

Going Indoors at Outdoor Museums

Outdoor displays have their strengths, but they also have their limitations. Not every idea can be effectively communicated outside. At a museum of Roadside America the interiors of period buildings displayed would be vital to what was communicated overall. Inside the restored gas-station service bay the

Figure 6.15. Closed gas station, Ola, Arkansas, 2007. Multiple adaptive reuses can be a sign of wise stewardship. Here a gasoline station closed, served briefly as a church, and then became a retail shop in a display of roadside impermanence.

tools of the auto mechanic would be displayed and perhaps a car undergoing repair. Mechanics might actually be seen working on cars. In the reconstituted roadside cafe, food preparation might be viewed and indeed the "fast food" of the typical quick-service restaurant of the past might actually be offered to visitors. Reconstituted motel rooms might be fully furnished and actually rented by the night. However, outdoor display will also need to be reinforced by indoor exhibits in special-purpose buildings. There is the matter of introducing visitors to what lies outdoors, and there are issues that period building ensembles alone can not fully assign. For example, the pesky matter of sprawl is perhaps best considered through interactive cartography and photography (especially satellite photography) displayed indoors in specially contrived settings. Certain aspects of Roadside America, particularly the driving experience, will only with great difficulty be brought to an outdoor museum. As desirable as it might be, it will simply be impossible to put visitors into vintage cars on vintage roads to simulate the motoring experiences that typified motorists in the past. Lessons on motoring might be had through computerized interactive games.

The Importance of Signs

Roadsides of all periods have registered on motorist sensitivities mainly through visual display. Signs have been especially important both for controlling traffic and for promoting commerce. Place-product packaging cues travelers to commercial services, with signs playing a crucial role. Building massing, architectural styling, color schemes, driveway and parking-lot layout, and, most important of all, logos forcefully displayed on advertising signs serve to identity local, regional, and national networks look-alike stores. The shared image is calculated to creating and preserving brand loyalty among customers, who arrive and depart mainly by automobile.[29] The high-recognition value of the colors yellow and red gave an advantage to the Shell Oil Company's network of gas stations. McDonald's golden arches proved beneficial to the chain's development beyond all expectations. Place-product packaging would be a major theme for museum visitors to explore. Outside, abundantly displayed signage would demonstrate commercial Roadside America's essential visuality. Inside, the history of different brands, and indeed the origin and evolution of their sign signatures, would be more fully elaborated. Outside place-product packaging could be demonstrated. Inside it might be more fully explained.

The display of signs would surely anchor any museum celebrating the history of Roadside America. Signs were fundamental to how the commercial roadside functioned. True, any outdoor museum would want to display and interpret the distinctive building types that characterized Roadside America over time—buildings that clearly looked like gas stations, drive-in restaurants, or motels. And the "ducks" of Roadside America would also need to be included—the fanciful teepees, windmills, and other fully iconic pieces of roadside kitsch that today carry such strong nostalgic implications. But, as we have argued, Roadside America throughout its evolution was actually dominated by "decorated sheds." And what they were decorated with was mainly signs. Traffic signs would also deserve careful inclusion. Traffic signs have been for motorists the principal means of programming the road experience. Motorists build up and validate expectations in driving or motoring from place to place with the help of signs. But they also bring to road travel full governmental control, especially over traffic movement (figs. 6.16 and 6.17). An outdoor museum of the American Roadside would substantially be a sign museum.

We have mentioned roadside blight, including that of billboard art. But a museum of Roadside America needs also to explore roadside beauty, including important attempts in the past to encourage roadside beautification, not just by removing things that were thought to be unsightly, such as billboards, but most especially through landscaping. From the very beginning, motoring was viewed as a means of accessing the nation's scenic beauty. Even commercial interests were involved in that conceptualization, promoting, as they did, the scenic values of motor travel. General Motors' once-evocative slogan—"See the USA in your Chevrolet"—still echoes. Bus transportation certainly took scenic roadsides to account, with Greyhound, for example, designating its buses as "Scenic Cruisers" in the 1980s when elevated passenger decks and large windows permitted generous views of roadside landscapes.

Researching Roadside History

Perhaps the most successful museum programs in the United States today combine artifact collecting, display, and interpretation with research. The research library is vital, and the conference center is also important in this regard. The Henry Ford Museum and Greenfield Village in Dearborn, Michigan, and Old Sturbridge Village in Massachusetts come immediately to mind. At Dearborn the library contains archival material from the Ford Motor Company,

Figure 6.16. Fruit stand south of Dupont Center, Florida, 2002.

as might be expected given that Henry Ford founded the museum. The library's many other holdings emphasize U.S. history generally and include, by way of example, the photograph archive of the Detroit Publishing Company, the nation's premier publisher of postcard art early in the twentieth century. The library at Sturbridge emphasizes nineteenth-century American history with an emphasis on rural vernacular architecture and the tools and techniques of farming during that period. Libraries are intended to reinforce museum curation, which makes for increased accuracy in exhibits and in exhibit interpretation. At Sturbridge the library also guides its "living history" program whereby gaps in knowledge are filled through "living history" agendas—experiments with tools and ways of doing that enable researchers to reconstruct physically what might have been. With a museum of Roadside America, a library collection would logically focus on the vernacular architecture of roadside commerce, the history of outdoor advertising, the history of road building, the history of motoring, and so on.

Period trade journals of industries that have contributed to roadside commerce—the petroleum, fast food, and lodging industries, for example—would also need to be included, as well as trade journals oriented to grocers (especially the developers of the early supermarket chains), owners of auto dealerships, and

Figure 6.17. Signs at the intersection of State Road 204 and I-95, south of Dupont Center, Florida, 2002. Government pronouncements and commercial enticements compete for attention near the interchange.

the developers of shopping centers. Trade journals give insight into commercial intentions and provide outlines of the business strategies variously adopted and abandoned over time. Not to be overlooked are travel books, travel magazines, and travel guides. Their articles as well as in advertisements provide historical documentation of the rise of motoring as a recreational pursuit. Publications by and for civil engineers, urban planners, architects, and all the other professionals directly involved in actually creating roads and roadsides as material culture should also be included in the library.

Popular culture—the fiction, films, and even postcard art that reduced Roadside America into something readily and easily celebrated both as reality and as fantasy—should likewise be incorporated. Novels and short stories explore the iconography of Roadside America, particularly "open road" literature, are worth preserving in such a museum, as well as the many travelogues that included auto tours and were produced for commercial movie houses. As we have previously explored, many Hollywood movies were fully "road movies." Postcard images are especially important in visualizing Roadside America's past. Few were the gas stations, roadside restaurants, or motels that attracted serious artistic attention; but many were the roadside businesses that paid for and distributed advertisements in postcard form. We have liberally used postcard images in

Figure 6.18. Postcard advertisement for General Motors, Chevrolet Division, "Quality Used Cars," circa 1955.

illustrating this book. Allow us to include one more, a card issued by General Motors' Chevrolet Division to promote its OK Used Cars and Trucks (fig. 6.18). Would an outdoor museum dedicated to the history of Roadside America be complete without a used car lot?

Of course, a research library need not solely comprise hard materials such as actual postcards. It could also be digital. Again, the computer age looms. Library sources would not be used solely to document exhibits and thus to direct their interpretation. They could be used, as well, as the basis for interactive display, and the "virtual" dimension of a museum could be enhanced in augmenting or complementing "real" displays, even to the extent of making the museum visitor a kind of researcher. Additionally a research library need not be restricted to materials fully edited or otherwise carefully crafted, such as recorded reminiscences, or oral history.[30] Oral historians, using various interview and participant observation technique, probe the lives of individuals and indeed of people across whole communities to outline the ordinary, the commonplace understandings that are too often missed in other forms of documentation. How, for example, did a roadside retailer get started, and what were his or her expectations? What prompted change, and what brought success or even failure? Looking beyond the experiences of the roadside entrepreneur to the average consumer of roadside services, things that should be demonstrated include showing what was travel by car was like, what its pleasures and its difficulties were, and why it was undertaken.

Again, no museum should only "celebrate" the past, at least in the word's narrowest definition. Not just the successes and pleasantries deserve attention. Necessarily a museum of Roadside America would confront the myth of the "open road." Although car ownership and use, and thus the rise of Roadside America, had very much to do with affluent Americans enjoying enhanced degrees of geographic and social freedom, motoring has been anything but the individualistic, freedom-enhancing experience that early motorists craved. Roadside America has never been a laissez-faire utopia for libertarians. Indeed nowhere has governmental or community intervention become more evident than on and along U.S. streets and highways —everything from road building to traffic control to land use control is very much a community endeavor.[31]

The "open road" myth still sustains strong and often unquestioning support for cars and highways as the nation's foremost transportation mode. Part of the museum curator's challenge to that myth is the extent to which certain Americans were denied automobility's fullest freedoms. Through the twentieth century, many roadside businesses were closed to African Americans. The Civil Rights Movement of the 1960s definitely targeted roadside venues—restaurants and motels most especially—in combating racial discrimination. Gender issues also need assigning. In the earliest days of motoring, men were clearly favored over women when it came to providing motoring products and services. The typical motorist was once considered to be male, as well as white. What happened (or did not happen) along U.S. roadsides helped wrought important social change, some would say even revolutionary change, as the twentieth century unwound. Degrees of promiscuity—as tolerated if not encouraged in the back seats of cars as well as in the so-called hot pillow joints (motels that rented rooms by the hour)—greatly changed American sexual mores. It was a function of the increased anonymity that quickly came to characterize Roadside America as the "stranger's path."

Sponsorship and Funding

Again, it is not our intention to advance a specific plan for an outdoor museum. Our intent is to promote an idea and to stimulate thinking about how public memory of road and roadside history might be better promoted—a history heretofore largely overlooked in telling the American story. There remains the issue, however, as to how such a museum might be financed, irrespective of what it might actually be. Such a project, at least one conceived and executed on relatively a large scale, would need to be financially feasible, but the question remains of who would pay for it. Certain precedents come to mind—some successful and some not.

Public responsibility executed at local levels brought Old Salem into being in Winston-Salem, North Carolina, and Heritage Park to fruition in Calgary, Alberta. State involvements brought Lincoln's New Salem and Old World Wisconsin to the fore as provincial action did for Historic Sherbrooke in Nova Scotia. It might be emphasized, however, that in each of those instances, private organizations actually launched the planning and public promotion that ultimately brought government in as a primary sponsor. Congress, through the auspices of the National Park Service, created Steamtown USA, a tribute to railroading and its historic contributions to life in America. Certainly automobility has exerted as much influence, if not more influence, over the American experience as the railroads and certainly over the past century. Unlike in Canada, it is only private funding that sustains the majority of large outdoor museums in the United States. Both the Henry Ford Museum and Greenfield Village and Old Sturbridge Village are operated by not-for-profit foundations, having been originally funded by the generosity of individuals. However, today most history museums, even the wealthiest of them, face shortfalls in annual income. They struggle to maintain services. This reflects declining visitor numbers, in part a function of changing vacation patterns in the United States. Fewer families, especially those with children, take long motor trips for pleasure, and other sorts of recreational travel having become more popular. Much of today's tourist dollar is siphoned off by theme parks, which have placed themselves in direct competition with museums of all kinds. Admittedly the times may not be auspicious for a new kind of history-museum initiative. But the early planning and the early promotion can certainly more forward.

There are many potential sources of funding for an outdoor museum of Roadside America. Trade associations might prove crucial, especially those concerned with automobile manufacture, road construction, and retailing in general—especially the selling of cars, petroleum, food, and lodging along American roads.[32] Indeed specific corporations might prove willing to subsidize specific exhibits that showcase their own corporate histories. Trade unions might be another source. But, given the recession conditions that prevail at the time of this writing, trade associations and trade unions, and even some of the nation's largest corporations, especially the car companies, have been hard pressed to sustain even normal business activities, let alone pursue museum philanthropy.

To our knowledge the only roadside museum attempted to date was the work of Suffolk County, New York, under the aegis of its Department of Parks. The initiative died aborning in 1987. The proposed museum, to be located east of New York City on Long Island, originated when preservationists undertook to preserve the Big Duck—the iconic roadside feature now used by architects and others to characterize all programmatic architecture, and not just that which is roadside-related. The idea drew support from the New York Council on the Arts among other organizations but was too large for available funding. What was proposed was an ensemble of some fifteen buildings arrayed as an early-twentieth-century roadside typical of Long Island. The intended site for the museum was an existing park, but the plan encountered legal snags, including strict New York State land-use regulations concerning natural areas (a surrounding pine barren in this case), and loss of a donated diner as a result of a lawsuit.[33]

* * *

Has the time come to contemplate seriously an outdoor museum dedicated to telling the story of Roadside America? Certainly it is time to give serious thought to early Roadside America as a most significant aspect of our history, the important physical outgrowth of which pervades the nation's geography almost everywhere today. Americans long ago bought into motoring, and it has changed their lives and even the places they call home. It is time that we examined critically our automobile dependence, especially its environmental aspects—not just on nature, but on built environment also. How did we get to where we are today, and what should we be doing about it? Remembering how things got to be is an important focus, and remembering how Roadside America evolved over time seems more important than ever. But there is the elusiveness of Roadside America, a result of its fundamental ephemerality. It is difficult to remember how things were, and thus how things got to be, when it has all been so fundamentally changeful. We need something to anchor our memories, something that gives us firsthand experiences at (or approaching) the actual geographic scale of how things once were. A hands-on ability to confront the history of Roadside America is necessary. We know what Roadside America, as celebrated in literature, art, and film, has meant symbolically. Studied by historians and other scholars, its evolution both as actuality and as metaphor has been well outlined. But we need to see for ourselves. The outdoor museum can tell stories at the scale of landscape and place. Uncertainties will certainly plague such a project, but the time has come to give it careful thought and perhaps even to start careful planning.

CHAPTER SEVEN
THE ROAD CONTINUES

Those who train their talents on cultural memory usually choose edifying qualities to assert the need for special stewardship—whether it be a matter of aesthetics or a matter of fundamental historical centrality. Roadside America may or may not qualify on grounds of beauty. However, it clearly does deserve attention on the basis of historical significance. Roadside America may fail tests of nobility and heroism, or, for that matter, the test of cultural essentiality, but it has been fully persistent in American life over the past century, and fully pervasive over the past half-century. Roadside America has introduced itself into nearly every aspect of contemporary life, either directly or indirectly.

How then will we remember Roadside America, especially its early years? The question also arises as to whether Americans will recall accurately the early infatuation with its conveniences, its seeming liberation, and its fashionable modernity, and thus its popular invitation to enhanced personal identity and status. How will they remember that early appeal and the template that that appeal set for nothing less than the wholesale reorganization of the nation's geography? America's roadsides of even the recent past are rapidly evaporating, submerged by ongoing redevelopment. Doing nothing to preserve at least something of the earliest material culture of Roadside America will not aid remembering, but bring forgetfulness. Roadsides, like all kinds of places, change. And today's roadsides are programmed to change; its architecture and its landscape configurations are altered constantly in response to rapidly evolving marketing strategies, technological innovations, and the ever-accelerating fads and fashions of a consumer society.

One way to remember is to behold the present scene and reason back from it. The chief advantage of such a stance is that its starting point is verifiable, warts and all. Remembering back from the present, however, clearly invites selective amnesia and perhaps even fabricated history—the past distorted both through omission and commission. Thus, as David Lowenthal, warned, remembering the past is easily, and all too readily, conceived as contrived "heritage" rather than as actual "history." Heritage involves partial and often distorted remembering designed more to advocate on behalf of some present-day course of action (or inaction) rather than accurate storytelling about the past—history as it actually might have been. It produces a stilted look backwards that is calculated more toward advocating a desired future based on a presumed past. Often the myths, traditions, and nostalgic stances of heritage makers are intended to aid the afflicted or people or communities in search of greater security through a sense of shared community. Across the globe that search, as often as not, has been based on perceived ethnic and religious commonalities.[1]

Even the seemingly socially benign roadside can be made to carry heritage implications. Pictured here from the 1950s is Cherokee, North Carolina, a place configured not so much to celebrate a cultural heritage as to commodify that heritage (fig. 7.1). Merchants here have pitched a local culture to motorists through roadside attractions that have coalesced as a commercial strip, a thoroughly American thing to have done, particularly in those years just after World War II. But the local "Cherokee" experience, whatever it might have been, did not develop the teepee (note the iconic building programmed to look like one). In roadside terms that building is very much a "duck." But it is not a Cherokee duck. Other buildings stand as decorated sheds with signs and logos suggestive of a Native American past, if not a Cherokee past—all calculated to meet tourist expectations as to what the Cherokee experience might have been. However, the symbols at work were largely of other Indian nations as far way as the Great Plains. Like so much along early American roads, it engendered commerce through games of make-believe. This place spoke not so much about history as about commercial opportunity and customer satisfaction.

Lowenthal, in warning about false history, questioned historic preservation as a kind of remembering, and he questioned history museums also, especially outdoor museum contrived as landscape and place. In preserving material culture, how easily many museums sustain incomplete if not altogether false histories. For one thing, a respect for endurance is advanced over ephemerality. Notions of stability tend to be advanced over notions of change. In the outdoor museum,

Figure 7.1. Postcard view of Cherokee, North Carolina, circa 1950. Signlike buildings, including the teepeelike structure on the left, wrought false testimony as to what Cherokee life was or once had been. But it resonated well as a roadside attraction, providing visitors with what they expected to see—and not necessarily what they ought to see—in generating income and community affluence among a population that has been variously "othered."

the past tends to become a set piece. Disrupting the flow of change easily invites distorted remembering, with the accumulated debris of preservation too readily smothering the search for history under a cloak of heritage.[2] But to reject totally the use of material culture (including that defined at architectural and landscape scales) as a means of looking backward over time seems excessive. It is one thing to insist on reason, rather than on therapy, in reviewing the past, but this is short-sighted and completely depreciates the use of material culture as a means of doing so. In Cherokee, North Carolina, important lessons might be learned from remembering how local businessmen sought to capitalize on cultural traditions through roadside commercial development. Important lessons might be told as to how a kind of fake history came to be represented and why it was that local residents, as well as merchants, were so easily led down that path.

Preservationists in the United States became more responsive to issues of landscape with the rise of the district concept, especially after passage of the Historic Preservation Act of 1966, which encouraged historic district designation. There is still doubt, however, as to whether many preservationists today would advocate preserving something as ordinary as a commercial-strip historic district, even if one could be found with serious time-depth. Many preservationists still look very much askance at Roadside America, as if with blinders on. Their way of defining significance remains rooted in architectural history's original emphases—the prizing of the grand over the mundane.

Nationwide, the preservationist's antipathy toward automobile-generated landscapes and places was heightened substantially when construction of a nationwide interstate freeway system began in the 1950s. This was especially so after interstate freeways were approved for the nation's inner cities, resulting in substantial disruption to traditional urban fabrics. The automobile became the enemy more than ever and very clearly also became the main rationale for advancing preservation values. Historic preservation was promoted as the antithesis to both the highway engineer's destructiveness and the commercial crassness of the roadside merchant, not to mention the seeming lack of imagination brought to suburban subdividing among other forms of auto-oriented land development by realtors, contractors, and architects. Largely lost in this reaction was meaningful concern for early roadside evolution, particularly the highly opportunistic early architecture of motoring as well as the roads themselves along which it all was arrayed. As such the early, truly historic landscapes and places of early motoring were thought not to have a history or even to constitute history—at least significant history. But we now know—or at least we ought to know—that we, as Americans, live primarily in a world derived from those early landscapes and places, which now are mostly lost.

It is true that many preservationists today do look beyond discreet pieces of architecture, and even small building ensembles, to broader preservation options (especially the historic district) that might encompass whole landscapes at the scale of entire urban neighborhoods.[3] Nonetheless, the traditional focus on individual buildings continues, aided and abetted by the National Register of Historic Places, perhaps the most important instrument for identifying historical significance in the built environment. Originally the National Register mainly designated buildings as historically or architecturally significant, and not places at all (at least not places defined in a landscape sense). Once it became a primary tool for allocating financial incentives for preservation, especially through modified tax codes beginning in the 1980s, the keepers of the register embraced more fully the historic district idea whereby quantities of significant buildings, along with neighboring supporting infrastructure otherwise lacking in significance, might be made eligible as well. But it was very much an afterthought. Whereas it is relatively easy to assign significance to a building through association with a historically important person, including a building's architect, or to events or activities, it is not so easy to do so with an entire landscape, especially when that landscape has value mainly for its commonplaceness.

Coming to fore recently is the historic corridor and the recognition that the architectural significance of insignificant buildings and a linearly arrayed infrastructure can be identified and interpreted. Things that are dispersed geographically rather than clustered can still have importance. The National Register has also embraced the corridor idea. Thus have highway transects come to the preservationist's attention, which is perhaps a requisite for recognizing roadsides, or their components, as meriting careful attention also. Nonetheless that attention tends today to focus on buildings largely isolated from their past surrounds, things isolated from one another not only geographically but temporally.

Where significant roadside buildings survive in architectural ensembles, historical districting might apply, possibly to supplement a historic corridor's definition. The bulk of such survivors today are largely restricted to small-town centers, especially along the former growth edges of small-town downtowns or Main Streets during the 1910s or 1920s (see figs. 6.8 and 6.9). Rarely are they out along highways that are peripheral to small towns—commercial strips that atrophied aborning, for example, from the 1940s, 1950s, or even 1960s. And rarer still are they found out along the commercial strips of big-city suburbs, and certainly not from the 1970s on. As for Roadside America, it could be argued that relatively little that is historically significant survives. Survival has not been the nature of the beast—Roadside America being ever changeable.

It should also be noted that many preservationists taking up the cause of landscape preservation today tend to focus on "designed landscapes" such of parks and gardens, as behooves those with backgrounds in landscape architecture as opposed to architecture. Some focus on rural landscapes—places spared modern urbanization and thus variously deserving protection on the grounds of historical, architectural, and/or natural ambiance.[4] Consequently the roads and roadsides (or road margins) most appreciated by preservationists today may well be those found among the rural "byways," as they are officially designated in many states, that celebrate the scenic. They prize the undeveloped over the developed. They do not prize roadsides that were developed as what might be called "buyways"—commercial Roadside America.[5]

Lastly advocates of roadside memory might turn to the nation's museums, particularly its outdoor or "living history" museums. The necessity of seeing the whole of a place as it might have been, and not just its most stylish or historically most significant parts, lends itself to thinking at the landscape scale. Most outdoor museums in the United States presently celebrate pioneer, family farm, and small-town or village life in the past. Most of them tend accordingly to be promote heritage, even the best of them, such as Henry Ford's Greenfield Village. Ford, perhaps more than any other, promoted the affordable automobile such that automobility's popularity might revolutionize U.S. geography. But, as he did so, he also nostalgically relished the past that automobility would surely destroy. Americans, he evidently thought, needed to remember traditional values while embracing new ones. His museum, initially at least, was not about automobiles.

Preserving History In Place

Historic preservation remains the primary foil for saving old buildings and indeed entire landscapes in order to recycle them for future use. It involves more than just remembering. More specifically preservation has to do with recycling old things into new uses. It has to do with retaining the resource value of old things, often through their reuse in totally new and innovative ways—ways totally beyond the purview of their original builders and even subsequent owners. The historic preservation movement has made major strides over the past few decades, something that was difficult to foresee when the geographer Peirce F. Lewis, writing in the mid-1970s, declared that the movement was "a thundering failure."[6] Up to then, preservationists had proven totally incapable of stopping the damage wrought by automobility. The automobile was making devastating inroads in and around big-city downtowns. Important landmark buildings were disappearing almost daily, but so also were ordinary buildings, which were being demolished wholesale, and traditional urban fabric—block after city block—was leveled, mostly for parking.[7]

Of course, there were reasons for it. Americans loved their cars. They also found favor in newness, being forward looking and not backward glancing as a society. The past was clearly for the rearview mirror—and was something to be left behind. Indeed, Lewis argued, history was something most Americans viewed with degrees of hostility. "Reverence for the past, after all, is contrary to the very essence of the American dream," he wrote, "the dream of progress, of growth, of a better future."[8] And apparently nothing was more progressive than automobility and the convenience that it offered, although everywhere that convenience seemingly produced landscapes and places that were unimaginative if not banal.[9]

Why had historic preservationists not accomplished more? Perhaps theirs was a movement simply too undeveloped and preservation as an ideal simply too new. The issue that preservationists had not yet fully answered, of course, was cost. Could the rehabilitation of old buildings be made to pay, and could rehabilitation be made profitable in ways respectful of traditional cultural values? Revitalization in an historic district, for example, could be a double-edged sword, especially when initiatives at saving old things extended to creating new things, destroying in the process important aspects of the past. Today it is preservation's recent economic successes that sustain the movement. Historic preservation has advanced through economic pump priming, such as financial incentives that include tax abatements, tax deferments, and tax credits extended to property owners, as well as outright assistance packages such as start-up loans and loan guarantees to business owners. Also important, government-private partnerships can involve such initiatives as streetscape improvement and building-facade upgrading in commercial areas. And a new flexibility has been introduced into zoning and building codes including those that govern historic district designation, the promotion of enterprise zones, and the promotion of tax-increment financing districts.

Central to this process, the Federal Rehabilitation Investment Tax Credit program allowed, beginning in the 1970s, a 20-percent tax credit for the rehabilitation of commercial or income-producing properties listed on the National Register of Historic Places and a 10-percent tax credit for the rehabilitation of those buildings built before 1936. Between 1976 and 1986 (the year the law was modified, making it less effective), some $1.5 billion in private investment was funneled into building rehabilitation through the program, effecting some 23,000 properties nationwide. The program created an estimated 120,000 housing units of which more than 15 percent represented low- and moderate-income housing.[10] Many states established their own tax-credit programs to reinforce federal initiatives. In Rhode Island developers receive a reimbursement for 30 percent of their restoration costs, with eligibility hinging on the listing of properties in the National Register.[11] In 2009 the National Register of Historic Places, administered by the National Park Service, listed more than 1.4 million buildings and objects.[12]

More than 2,000 local historic district commissions operate in the United States.[13] This is quite an accomplishment given that the very earliest of them, established in places such as Charleston, South Carolina, date from only the late 1920s. In Chicago in 2008, for example, there were 50 historic districts (containing over 9,000 properties). Designated as well were 259 individual landmark structures.[14] Recent studies show that property values in designated historic districts tend to be some 25 percent higher than in equivalent areas not designated or zoned as historic.[15] Historic districting is seen to bring stability to neighborhoods, thus sustaining architectural character and diversity. But it might or might not strengthen an area's traditional social fabric. Rising property values tend to inflate living costs, making historic districts less affordable to people on limited incomes. Historic districting, in other words, usually leads to gentrification and population turnover.

The National Trust for Historic Preservation operates a Main Street Program designed to assist commercial-property owners with building renovation in large and small locations. The program's purpose is to help reverse business decline in the nation's traditional business districts, places seen as undermined by automobility, specifically through the rise of competing suburban shopping centers and commercial strips. Clearly the National Trust views (as preservationists generally do) the automobile as transgressor—the foul instrument of unwanted change. More than sixteen hundred communities in some forty states have Main Street programs. Some $15.2 billion have been invested in these communities accordingly, involving some seventy-nine thousand building renovations, some fifty-two thousand new business startups, and the creation of some two hundred thousand new jobs.[16]

Nonetheless, despite the apparent successes scored in recent decades by the preservation movement, it is doubtful that the financial and other tools that were developed will prove adequate to preserving Roadside America. Today's commercial strips in big-city suburbs, for example, are especially changeful. Escalating land values there excites tremendous pressure on property owners either to redevelop or to sell to those who will do so, with higher and higher building densities resulting and not just change. As we have argued, commercial roadside infrastructure tends to be programmed for impermanence. That is its very nature. Short-term stability on the roadside is difficult to achieve, let alone permanence. In places such as Amesburg, Massachusetts, where a historic preservation plan was recently adopted, automobility, and the changes to local landscapes precipitated by it, loomed as a pervasive problem. Automobile-affected landscapes were not seen to offer preservation opportunity. The rural byway, on the other hand, was thought to be fully ideal. In Amesbury the automobile has been seen as destroying valuable landscape resources, replacing them with "characterless uniformity."[17] Preservationists there have targeted not only the town's traditional downtown and the town's older residential neighborhoods for attention, but, more especially, outlying farmland. "The most important and most vulnerable historic landscapes are farmsteads," the authors of the plan wrote. "Other historic landscapes include archeological sites, river landscapes, and historic parks and recreation areas." Recommendations included "creation of an 'Amesbury Greenbelt' to integrate and promote the goals of open space conservation, natural resource protection, and highway preservation,"[18] which also involved the protection of roadsides from commercial development.

Such sentiment echoes various national initiatives designed to conserve landscape as scenery, scenery viewed as something to be protected mainly from automobile-related intrusion. For example, Scenic America, a relatively new organization established to promote "a national movement to preserve and defend our irreplaceable scenic resources," advocates the elimination of "billboard blight" and the mitigation of other landscape intrusions such as cell-phone towers and overhead power lines. The organization seeks "to protect the scenic character of the nation's highways and byways" and "to promote context-sensitive highway solutions" regarding road construction.[19]

Thus we say again that it is not certain that many historic preservationists are overtly alert today to the historical significance of the automobile as a fundamental player in forming the American built environment over the past century. Considered mundane by most Americans at the time of their forming, automobile-affected landscapes excited little appreciation beyond their novelty and what they spoke about the future. Automobile use, and the landscapes and places that it created, came to dominate life so quickly that very early on automobility became something taken for granted and hardly worth serious thought.

Motoring's origins in pleasure trips substantially obscured the seriousness of the automobile's social, economic, political, and environmental impacts.[20] With clear social status implication, motoring was first an elite sport, an embrace of speed and exhilaration that only money could buy. With relatively cheap, mass-produced motorcars provided by Henry Ford among others, motoring's implications for enhanced personal identity through mobility (social as well as geographic) quickly diffused to the middle classes. The U.S. economy came to be dominated by the manufacturing of, the selling of, and the servicing of automobiles. Affected by automobility, politics, especially the nation's foreign policy, came to emphasize petroleum-based energy. Problems derived from petroleum dependence, including climatic change, now threaten our planet as a physical and biological system.

Again, built environment in America was literally remade around the automobile, and the geography of metropolitan areas was turned inside-out with the rise of the new automobile suburbs. Values that were fully centered on the automobile emerged early in the twentieth century to revolutionize life in the United States. But much of the material evidence, especially that of Roadside America, was allowed to disappear. What remains should command value not just as mere artifact, but as historical record. Instead, early automobile-oriented buildings tend to be ignored, if not considered things to be appropriately replaced. Roadside relics tend not to be viewed as historical resources or, for that matter, the stuff out of which heritage ought to be constructed. By and large attention today remains focused on architecture that is pre-automobile in origin and on landscapes, like parks and gardens, that today are not associated with automobiles.[21]

Re-creating History As Place

Thus do we return to the idea of a roadside museum—albeit perhaps one that would be ensconced in a historic district or even as part of a heritage corridor and one that would be aided by an array of well-established financial incentives for preservation. With the museum the idea is not so much to preserve as to instruct, at least as most museum curators today view their work. A museum oriented to roadside history might not serve just to educate Americans generally, but also historic preservationists by reminding them of the roadside's past importance and of the automobile and automobile-affected landscapes and places in the American experience. As Peirce F. Lewis asserted decades ago, the first argument for successful historic preservation is not economic. Rather it has to do with what he called "cultural memory." "Any healthy society," he wrote, "needs to know where it is, and to know that, it must know where it came from. We must, in short, have a sense of history." But, he added, "we can not have that sense of history unless we have reminders—tangible, incessant reminders—of the kind of environment in which our forefathers worked and played and lived out their lives."[22] It is in the museum, we suspect, that such challenges, regarding Roadside America at least, may be best met.

What might be advocated is an outdoor (or open air or living-history) museum that treats America's past automobility in terms of changing roads and roadsides—something, we think, best done through some kind of landscape display. Outdoor museums constructed at the landscape scale enable visitors to visualize the past as more than a single building, or for that matter a single room in a building. They enable visitors to think back in a context simulating if not replicating real-life proxemics.

Motoring has for a century been central to life in the United States, and motor vehicles have long assumed degrees of centrality in museum exhibits. Witness the arrival of Dwight Eisenhower's World War II command car at the then new Eisenhower Museum in Abilene, Kansas, in the 1950s (fig. 7.2). Was the museum thought incomplete without referencing Ike and automobility? One could assume this was so, as it was during the Eisenhower presidency, of course, that the nation's modern interstate freeway system was established, and Eisenhower's interest in roads went back at least to 1919, when he accompanied a convoy of military vehicles on a coast-to-coast demonstration run on the Lincoln Highway.[23]

Our core concern is how the past might best be presented so that America's early embrace of the automobile is effectively understood in landscape terms. We actually lean toward a large gesture. Consider a place such as Scranton, Pennsylvania's Steamtown, the work of the National Park Service, which was opened to interpret the nation's railroad age.[24] There old railroad shop and yard facilities have been partially reconstituted as a national museum of railroading (see fig. 5.23). There visitors not only see but experience things firsthand from the past, and in ways that were important in the past, such as riding on steam-engine excursion trains. Steamtown challenges visitors to explore issues vital to

Figure 7.2. Postcard view, Eisenhower Center, Abilene, Kansas, 1957. The card's caption reads: "Command car of General Dwight D. Eisenhower being unloaded in front of Eisenhower Museum, March 1957. Purchased by friends, it was in use by the General during World War II."

understanding railroading and its role in creating landscapes and places and to understanding its historical impact on life in America. Understanding itself may be abstract, but it is always rooted in that seen or touched or heard, and at the scale of life as actually lived. What equivalences might we seek in a National Museum of the American Roadside?

Such a museum would enable exploration of twentieth-century modernism, at least the modernism of automobile technology as applied to landscape and place.[25] Change is modernism's fundamental aspect. There is no better circumstance to demonstrate change—to represent it vividly in landscape terms—than through road and roadside displays that showcase just how the changes wrought by the automobiles' use were confronted, who benefited the most and the least by the new automobility and why, how memories of early roads and roadsides in America could inform our sense of who we were as a people and who we are today, and just what does and does not constitute progress, since progress is what modernism presumably has been all about.

Modernism has been amplified in ways compelling to the senses. Impermanent as it was, Roadside America remained very colorful (some critics said chaotic) for its relative gaudiness. Early writing that focused on Roadside America, as we have seen, tended to be highly critical.[26] Popular tastes substantially submerged the cultivated tastes of America's gentry classes. Where better to illustrate the rise of popular culture than with examples of changing roadside display? The roadside has been, in first approximation, a kind of advertising venue designed to attract attention and persuade.[27] It is the stuff of advertising—that which primes consumption—that remains the critical engine of U.S. capitalism. Americans in the twentieth century increasingly defined both personal and collective identity around products and services advertised. Important issues concerning capitalism in the United States, including the valuing of private property—but also the very nature of change in the United States—can be explored through roadside signs and signlike buildings.[28]

Roadsides everywhere evolved to be accessed quickly with minimum delay. Driveways and parking lots (usually private spaces carefully orchestrated with public rights-of-way) refined space—and the resulting geography was meant not so much for pedestrians as for motorists. It was space that came to be substantially regulated through exercise of government police powers: through zoning ordinances, building codes, and sign ordinances. It was not chaotic at all. Government forcefully took jurisdiction over traffic regulation. We pride ourselves as a nation of freedom-loving individuals. Perhaps nothing has symbolized freedom of action more that the ideal of the *open road*. And yet nowhere in America is life more regulated than on and along our streets and highways. Numerous American myths stand ready to be explored through the lens of road and roadside, a lens configured in museum format.

Automobility fostered new kinds of spaces and places.[29] But it also fostered new meanings for old places. Increasingly U.S. geography has been privatized, and the uses of public space have been increasingly devalued over time. Main Street with its public sidewalks has given way to the shopping mall with private spaces performing presumed public functions. People travel cocooned in metal and glass, substantially distanced and isolated from one another. Americans live increasingly in neighborhoods segregated by income, and the car and the garage are mechanisms for social connection. Where better to question such happenings than in a road and roadside museum?

Petroleum underpins automobility.[30] We fight wars over the control of petroleum resources. Who we are as a nation, and the image we thus present to other nations accordingly, has come to hinge on sustaining automobile-oriented habits: not just fueling our vehicles, but paving our roads and parking lots. Asphalt parking lots dominate land use even today (by areal extent at least) in most small-town and big-city downtowns, and certainly in suburban shopping areas.[31] Yet, no one could wish for a parking lot museum. Not only have very new geographies been created, but, in their creation, the environment has been greatly changed—not just built environment, but "natural" environment also, that is, our fundamental physical and biological surrounds. Where better to explore such issues than in a museum devoted to roadside history? Such a museum would not serve just for celebration, but for critical analysis as well. It would not serve romanticization, but understanding.

Material culture of the past can energize questioning. Display of material culture can be an effective means of arousing questions and thus encouraging discussion. Pictured here is an indoor exhibit of an outdoor place at the National Museum of Transportation outside St. Louis, Missouri (fig. 7.3). The exhibit not only reminds viewers of a widely known local landmark (notorious throughout

Figure 7.3. The Coral Court Motel exhibit, National Museum of Transportation in suburban St. Louis, Missouri, 2009. Perhaps suggestive of what a museum of Roadside America might display, the exhibit is nonetheless highly contrived. Although authentic, the things displayed have not only been lifted from their original setting, but are exhibited in a confined space. Viewers, held behind a barrier, thus view them essentially as being in a contained two-dimensional field rather than in an open, life-sized space.

much of its life as a "hot pillow joint" with crime connections), but an important kind of place in the highway scheme of things. Roadside history is not just about the up and up, but the untoward as well. It potentially covers the whole of human experience. Interest in material culture lies not so much in mere "thingness" as in what things symbolize or signify.

At heart a museum's value lies not just in collecting and warehousing things, but in interpreting them and thus giving them life through meaning. The past is made tangible, with things displayed serving as a figurative bridge to life otherwise little known or unknown, and the lay public as well as professionals can readily be smitten by it. Material culture, especially in a museum, often unleashes deep personal interest among observers, albeit sometimes limited to a delight in the antiquarian.[32] Even emotionally detached students often succumb to an object's allure when they fixate on "human efficacy," as the historian Thomas J. Schlereth called it.[33] Curators, usually by their manner of presenting things, have been accused of deliberately stimulating among museum visitors "object fetishism," to borrow further from Schlereth.[34] Exhibits become more than the sum of their parts however studiously they are fashioned, and they are capable of setting off unforeseen interactions among visitors and even among curators themselves.[35]

In the outdoor history museum, buildings are not displayed as isolated objects, but as part of building ensembles that are suggestive of past landscapes or places and are potentially capable of stimulating distinctive understandings about how life was once lived at the geographic scale. An outdoor museum (cum district/cum corridor) with emphasis on the material culture of automobility would serve if properly structured and interpreted to teach lessons about technology and its impact, including the unintentional. Initially the automobile came unobtrusively in small numbers and with seemingly little immediate impact on traditional ways of organizing landscapes and places. It came promising exhilaration, pride of ownership, and, of course, convenience. Those who could afford an automobile found life invigorated, if only through the excitement of speed—the car was at first considered very much a sporting device. Even as auto use spread to the masses and as roadside services came increasingly to the fore, landscape change remained for the most part relatively slow and inconsequential. But it accelerated quickly, and not just in the cities, but in the nation's small towns and even down on the farm.

Having bought into the new automobile technology and having abided its environmental and geographic impacts unquestioningly, Americans became, in a sense, trapped by the largely unintended consequences of their actions and inactions. Commerce invaded residential neighborhoods. Parking lots invaded traditional downtowns. Cities were made to sprawl outward and devoured countryside. Whole categories of rural structures, such as schools and churches, were consolidated and relocated into towns. Functions in very small places were transferred up the urban hierarchy to larger places, ultimately to benefit mainly the nation's metropolises. And it all seemed so natural, as if it could not have happened any other way. Not all, perhaps, but many of those stories could be told effectively in an outdoor museum. Certainly the impact wrought in rural and small-town America could be effectively assigned, if only through amending already existing village- and farm-oriented museum venues.

A museum of Roadside America would necessarily need to focus on Americans as consumers, specifically on their growing appetite for products and services and the way it serves to energize roadside selling, and vice versa. Not without its apparent benefits, roadside selling helped energize a national culture of entertainment and leisure. Perhaps it will be this dimension of Roadside America that will prove most significant in attracting visitor interest. No one says that thinking about the past should not be fun, at least to start with. Serious attention can always come later, including concern with the unseemly and untoward as problems variously left solved or unsolved.

Besides their educational implications, museums by their very nature also serve as entertainment zones. And what in the recent past has been more entertaining than Roadside America? There was the spectacle of odd-looking buildings, colorful advertising signs, and, at night, the vivid use of light. The opportunity to consume, whether it was goods or services, was created, along with a lifestyle built around speed, convenience, and a sense of individual prerogative. For Americans motoring on vacation, the roadside worked as theater, the passing landscape made a visual panorama. Tourists became an audience seeking suspension of the routine as they sought to place themselves in uncommon situations. Thus did quirky roadside attractions, including museums, came to the fore all across the nation beginning in the 1920s, but especially in resort areas. For everyday consumers there were attracting "ducks" and "decorated sheds" in every locality, shopping made perhaps more exciting for some if not most.

The "fun and funky" of Roadside America continues to draw its many fans, including those who think of roadside history primarily in those terms (figs. 7.4 and 7.5). Many self-styled "commercial archeologists" are smitten with a kind of fantasy-world nostalgia for America's roadside past, a past substantially defined in terms of "gee whiz. Look at that." Such characterization is not meant to demean. A museum dedicated to understanding the history of Roadside America would do well to vigorously embrace such an orientation. It would provide an essential spark, giving such a museum its own clear personality and thus setting it apart from other kinds of museums. It would serve to attract its own kind of visitors, including car enthusiasts and, we might add, aficionados of popular culture generally. But the material culture of classic Roadside America included more than kitsch or silliness. The roadside was about serious business, although often was that enterprise cloaked in clowns' garments.

Figure 7.4. The Miracle of America Museum, Polson, Montana, 2009. Located on U.S. 93 to intercept tourists traveling the Glacier National Park and other scenic spots nearby, this museum perhaps typifies the winsome mix of didacticism and entertainment that has come to characterize many a roadside tourist attraction. The proprietor's advertising assures: "Great Family Fun." But it also promises promotion of conservative political and religious views, and its artifacts are intended "to show how the ingenuity and creativity of mankind, particularly under the free enterprise system, has benefitted society."

Figure 7.5. "Gallery" on the Zion–Mt. Carmel Highway in today's Zion National Park, a park that visitors can access by car, experience visually by car, and leave by car, never having gotten out of a car. Literally "framed" for motorists on the highway were spectacular scenic views.

Caution: Speed Bumps Ahead

Most of us, preoccupied with everyday life today and still fundamentally forward looking, are forgetful of the past. We need reminding of our roots—our history—lest we neglect the lessons that history teaches. And in our current world of automobile dependence, understanding our roots should involve careful consideration not just of America's love affair with cars, but consideration of what that love affair wrought as built environment. Our surroundings, after all, do not just reflect social, political, and economic ways of thinking and doing, but, as geography, help form society, politics, and economy in fundamental ways. Roadside America, an important part of that equation, is as important a historical consideration as the conquest of a continent defined as wilderness, the sustenance of independence through land ownership (especially the family farm), and the honing of national power through industry and urbanization energized initially through railroading—to mention again some of the emphases that have traditionally dominated history museum development in the United States.

Americans need reminding of how automobility first arrived. Yes, there was much clowning around, perhaps too much, when it came to configuring distinctive landscapes on the margins of the nation's evolving roads and highways. Much of the early roadside was flimsy, overtly crass, and otherwise open to derision, especially from those with elite fashionable tastes. But popular culture ultimately triumphed, in part led by what entrepreneurs were creating as Roadside America. Old values were enjoined anew. New values were added to the U.S. lexicon of worth. Americans prized speed and mobility and rewarded convenience. They responded to persuasive messages that were delivered forcefully, and they sustained self-perceptions formed around the advertisement of goods and services. And Americans relished doing so in environments suggestive of leisure and entertainment, all the while taking it all for granted.

We need to be reminded of how it all began, what was lost along the way, and what might have been—"the roads not taken," so to speak. Automobility came with options—various avenues that might have been followed but were not. Why were only some options pursued and pursued, many critics claim, so blindly? American-style automobility was not a natural outcome. One has only to look to landscapes and places affected by automobile use in other parts of the world. Many similarities are to be found, perhaps more similarities than differences. But there are important differences. Automobility in the United States was planned, sold, and then bought for reasons. What were those reasons, and what are the consequences for life today?

Exploring such issues as museum program—the effects of modernism, the privileging of the visual, America's quest for speed and convenience, changing social values, the enhancement of the private over the public, and lingering petroleum dependence, for example—should be made fundamental to understanding who we are as a nation today. All are themes that can be brought together in our collective remembering of roads and roadsides in America life. Fostered on the roadside, a new sense of space arose. A more abstracted world of sight in which exaggerated size, color, and, at night especially, the intense use of light entered forcefully. It was a world of technological progress that most Americans could readily "buy into" (quite literally), and thus participate. A world of accelerated ephemerality rooted in rapid technological change evolved. Roads no longer merely led to places, but fostered an important new kind of place: Roadside America. Indeed, the roadside became, we would argue, the most important kind of place yet devised in the American experience. And so it continues.

Words of caution are in order. A museum of Roadside America, if that is what someone someday chooses to create, will not be without its problems. Museums of whatever form or purpose tend to violate, by their very nature, conventional notions of history and even memory. They are invitations to one or another heritage belief. Confronting the past through three-dimensional "lived" experience is especially problematic. Most Americans consider history not as something immediately personal, but as something quite distanced—something fully "past." Constructing landscapes (or "museumscapes" if you will) that are intended to re-create mimetically past historical scenes collapses the distance between history and personal being. Or, put another way, it leads visitors to such scenes to conflate the firsthand experiencing of a museum with actual historical knowledge.[36] Care must be exercised.

Museums are never neutral in what they present. As the historian Randolph Starn warned: "They collect and conserve, classify and display, research and educate, they also deliver messages and make arguments."[37] The act of mere display tends to sacralize an object, elevating it to a high level as discursive subject. As such, museums, like commercial roadsides, contribute to modern society's tendency to embrace spectacle. Thus curatorship in outdoor museums can all too easily take on "theme park" implications. The corporate-owned theme park has but one objective—to offer entertainment for profit pure and simple.[38] That of the museum, on the other hand, is idealized more as education through preservation and interpretation, revenue generation being more a means to an end than an end in itself.

In theme parks history is readily sanitized, making the past more palatable to customers who come mainly seeking pleasure. Often the past is presented as a kind of "hyper-reality," with historical stereotype through hyperbole being favored.[39] Visitor reactions are often focused and simplified through enhanced visual impact, for example, which is the fundamental trick of roadside entrepreneurship. Museum curators, on the other hand, presumably strive for accuracy and authenticity, if not critical analysis. Good intentions can easily go astray, however. As one observer put it: "While their educational intentions are much loftier and their financial expectations more modest, open-air museums can easily slip into creating themed scenes and experiences."[40] How might one keep a museum of Roadside America from succumbing completely to many of the commercial enthusiasms, which as strategies for attention-getting most especially contributed to roadside success?

Material culture—the well from which museums spring—is the most liberal of resources. Relics tend to impress, especially when they stand unmediated by intercessors separating them from a viewer—when the spoken or written word, for example, does not intercede. The word, in whatever form, is poised between that which is observed and the observer who uses the word. But seeing or viewing does not always generate word thought. Often it merely excites or titillates. In the outdoor museum, it necessary to ensure that pure titillation does not end the experience. On first encounter, perhaps it is best to engage the exciting and titillating before seeking deeper understanding. Or it may be best merely to arouse interest and then engage reflection, especially before someone else (an exhibit's curator, for example) begins to tell the visitor what to think.

Confronting material objects, especially buildings and building ensembles, can transport observers away from their own culture's assumptions to make, as Jules David Prown puts it, "affective contact" with people from the past. New comprehension is thereby invited without labeling or curatorial dialogue. But the experience must be handled carefully so as not to distort, fabricate, or mislead. Putting buildings, for example, in appropriate physical relationship to one another, and at a proper geographic scale, is one form of important control. Not extrapolating unduly from the object itself—not forcing from it an unwarranted symbolic meaning—is another. Attempting to use buildings as they might have been used in the everyday past is still another.

John B. Jackson, perhaps more than any other, is responsible for what now passes academically as landscape study. But what he encouraged scholars to do was to get out in the real world and see things firsthand. Historians, especially, needed to leave their dusty archives and use the material culture of the everyday as reference points for understanding change.[41] And he himself did just that, for years riding a motorcycle from his home in Santa Fe, New Mexico, to teaching assignments at the University of California at Berkeley and at Harvard University in Cambridge, Massachusetts. Jackson, while affecting scholarship, wrote mainly for an educated lay audience. He was more concerned to generate interest in landscape history among ordinary Americans than among scholars. Looking at and thinking about landscape liberated the mind to new understandings, to the asking of new questions—something that archival searches in response to old questions, for example, did not do. It was while out looking at things that we, as budding scholars, first thought to study Roadside America. The U.S. roadside was everywhere, but few Americans, whether scholars or lay people, were focused intellectually on it. Perhaps we have helped to change that myopia somewhat.

Certainly it is through direct confrontation with our everyday world that we continue our work.

Landscapes observed for interest and edification can be of several kinds. Regarding Roadside America, they can be the currently evolving roadsides of our own locales, or of distant locales we have visited. For historical understanding, however, we can turn only to relics, to built environments surviving from the past or to buildings and spaces in museums that one way or another stand as replications or simulations of the past. Museums are publicly acknowledged to be places for reflection. The public and museum curators have known this longer than have the members of most academic disciplines, especially academic history. Indeed, only in recent decades have academic historians taken serious note of what history museums do, and how they do it. Only in recent decades have history departments begun to educate a distinctive class of "public historian," scholars specifically intended for museum, preservation, and related professional careers. History museums stand as places where people are expected to learn in ways important to themselves and to the communities where they live, and not in ways necessarily important to established scholarship.[42]

A museum of Roadside America would necessarily rely on scholarly insight for interpreting the material culture. But curatorship would also seek to plumb the personal in its visitors by portraying historically significant things not only accurately, but in ways that facilitate visitor comprehension. It would become a matter of helping visitors insert themselves into imagined pasts in ways appropriate to understanding their lives today. On a recent visit to the National Museum of Transportation near St. Louis, one author found himself at the recently installed Coral Court display. He was strongly reminded of the evocative power latent in museum exhibits. While he positioned himself to take a photograph (see fig. 7.3), another visitor eagerly interrupted his concentration. She volunteered how she and her husband had spent their wedding night at Coral Court, leaving the next day by car on their honeymoon. She had no idea at the time that the motel enjoyed a checkered reputation. They had taken Coral Court at the time to be an innocent, safe, comfortable, and convenient place for lodging. The display very much resonated in personal terms for her.

Some of what visitors learn in a museum can even shock. With luck much will surprise. And that is what a museum of the American roadside ought to do to be most effective—surprise and even unsettle if not shock. Numerous authors have emphasized automobility's negative aspects, especially after its embrace became so exaggerated through the rejection of other transportation options such as mass transit in the nation's booming metropolises. Brian Ladd in his book *Love and Hate in the Automotive Age* draws attention to what too many motorists learned long ago the hard way. Mass mobility achieved only via cars and trucks is in its overall impact more confining and limiting than liberating. Today commuting in large metropolitan areas binds the typical commuter into the tight space of a car over quite long periods of time, which add up to a substantial portion of one's life.[43] The debasement of the natural environment via engine emissions, for example, is a negative implication of automobility very much in public mind today as a result of global warming. Oil spills in places such as the Gulf of Mexico increasingly alarm people.

More subtle, perhaps, are the social changes the automobile has caused in American society over the past century, many of them fully problematical also—for example, a persistent if not increasing social segregation defined along lines of race and ethnicity, but also social class and status.[44] Automobility sustained the flight of affluent white Americans to the suburbs, leaving impoverished inner-city neighborhoods in its wake. Today the gated community is fully symptomatic of class division geographically sustained through automobile dependence. Visitors to a museum of Roadside America, should one be built, would want to look at automobility from the viewpoint of a balance sheet, to weigh, in other words, the automobile's social pluses and minuses.

* * *

Outdoor museums have grown relatively commonplace since the mid–twentieth century, and many having taken on the challenge of re-creating a distinctive kind of place important in the American past. If an actual place is not preserved, then museums can offer place simulations, places created in the image of the geographic past.[45] Concern with "material life" (a broader and perhaps more useful concept than what "material culture" alone implies) is a growing concern among historians reaching out to understand and indeed participate in museum curatorial work. Using things by way of demonstrating their meaning is central to the concept. Nonetheless physicality remains central. Things as objects remain the focus. It is around things that stories through doing (or demonstrating or using) are made to evoke the past.⁴⁶ The history of consumerism has lately become a guiding interest in many American museums, making automobility potentially a core topic to be covered. It is certainly a topic waiting its turn for full attention.⁴⁷ Simulated consumption of roadside services, for example, might be one kind of storytelling activity that museum visitors might be expected to participate in firsthand.

The historic district and the more recent heritage corridor have come to the fore among preservationists as important tools for preserving the material culture of the past, extending preservation efforts from the merely architectural to a geographic scale of concern. Preservation also embraces simulation of the past. But it is not re-creation that is intended as functioning displays as in museums, but revitalization that is intended to nurture life as it is ongoing today and tomorrow. The architectural historian Richard Longstreth may be correct in asserting that Roadside America has been of little interest to historic preservationists because of its sprawling, substantially amorphous nature. Roadside America, taken as a kind of landscape or place, violates the preservationist's penchant, at least until recently, for neatly circumscribed landmark structures.⁴⁸ Ever changeful, and thus without clear historical "hooks" to grab the preservationist's attention, Roadside America appears to most of them not only underwhelming as physical actuality, but too much the child of *recent history,* a past too recent, perhaps, actually to have a history. Although roadside buildings survive as isolates from the past, few roadside landscapes do so in ways fully suggestive of a historic place worth revitalizing.

The distant past figures little in accessing the typical American roadside. The recent past figures powerfully. This can be good, however, at least so far as museum development is concerned. The best museums are those that assign a significant set of contemporary problems, and their purpose is not to assert avenues of problem-solving so much as to make visitors aware of problems. Looking at the recent past certainly carries a sense of relevancy, and perhaps a sense of urgency as well—something that tends to be missing in museums that are organized around distant periods. In his assessment of what made museums influential, the historian Kenneth Hudson concluded that it was timing. Successful curators assigned the right issues at the right time. Museums were influential, he wrote, when the "time was ripe for that influence."⁴⁹ The sprawling, amorphous nature of Roadside America, and especially its impact on life in the United States today, seems to be a ripe topic.

APPENDIX

Elements Appropriate to an Outdoor Roadside Museum
1910s: Roadside America as a Commercial Extension of Main Street

- Battery recharging station for electric vehicles
- Billboards and roadside "snipe" signs
- Bicycle shop with car sales, including steam-powered vehicles
- Blacksmith shop converted to car repair with curbside gas pumps
- Brick and macadam pavements
- Hotel with dining room, men's bar, women's restroom, and auto-club office (emphasizing road maps and travel brochures)
- "House" Gas Station
- Livery barn reoriented to car storage
- Lunch wagon
- Popcorn and peanut vendor truck
- Storage garage with car-washing floor and lubrication floor/greasing pit
- Self-standing multiple-story Ford dealership with sales floor and repair garage on lower level and Model T "car-kit" assembly floor above
- Traditional multiple-story storefront containing a car and truck dealership (with sales floor, repair garage, and curbside pumps out front at ground level) with offices on the upper floor (one to be dedicated to a traffic courtroom as typically overseen by a justice of the peace)
- Traditional single-story storefronts containing a lunch-counter cafe and a confectionary store
- Taxicab stand

- Traffic signage
- "White way" street lighting

1920s: Roadside America as Evolving Inner-City Thoroughfare and New Peripheral Commercial Strip

- Billboards and electric signs
- Car and truck dealership with showroom, repair garage, and used-car lot
- Concrete-ribbon and concrete-slab pavements
- Drugstore with soda fountain service at the curb
- "House-with-canopy" gas stations with outside lubrication floors/greasing pits
- Ice cream vendor truck
- Street-side food stands, one with drive-up window
- Traditionally styled "Super Service Station" with enclosed service bays
- Roadside souvenir stand (blankets, moccasins, and so on) with petting zoo
- Roadside tourist attraction (perhaps a snake farm)
- Tourist camp with cabins added, "mom-and-pop" operated
- Tourist court, "house-with-canopy" gas station, and cafe complex, "mom-and-pop" operated
- Tourist home
- Traditional single-story "taxpayer" storefronts with enlarged on-street parking in front containing an auto parts store among other auto-related retail venues
- Traffic signage

1930s and 1940s: Roadside America as Evolving Peripheral Commercial Strip

- Billboards, "snipe" signs, and edge-of-town community booster signs
- Car and truck dealership with sales floor, repair garage, body shop, and used-car lot
- Concrete and asphalt pavements

- "Goggie-style" coffee shop franchised by national chain
- Highway contractor construction yard (with emphasis on road building)
- Historical markers and roadside memorials
- Drive-in restaurants with carhops
- Modernistic "oblong box" gasoline stations
- Motor court in Spanish Revival architectural style
- Rest park (with emphasis on roadside beautification)
- Roadside farm-produce stand (with emphasis on truck gardening)
- Roadside souvenir stand (blankets, moccasins, and so on) with pony rides
- Roadside tourist attraction (a small fun park, perhaps)
- Traffic signage
- Trailer park
- World War II Quonset hut containing an auto parts store with off-street parking

1950s: Roadside America as Evolving Peripheral Commercial Strip

- Asphalt pavements
- Billboards, "snipe" signs and edge-of-town community booster signs
- Bus station
- Car wash
- Chicken-dinner restaurant with parking lot
- Entry to drive-in movie theater
- Farm implement store, repair garage, and used-equipment lot
- Highway maintenance office and garage, including material storage yard
- Icehouse with convenience grocery
- Motor court franchised by motel chain
- "Oblong box" gasoline station extended to contain highway cafe
- Putt-putt golf course
- Revival-style "oblong box" gasoline stations
- Residential subdivision sales office with billboards and subdivision entry gate
- Roadside tourist attraction with souvenir gift shop ("dinosaur land," perhaps)

- Salvage yard
- "Small box" gasoline station for independent gasoline dealer (with gasoline storage tanks, billboards, and overhead pennants flying)
- Small shopping center with off-street parking in front containing an auto-insurance agency (with emphasis on highway safety) among other auto-related retail venues; the anchor store (signed as supermarket) containing indoor museum displays
- Tire store for national chain
- Truck stop
- Traffic signage
- Used-car lot
- Walk-up hamburger restaurant franchised by national chain
- Walk-up soft ice-cream stand franchised by national chain

For a discussion of the respective roadside venues listed above, see Chester H. Liebs, *Main Street to Miracle Mile: American Roadside Architecture* (Boston: Little Brown, 1985); John A. Jakle and Keith A. Sculle, *The Gas Station in America* (Baltimore: Johns Hopkins University Press, 1994); John A. Jakle, Keith A. Sculle, and Jefferson Rogers, *The Motel in America* (Baltimore: Johns Hopkins University Press, 1996); John A. Jakle and Keith A. Sculle, *Fast Food: Roadside Restaurants in the Automobile Age* (Baltimore: Johns Hopkins University Press, 1999); Richard Longstreth, *The Drive-In, the Supermarket, and the Transformation of Commercial Space in Los Angeles, 1914–941* (Cambridge, MA: MIT Press, 1999); John A. Jakle, *City Lights: Illuminating the American Night* (Baltimore: Johns Hopkins University Press, 2001); John A. Jakle and Keith A. Sculle, *Signs in America's Auto Age: Signatures of Landscape and Place* (Iowa City: University of Iowa Press, 2004); John A. Jakle and Keith A. Sculle, *Motoring: The Highway Experience in America* (Athens: University of Georgia Press, 2008); John A. Jakle and Keith A. Sculle, *America's Main Street Hotels: Transiency and Community in the Early Auto Age* (Knoxville: University of Tennessee Press, 2009).

NOTES

1. The Journey Begins

1. Coauthored books include *The Gas Station in America* (Baltimore: Johns Hopkins Univ. Press, 1994); *The Motel in America*, with Jefferson S. Rogers (Baltimore: Johns Hopkins Univ. Press, 1996); *Fast Food: Roadside Restaurants in the Automobile Age* (Baltimore: Johns Hopkins Univ. Press, 1999); *Lots of Parking: Land Use in a Car Culture* (Charlottesville: Univ. of Virginia Press, 2004); *Signs in America's Auto Age: Signatures of Landscape and Place* (Iowa City: Univ. of Iowa Press, 2004); *Motoring: The Highway Experience in America* (Athens: Univ. of Georgia Press, 2008); and *America's Main Street Hotels: Transiency and Community in the Early Auto Age* (Knoxville: Univ. of Tennessee Press, 2009).

2. John B. Jackson, "Other-Directed Houses," *Landscape* 6 (Winter 1956–57): 31.

3. [James Agee], "The Great American Roadside," *Fortune,* Sept. 1934, 53.

4. David Blanke, *Hell on Wheels: The Promise and Peril of America's Car Culture, 1900–1940* (Lawrence: Univ. Press of Kansas, 2007), 17.

5. Darrell A. Norris, "Roadside America: A Twilight Landscape," *Pioneer America Society Transactions* 9 (1986): 39.

6. Since 1993 the Society for Commercial Archeology has published the *SCA Journal*, a quarterly magazine devoted to celebrating relics of Roadside America.

7. Norris, "Roadside America," 40.

8. Douglas W. Rae, *City: Urbanism and Its End* (New Haven: Yale Univ. Press, 2003), 60.

9. Ibid., 228.

10. See John A. Jakle, "Landscapes Redesigned for the Automobile," in Michael P. Conzen, ed., *The Making of the American Landscape,* 294 (Boston: Unwin Hyman, 1990).

11. Jakle and Sculle, *Motoring*, 19.

12. Ibid., 29.

13. See Joseph Interrante, "The Transformation of America," in David L. Lewis and Laurence Goldstein, eds., *The Automobile and American Culture*, 89–104 (Ann Arbor: Univ. of Michigan Press, 1983).

14. See Jakle and Sculle, *Lots of Parking*, 10–11.

15. Rae, *City*, 229.

16. See James J. Flink, "Three Stages of American Automobile Consciousness," *American Quarterly* 24 (Oct. 1972): 451–73.

17. Lewis Mumford, *The Highway and the City* (New York: Harcourt, Brace & World, 1964), 244–45.

18. Robert Lynd and Helen Lynd, *Middletown: A Study in Modern American Culture* (New York: Harcourt, Brace & World, 1956), 251–63. Also see David L. Lewis, "Sex and the Automobile: From Rumble Seats to Rockin Vans," in Lewis and Goldstein, eds., *The Automobile and American Culture*, 123–33.

19. *Recent Social Trends in the United States*, vol. 1 (New York: McGraw-Hill, 1933), 177; quoted in Blanke, *Hell on Wheels*, 49.

20. Peter Freund and George Martin, *The Ecology of the Automobile* (Montreal: Black Rose Books, 1993), 7.

21. See K T. Berger, *Where the Road and the Sky Collide: America through the Eyes of Its Drivers* (New York: Henry Holt, 1993), 368.

22. For a discussion of roadside signage and roadside visualization in motoring, see John A. Jakle and Keith A. Sculle, *Signs in America's Auto Age: Signatures of Landscape and Place* (Iowa City: Univ. of Iowa Press, 2004), 117–43.

23. Barney Warf, *Time-Space Compression: Historical Geographies* (New York: Routledge, 2008), 153–55.

24. See David Harvey, *The Urbanization of Capital: Studies in the History and Theory of Capitalist Urbanization* (Baltimore: Johns Hopkins Univ. Press, 1985); and Neil Smith, *Uneven Development: Nature, Capital and the Production of Space* (Oxford, UK: Blackwell, 1996).

25. For an introduction to the landscape concept, see John Brinkerhoff Jackson, *Landscape in Sight: Looking at America*, edited by Helen Lefkowitz Horowitz (New Haven: Yale Univ. Press, 1997); D. W. Meinig, ed., *The Interpretation of Ordinary Landscapes: Geographical Essays* (New York: Oxford Univ. Press, 1979); John A. Jakle, *The Visual Elements of Landscape* (Amherst: Univ.

of Massachusetts Press, 1987); and George F. Thompson, ed., *Landscape in America* (Austin: Univ. of Texas Press, 1995).

26. For an overview on the concept of place, see Allan Pred, "Place as Historically Contingent Process: Structuration and the Time-Geography of Becoming Places," *Annals of the Association of American Geographers* 74 (1984): 279–97; Robert D. Sack, "The Consumer's World: Place as Context," *Annals of the Association of American Geographers* 78 (1987): 642–64; and Kathleen Stewart, *A Space on the Side of the Road: Cultural Politics in an "Other" America* (Princeton, NJ: Princeton Univ. Press, 1996).

27. John R. Stilgoe, *Outside Lies the Magic: Regaining History and Awareness in Everyday Places* (New York: Walker & Co., 1998), 6.

28. See John B. Jackson, "The Stranger's Path," *Landscape* 7 (Autumn 1957): 11–15.

29. Jane Jacobs, quoted in Richard Moe, "Adding Up to Noplace," *Historic Preservation News,* June/July 1994, 14.

30. See Edward Relph, *Place or Placelessness* (London: Pion, 1976).

31. Pierre Nora, quoted in Marita Sturken, *Tangled Memories: The Vietnam War, the AIDS Epidemic, and the Politics of Remembering* (Berkeley: Univ. of California Press, 1997), 11.

32. See Dan P. McAdams, *The Stories We Live By: Personal Myths and the Making of Self* (New York: Morrow, 1993).

33. David Thelen, "Memory and American History," *Journal of American History* 75 (Mar. 1989): 1117–29.

34. Kevin Lynch, *What Time Is This Place?* (Cambridge, MA: MIT Press, 1972), 36.

35. Ibid., 61–62.

36. David Lowenthal, *Possessed of the Past: The Heritage Crusade and the Spoils of History* (New York: Free Press, 1996).

37. L. P. Hartley, *The Go-Between* (London: Hamish Hamilton, 1953), 9. Also, see David Lowenthal, *The Past Is a Foreign Country* (Cambridge, UK: Cambridge Univ. Press, 1985).

38. David Lowenthal, "History and Memory," *Public Historian* 19 (Spring 1997): 35.

39. David Lowenthal, "The Timeless Past: Some Anglo-American Historical Preconceptions," *Journal of American History* 75 (Mar. 1989): 1264.

40. Ibid., 1266–67.

41. David Lowenthal, "The American Way of History," *Columbia University Forum* 9 (Summer 1966): 27.

42. See Jean Starobinski, "The Idea of Nostalgia," *Diogenes* 54 (June 1, 1966): 81–103.

43. See Robert Hay, "Sense of Place in Developmental Context," *Environmental Psychology* 18 (June 1998): 1–29; and Irving Altman and Setha M. Low, eds., *Place Attachment* (New York: Plenum Press, 1992).

44. See B. A. Brown, "Icon on Wheels: Supericon of Popular Culture," in Marshall Fishwick and Ray B. Browne, eds., *Icons of Popular Culture*, 47–62 (Bowling Green, OH: Bowling Green State Univ. Popular Press, 1970).

45. See Cynthia Golomb Dettlebach, *In the Driver's Seat: The Auto in American Literature and Popular Culture* (Westport, CT: Greenwood Press, 1976); David Laird, "Versions of Eden: The Automobile and the American Novel," in Leon Mandel, ed., *Driven: The American Four-Wheeled Love Affair* (New York: Stein & Day, 1977); and Laurence Goldstein, "The Automobile and American Poetry," in Lewis and Goldstein, eds., *The Automobile and American Culture*, 224–43.

46. J. N. Nodelman, "Reading Route 66," *Journal of American Culture* 30 (June 2007): 168.

47. John A. Jakle, *The Tourist: Travel in Twentieth-Century North America* (Lincoln: Univ. of Nebraska Press, 1985), 10.

48. Ronald Primeau, *Romance of the Road: The Literature of the American Highway* (Bowling Green, OH: Bowling Green State Univ. Popular Press, 1996), 7.

49. Ibid., 141.

50. Sinclair Lewis, *Free Air* (London: Cape, 1933).

51. John Steinbeck, *The Grapes of Wrath* (New York: Viking Press, 1939).

52. Jack Kerouac, *On the Road* (New York: Viking Press, 1955).

53. For a fuller assessment of Kerouac's work, see Paul Maher, Jr., *Jack Kerouac's American Journey: The Real-Life Odyssey of "On the Road"* (New York: Thunder's Mouth Press, 2007).

54. Vladimir Nabokov, *Lolita* (New York: Olympia Press, 1955); and John Updike, *Rabbit Run* (New York: Alfred A. Knopf, 1960) and *Rabbit Redux* (New York: Alfred A. Knopf, 1971).

55. Updike, *Rabbit Redux*, 398.

56. See Kristen Whissel, *Picturing American Modernity: Traffic, Technology, and the Silent Cinema* (Durham, NC: Duke Univ. Press, 2008).

57. See Raymond Lee, *Fit for the Chase: Cars and the Movies* (Secaucus, NJ: Castle Books, 1969).

58. Corey K. Creekmur, "On the Run and on the Road: Fame and the Outlaw Couple in American Cinema," in Steven Cohan and Ina Rae Hark, eds., *The Road Movie Book,* 90 (London: Routledge, 1997).

59. See Katie Mills, *The Road Story and the Rebel: Moving through Film, Fiction, and Television* (Carbondale: Southern Illinois Univ. Press, 2006).

60. See Barbara Klinger, "The Road to Dystopia: Landscaping the Nation in 'Easy Rider,'" in Cohan and Hark, eds., *The Road Movie Book,* 179–203.

61. Mark Alvey, "Wanderlust and Wire Wheels: The Existential Search of 'Route 66,'" in Cohan and Rae, eds., *The Road Movie Book,* 143.

62. John Steinbeck, *Travels with Charley in Search of America* (New York: Bantam, 1962).

63. For example, see William Least Heat Moon, *Blue Highways: A Journey into America* (Boston: Little, Brown, 1982).

64. See Gerald Silk et al., *Automobile and Culture* (New York: Harry M. Abrams, 1984). For an overview of all the cultural arts in relation to automobility in America, see Michael L. Berger, *The Automobile in American History and Culture* (Westport, CT: Greenwood Press, 2001).

65. Especially, see Ulrich Keller, *The Highway as Habitat: A Roy Stryker Documentation, 1943–1955* (Santa Barbara, CA: Univ. Art Museum, 1986).

66. Warren Belasco, "Motivatin' with Chuck Berry and Frederick Jackson Turner," in Lewis and Goldstein, eds., *The Automobile and American Culture,* 264.

67. Willie Nelson, "On the Road Again," 1979.

2. Observing Roadside America

1. "The Wayside Hen," *American Motorist* 9 (June 1917): 27.

2. For a concise introduction to federal highway initiatives, see Spencer Miller Jr., "History of the Modern Highway in the United States," in Jean Labatut and Wheaton J. Lane, eds., *Highways in Our National Life,* 88–119 (Princeton, NJ: Princeton Univ. Press, 1950); Phil Patton, *Open Road: A Celebration of the American Highway* (New York: Simon & Schuster, 1986);

Bruce E. Seeley, *Building the American Highway System: Engineers as Policy Makers* (Philadelphia: Temple Univ. Press, 1987); and John A. Jakle and Keith A. Sculle, *Motoring: The Highway Experience in America* (Athens: Univ. of Georgia Press, 2008).

3. See John A. Jakle, "Pioneer Roads: America's Early Twentieth-Century Named Highways," *Material Culture* 32 (Summer 2000): 1–22.

4. See Drake Hokanson, *The Lincoln Highway: Main Street across America* (Iowa City: Univ. of Iowa Press, 1988).

5. Miller, "History of the Modern Highway," 92.

6. For an introduction to America's fascination with toll highways and freeways, see Helen Leavitt, *Superhighway—Superhoax* (New York: Ballantine Books, 1970); and Tom Lewis, *Divided Highways: Transforming American Life* (New York: Viking, 1997).

7. James Flagg, *Boulevards All the Way—Maybe* (New York: Doran, 1925), 188.

8. Effie Price Gladding, *Across the Continent by Lincoln Highway* (New York: Bretanos, 1915), 111, 114, 160.

9. Austin F. Bement, "The Lincoln Highway Tour in 1916," in *The Complete Official Road Guide of the Lincoln Highway* (Detroit: Lincoln Highway Association, 1916), 31.

10. Newton A. Fuessle, "The Lincoln Highway—A National Road," *Travel* 24 (Feb. 1915): 26.

11. Charles Henry Davis, "The National Old Trails Road," *Travel* 25 (May 1915): 36.

12. Ibid. For a fuller treatment of the role played by the Daughters of the American Revolution, see Arline B. N. Moss, "Report of National Committee on National Old Trails Road," in *Proceedings, Thirty-Eighth Continental National Society, DAR*, n.p. (Washington, DC: Daughters of the American Revolution, 1929).

13. R. H. Johnston, "A Winter Tour New York to Savannah," *Travel* 13 (May 1908): 368.

14. Archer B. Hulbert, *The Cumberland Road* (Cleveland: Arthur H. Clark, 1904): 187.

15. "Small Town Car Owners in Majority," *Motor Travel* 15 (Nov. 1923): 23.

16. Lewis Atherton, *Main Street on the Middle Border* (Bloomington: Indiana Univ. Press, 1954), 37.

17. Mary King, *Quince Bolliver* (Boston: Houghton Mifflin, 1941), 22.

18. Hamilton Basso, *Court House Square* (New York: Charles Scribner's Sons, 1936), 77.

19. See John A. Jakle and Keith A. Sculle, *America's Main Street Hotels: Transience and Community in the Early Auto Age* (Knoxville: Univ. of Tennessee Press, 2009).

20. Sinclair Lewis, *Oil!* (New York: Grosset & Dunlap, 1926), 1, 5.

21. See Rudy J. Koshar, "Driving Cultures and the Meaning of Roads: Some Comparative Examples," in Christof Mauch and Thomas Zeller, eds., *The World beyond the Windshield: Roads and Landscapes in the United States and Europe*, 14–34 (Athens: Ohio Univ. Press, 2008).

22. Mrs. Gino Ratti, "The Alluring Road," *Hoosier Motorist* 13 (May 1925): 6.

23. John Steinbeck, *Travels with Charley in Search of America* (New York: Viking Press, 1962), 95.

24. Agee, "The Great American Roadside," 53–63, 172, 174, 177.

25. "Nomadic Americans," *Concrete Highways and Public Improvements* 12 (July 1928): 1.

26. Agee, "The Great American Roadside," 172.

27. John A. Jakle and Keith A. Sculle, *The Gasoline Station in America* (Baltimore: Johns Hopkins Univ. Press, 1994), 45–47.

28. "Three Gasoline Pumps to Every Mile of State Highway in United States," *Stanolind Record* 21 (Feb. 1940): 7.

29. George H. Lorimer, "Selling Scenery," *Saturday Evening Post*, Oct. 11, 1919, 28.

30. Gladding, *Across the Continent by Lincoln Highway*, 146.

31. Sinclair Lewis, "Adventures in Automobumming: The Great American Frying Pan," *Saturday Evening Post*, Jan. 3, 1920, 62.

32. Ibid.

33. Flagg, *Boulevards All the Way—Maybe*, 52.

34. Irvin S. Cobb, *Some United States* (New York: Doran, 1926), 290.

35. J. B. Priestley, *Midnight on the Desert* (New York: Harper, 1937), 88.

36. Kenneth L. Roberts, "Travels in Billboardia," *Saturday Evening Post*, Oct. 13, 1928, 186.

37. "The Roadside of Pennsylvania," *Roadside Bulletin* 4 (Nov. 1936): 9.

38. "Beauty and the Open Road," *Highway Magazine* 26 (May 1935): 138.

39. "A Report of Progress in Highway Beautification," *Highway Engineer and Contractor* 20 (June 1929): 45.

40. J. M. Bennett, *Roadsides: The Front Yard of the Nation* (Boston: Stratford, 1930), iii.

41. Sherwood Anderson, *Home Town* (New York: Alliance Book Corp., 1940), 33.

42. J. B. Jackson, "The New American Countryside: An Engineered Environment," *Landscape* 16 (Autumn 1966): 17.

43. Tom Wolfe, *The Kandy-Kolored Tangerine-Flake Streamline Baby* (New York: Pocket Books, 1966), 67.

44. Ibid., 5.

45. Erling D. Solberg, "Zoning for Roadside Protection," in W. Brewster Snow, ed., *The Highway and the Landscape,* 159–60 (New Brunswick, NJ: Rutgers Univ. Press, 1959).

46. Steinbeck, *Travels with Charley in Search of America,* 81.

47. Ibid.

48. George R. Steward, *U.S. 40: Cross Section of the United States of America* (Boston: Houghton Mifflin, 1953), 22.

49. Thomas R. Vale and Geraldine R. Vale, *U.S. 40 Today: Thirty Years of Landscape Change in America* (Madison: Univ. of Wisconsin Press, 1983), 7.

50. J. Todd Snow, "The New Road in the United States: Spatial and Behavioral," *Landscape* 17 (Autumn 1967): 14.

51. Larry McMurtry, *Roads: Driving America's Great Highways* (New York: Simon Schuster, 2000), 12.

52. John Brookes, *The Landscape of Roads* (London: Architectural Press, 1960), 13.

53. See William Least Heat Moon [William Trogdan], *Blue Highways: A Journey into America* (Boston: Little, Brown, 1982).

54. Thomas W. Pew Jr., "Route 66: A Ghost Road," *American Heritage* 28 (July 1977): 26.

55. Flagg, *Boulevards All the Way—Maybe,* 27–28.

3. Learning from Roadside America

1. [James Agee], "The Great American Roadside," *Fortune* 10 (Sept. 1934): 53.

2. *Exploding Metropolis* (Garden City, NY: Doubleday Anchor Books, 1957).

3. William H. Whyte Jr., introduction, *Exploding Metropolis*, xvii.

4. William H. Whyte Jr., "Urban Sprawl," *Exploding Metropolis*, 116–17.

5. Edmund K. Faltermayer, *Redoing America: A Nationwide Report on How to Make Our Cities and Suburbs Livable* (New York: Collier Books, 1969), 29.

6. Ibid., 17–18.

7. Ibid., 32.

8. Ibid., 173–74.

9. Ibid., 151.

10. R. Crumb, "A Short History of America," *CoEvolution Quarterly*, no. 24 (Winter 1979–80): n.p.

11. Christopher Tunnard and Boris Pushkarev, *Man-Made America: Chaos or Control?* (New Haven, CT: Yale Univ. Press, 1963), 324–26.

12. Peter Blake, *God's Own Junkyard: The Planned Deterioration of America's Landscape* (New York: Holt, Rinehart & Winston, 1964), 7.

13. Ibid., 24.

14. Ian Nairn, *The American Landscape: A Critical View* (New York: Random House, 1965), 5–7.

15. Peirce F. Lewis, "The Geographer as Landscape Critic," in Peirce F. Lewis, David Lowenthal, and Yi-Fu Tuan, *Visual Blight in America*, 2–3 (Washington, DC: Association of American Geographers, Commission on College Geography, Resource Paper No. 23, 1973).

16. John A. Kouwenhoven, *Made in America: The Arts in Modern Civilization* (Garden City, NY: Doubleday, 1962), 43.

17. See Peter G. Rowe, *Making a Middle Landscape* (Cambridge, MA: MIT Press, 1991), 218–19.

18. Ulrich Keller, "Highway Iconography," in *The Highway as Habitat: A Roy Stryker Documentation, 1943–1955* (Santa Barbara, CA: University Art Museum, 1986), 17.

19. Stewart Alsop, "America the Ugly," *Saturday Evening Post*, June 23, 1962, 8.

20. See Timothy Davis, "A Pleasant Illusion of Unspoiled Countryside," in Alison K. Hoagland and Kenneth A. Breisch, eds., *Constructing Image, Identity, and Place,* Perspectives in Vernacular Architecture 9, 228–46 (Knoxville: Univ. of Tennessee Press, 2003). Also see Timothy Davis, "The American Motor Parkway," *Studies in the History of Gardens and Designed Landscapes: An International Quarterly* 25 (Oct.–Dec. 2005): 219–49.

21. See John W. Houck, ed., *Outdoor Advertising: History and Regulation* (Notre Dame, IN: Univ. of Notre Dame, 1969); Lewis L. Gould, "First Lady as Catalyst: Lady Bird Johnson and Highway Beautification in the 1960s," *Environmental Review* 10 (Summer 1986): 77–93; Carl A. Zimring, "Neon, Junk, and Ruined Landscape: Competing Visions of America's Roadsides and the Highway Beautification Act of 1965," in Christof Mauch and Thomas Zeller, eds., *The World beyond the Windshield: Roads and Landscapes in the United States and Europe* (Athens: Ohio Univ. Press, 2008), 94–107.

22. [John B. Jackson], "The Operators," *Landscape* 15 (Winter 1965–66): 12.

23. E. Relph, *Place and Placelessness* (London: Pion, 1965), 136.

24. Nairn, *The American Landscape,* 12.

25. For a concise review of Jackson's writings on Roadside America, see Timothy Davis, "Looking down the Road: J. B. Jackson and the American Highway Landscape," in Chris Wilson and Paul Groth, eds., *Everyday America: Cultural Landscape Studies after J. B. Jackson,* 62–76 (Berkeley: Univ. of California Press, 2003).

26. [John B. Jackson], "Notes and Comments," *Landscape* 13 (Winter 1963–64): 2.

27. John B. Jackson, "Other-Directed Houses," *Landscape* 6 (Winter 1956); reprinted in John Brinckerhoff Jackson, *Landscape in Sight: Looking at America,* edited by Helen Lefkowitz Horowitz (New Haven: Yale Univ. Press, 1997), 186.

28. Ibid.

29. John B. Jackson, "Limited Access: The American Landscape Seen in Passing," *Landscape* 14 (Autumn 1964): 19.

30. Ibid.

31. See J. B. Jackson, *The Necessity of Ruins and Other Topics* (Amherst: Univ. of Massachusetts Press, 1980), 113–26.

32. Davis, "Looking down the Road," 72.

33. Robert Venturi, Denise Scott Brown, and Steven Izenour, *Learning from Las Vegas: The Forgotten Symbolism of Architectural Form* (Cambridge, MA: MIT Press, 1977).

34. Denise Scott Brown, "Learning from Brinck," in Wilson and Groth, eds., *Everyday America*, 54.

35. For a concise assessment of *Learning from Las Vegas*, see Geoffrey Broadbent, *Emerging Concepts in Urban Space Design* (London: Van Nostrand Reinhold (International), 1990), 245–52. For in-depth analysis, see Aron Vinegar, *I Am a Monument: On Learning from Las Vegas* (Cambridge, MA: MIT Press, 2008).

36. John Brinckerhoff Jackson, "The Future of the Vernacular," in Paul Groth and Todd W. Bressi, eds., *Understanding Ordinary Landscapes* (New Haven, CT: Yale Univ. Press, 1997), 152.

37. Ibid., 153.

38. Darrell A. Norris, "Interstate Highway Exit Morphology: Non-Metropolitan Exit Commerce on I-75," *Professional Geographer* 39 (Feb. 1987): 30–31.

39. Ibid., 24.

40. Craig Whitaker, *Architecture and the American Dream* (New York: Clarkson N. Potter, 1996), 252–53.

41. For example, see Brian J. L. Berry, "Ribbon Development in the Urban Business Pattern," *Annals of the Association of American Geographers* 49 (Mar. 1959): 145–55; and Andreas Grotewold and Lois Grotewold, "Commercial Development of Highways in Urbanized Regions: A Case Study," *Land Economics* 34 (1958): 236–44.

42. For example, see E. Eiselen, "The Tourist Industry of a Modern Highway: U.S. 16 in South Dakota," *Economic Geography* 21 (July 1945): 221–30; and J. M. Roberts et al., "The Small Highway Business on U. S. 30 in Nebraska," *Economic Geography* 32 (Apr. 1956): 139–52.

43. Grady Clay, *Close-Up: How to Read the American City* (New York: Praeger, 1973), 90–98. Also, see Kevin Patrick, "Transportation Corridors: The Development and Spatial Structure of Roadside Cultural Landscape," *Small Town* 22 (Jan.–Feb. 1992): 4–11.

44. John A. Jakle and Richard L. Mattson, "The Evolution of a Commercial Strip," *Journal of Cultural Geography* 1 (Spring/Summer 1984): 12–25.

45. Richard Longstreth, "The Forgotten Arterial Landscape: Photographic Documentation of Commercial Development along Los Angeles Boulevards during the Interwar Years," *Journal of Urban History* 23 (May 1997): 437–59.

46. Richard P. Horowitz, *The Strip: An American Place* (Lincoln: Univ. of Nebraska Press, 1985), 5.

47. Ibid., 11.

48. Ibid., 10.

49. Phil Patton, *Open Road: A Celebration of the American Highway* (New York: Simon & Schuster, 1986), 189.

50. For more on franchising, see Harry Kursh, *The Franchising Boom* (Englewood Cliffs, NJ: Prentice-Hall, 1968); Stan Luxemberg, *Roadside Empires: How the Chains Franchised America* (New York: Penguin Books, 1985); and Thomas S. Dicke, *Franchising in America: The Development of a Business Method, 1840–1980* (Chapel Hill: Univ. of North Carolina Press, 1992).

51. Gary Cross, *An All-Consuming Century: Why Commercialism Won in Modern America* (New York: Columbia Univ. Press, 2000), 17–18.

52. Thomas J. Baerwald, "The Emergence of a New 'Downtown,'" *Geographical Review* 68 (July 1978): 398.

53. See Joel Garreau, *Edge City: Life on the New Frontier* (New York: Doubleday, 1988).

54. Peter G. Rowe, *Making a Middle Landscape* (Cambridge, MA: MIT Press, 1991), 109–47.

55. Richard W. Longstreth, *City Center to Regional Mall: Architecture, the Automobile, and Retailing in Los Angeles, 1920–1950* (Cambridge, MA: MIT Press, 1997). Also see Richard W. Longstreth, "The Neighborhood Shopping Center in Washington, DC, 1930–1941," *Journal of the Society of Architectural Historians* 51 (Mar. 1992): 5–32; and Richard W. Longstreth, "The Diffusion of the Community Shopping Center Concept during the Interwar Decades," *Journal of the Society of Architectural Historians* 56 (Sept. 1997): 268–93; Nancy E. Cohen, *America's Marketplace: A History of Shopping Centers* (Lyme, CT: Greenwich Publishing Group, 2002).

56. Chester H. Liebs, *Main Street to Miracle Mile: American Roadside Architecture* (Boston: Little, Brown, 1985).

57. Ibid., 43.

58. Ibid., 39–73.

59. On gas stations, see Bruce Lohof, "The Service Station in America: The Evolution of a Vernacular Form," *Industrial Archaeology* 11 (May 1974): 1–13; John A. Jakle, "The American Gasoline Station, 1920 to 1970," *Journal of American Culture* 1 (1970): 521–42; Daniel Vieyra, *"Fill'er Up": An Architectural History of America's Gas Stations* (New York: Collier Books, 1979); John Margolies,

Pump and Circumstance: Glory Days of the Gas Station (Boston: Little, Brown & Co., 1993); John A. Jakle and Keith A. Sculle, *The Gas Station in America* (Baltimore: Johns Hopkins Univ. Press, 1994).

On motels, see Warren J. Belasco, *Americans on the Road: From Autocamp to Motel, 1910–1945* (Cambridge, MA: MIT Press, 1979); John A. Jakle, "Motel by the Side of the Road: America's Room for the Night," *Journal of Cultural Geography* 1 (Fall 1979): 519–33; Mary Anne Beecher, "The Motel in Builder's Literature and Architectural Publications: An Analysis of Design," in Jan Jennings, ed., *Roadside America: The Automobile, Design, and Culture*, 115–24 (Ames: Iowa State Univ. Press, 1990); John A. Jakle, Keith A. Sculle, and Jefferson S. Rogers, *The Motel in America* (Baltimore: Johns Hopkins Univ. Press, 1996).

On restaurants, see John Baeder, *Diners* (New York: Harry N. Abrams, 1978); Bruce A. Lohof, "Hamburger Stand: Industrialization and the American Fast Food Phenomenon," *Journal of American Culture* 2 (Fall 1978): 519–33; Paul Hirschorn and Steven Izenour, *White Towers* (Cambridge, MA: MIT Press, 1979); John A. Jakle, "Roadside Restaurants and Place-Product-Packaging," *Journal of Cultural Geography* 83 (Fall–Winter 1982): 76–93; Philip Langdon, *Orange Roofs, Golden Arches: The Architecture of American Chain Restaurants* (New York: Alfred A. Knopf, 1986); Thomas Hine, *Populuxe* (New York: Alfred A. Knopf, 1987); Alan Hess, *Googie: Fifties Coffee Shop Architecture* (San Francisco: Chronicle Books, 1985); Richard J. S. Gutman, *American Diner: Then and Now* (New York: HarperPerennial, 1993); Jeffrey Tennyson, *Hamburger Heaven: The Illustrated History of the Hamburger* (New York: Hyperion, 1993); Michael Karl Witzel, *The American Drive-In: History and Folklore of the Drive-In Restaurant in American Car Culture* (Osceola, WI: Motorbooks International, 1994); Jim Heimann, *Car Hops and Curb Service* (San Francisco: Chronicle Books, 1996); Michael Karl Witzel, *Drive-in Deluxe* (Osceola, WI: Motorbooks International, 1997); W. Anderson, *Where Have You Gone, Starlight Café? America's Golden Era Roadside Restaurants* (Bath, ME: Anderson & Sons, 1998); John A. Jakle and Keith A. Sculle, *Fast Food: Roadside Restaurants in the Automobile Age* (Baltimore: Johns Hopkins Univ. Press, 1999); Jim Heimann, *California Crazy and Beyond: Roadside Vernacular Architecture* (San Francisco: Chronicle Books, 2001).

On signage, see Lisa Maher, *American Signs: Form and Meaning on Route 66* (New York: Monacelli Press, 2002); Catherine Gudis, *Buyways: Billboards, Automobiles, and the American Landscape* (New York: Routledge, 2004); John A. Jakle and Keith A. Sculle, *Signs in America's Auto Age: Signatures of Landscape and Place* (Iowa City: Univ. of Iowa Press, 2004). For more on the signs of Las Vegas Strip, see Alan Hess, *Viva Las Vegas: After Hours Architecture* (San Francisco: Chronicle Books, 1993); Jeffrey Brouws, *Readymades: American Roadside Artifacts* (San Francisco: Chronicle Books, 2003).

60. On drive-in movie theaters, see Kerry Seagrove, *Drive-in Theaters: A History from Their Inception in 1933* (Jefferson, NC: McFarland, 1992); Don Sanders and Susan Sanders, *The American Drive-in Movie Theatre* (Osceola, WI: Motorbooks International, 1997); Elizabeth McKeon, Linda Everett, and Liz McKeon, *Cinema under the Stars: America's Love Affair with the Drive-in Movie* (Knoxville: Cumberland House, 1998). On supermarkets, see James Mayo, *The American Grocery Store: The Evolution of an American Space* (Westport, CT: Greenwood Press, 1993); Richard Longstreth, *The Drive-in, the Supermarket, and the Transformation of Commercial Space in Los Angeles, 1914–1941* (Cambridge, MA: MIT Press, 1999). On car dealers, see Robert Genat, *The American Car Dealership* (Osceola, WI: MBI, 1999). On parking, see John A. Jakle and Keith A. Sculle, *Lots of Parking: Land Use in a Car Culture* (Charlottesville: Univ. of Virginia Press, 2004).

61. See J. J. C. Andrews, *The Well-Built Elephant and Other Roadside Attractions* (New York: Congdon & Weed, 1984); Karal Ann Marling, *The Colossus of Roads: Myths and Symbols along the American Highway* (Minneapolis: Univ. of Minnesota Press, 1984); David Gebhard, "Programmatic Architecture: An Introduction," *SCA Journal* 13 (Spring–Summer 1995): 2–7; John Margolies, *Fun along the Road: American Tourist Attractions* (Boston: Bulfinch, 1998); Tim Hollis, *Dixie before Disney: 100 Years of Roadside Fun* (Jackson: Univ. Press of Mississippi, 1999).

62. Relative to the fast-food (or quick-service) industry, examples include Max Boas and Steve Chain, *Big Mac: The Unauthorized Story of McDonald's* (New York: Mentor Books, 1976); Robert L. Emerson, *Fast Food: The Endless Shakedown* (New York: Lebbar-Friedman, 1979); Marshall Fishwick, ed., *Ronald Revisited: The World of Ronald McDonald* (Bowling Green, OH: Bowling Green State Univ. Popular Press, 1983); John F. Love, *McDonald's behind the Arches* (Toronto: Bantam Books, 1986); David Gerard Hogan, *Selling Them by the Sack: White Castle and the Creation of American Food* (New York: New York Univ. Press, 1997).

63. For Route 66, see Quinta Scott and Susan Croce Kelly, *Route 66: The Highway and Its People* (Norman: Univ. of Oklahoma Press, 1988); Michael Wallis, *Route 66: The Mother Road* (New York: St. Martin's Press, 1990); Quinta Scott, *Along Route 66* (Norman: Univ. of Oklahoma Press, 2000); Gerd Kittel, Alexander Bloom, and Freddy Langer, *Route 66* (New York: Thames & Hudson, 2002); Arthur Krim, *Route 66: Iconography of the American Highway* (Santa Fe, NM, and Staunton, VA: Center for American Places, 2005); Peter B. Dedek, *Hip to the Road: A Cultural History of Route 66* (Albuquerque: Univ. of New Mexico Press, 2007).

64. For the Dixie Highway, see Claudette Stager and Martha Carver, eds., *Looking beyond the Highway: Dixie Roads and Culture* (Knoxville, TN: Univ. of Tennessee Press, 2006). For the Lincoln Highway, see Drake Hokanson, *The Lincoln Highway: Main Street across America* (Iowa City: Univ. of Iowa Press, 1986); Brian A. Butko, *Pennsylvania Traveler's Guide: The Lincoln Highway* (Mechanicsburg, PA: Stackpole Books, 1996); Brian A. Butko, *Greetings from the Lincoln Highway: America's First Coast to Coast Road* (Mechanicsburg, PA: Stackpole Books, 2005). For the old National Road, see Thomas J. Schlereth, *U.S. 40: A Roadscape of the American Experience* (Indianapolis: Indiana Historical Society, 1985), revised as *Reading the Road: U.S. 40 and the American Landscape* (Knoxville: Univ. of Tennessee Press, 1997); Karl Raitz, ed., *A Guide to the National Road* (Baltimore: Johns Hopkins Univ. Press, 1996); Karl Raitz, ed., *The National Road* (Baltimore: Johns Hopkins Univ. Press, 1996). For U.S. 1, see Andrew H. Malcolm and Roger Straus III, *U.S. 1: America's Original Main Street* (New York: St. Martin's Press, 1991). For the Yellowstone Trail, see Harold Meeks, *On the Road to Yellowstone: The Yellowstone Trail and American Highways, 1900–1930* (Missoula, MT: Pictorial, 2000).

65. Especially see Jeff Brouws, Bernd Polster, and Phil Patton, *Highway: America's Endless Dream* (New York: Stewart, Tabori & Chang, 1997); Chuck Forsman, *Western Rider: Views from a Car Window* (Santa Fe, NM, and Harrisonburg, VA: Center for American Places, 2003); Jeffrey T. Brouws, *Approaching Nowhere* (New York: Chiefly, 2006).

66. Liebs, *Main Street to Miracle Mile*, 39–73.

67. Jakle and Sculle, *Gas Station in America*, 130–62.

68. For a discussion of landscape dereliction, see John A. Jakle and David Wilson, *Derelict Landscapes: The Wasting of America's Built Environment* (Savage, MD: Rowman & Littlefield, 1992). For a general overview focused on Roadside America, see Troy Palva, *Lost America: The Abandoned Roadside* (St. Paul, MN: MBI, 2005).

69. See Timothy Davis, "The Miracle Mile Revisited: Recycling, Renovation, and Simulation along the Commercial Strip," in Annemarie Adams and Sally McMurry, eds., *Exploring Everyday Landscapes,* Perspectives in Vernacular Architecture 6, 104 (Knoxville: Univ. of Tennessee Press, 2005).

70. Faltermayer, *Redoing America*, 175.

71. Alan Hess, *Viva Las Vegas: After-Hours Architecture* (San Francisco: Chronicle Books, 1993), 10.

72. Ibid., 122.

73. Peter S. Beagle, *I See by My Outfit* (New York: Ballantine Books, 1965), 171.

74. Kent McDonald, "The Commercial Strip: From Main Street to Television Road," *Landscape* 28, no. 2 (1985): 12–13.

75. Ibid., 14.

76. Ibid., 18–19.

4. Preserving Roads and Roadsides

1. Charles B. Hosmer Jr., *Presence of the Past: A History of the Preservation Movement in the United States before Williamsburg* (New York: G. P. Putnam's Sons, 1965), 29–35; and "Yorktown Battlefield," "Yorktown Monument," http://www.nps.gov/york (accessed Dec. 28, 2008).

2. Hosmer, *Presence of the Past*, 35.

3. Cited in Walter Muir Whitehead, foreword, in Hosmer, *Presence of the Past*, 9.

4. See Michael A. Tomlan, "Preservation Comes of Age," in Antoinette J. Lee, ed., *Past Meets Future: Saving America's Historic Environments*, 73 (Washington, DC: Preservation Press, 1992). The so-called Second Battle of the Alamo, the effort to save the mission, which later became a fortress in the revolution for Texas' independence, clearly exemplifies the religious values at play in historic preservation; see Michael Kammen, *Mystic Chords of Memory: The Transformation of Tradition in American Culture* (New York: Alfred A. Knopf, 1991), 241.

5. Hosmer, *Presence of the Past*, 21; and Peter H. Brink and H. Grant Dehart, "Findings and Recommendations," in Lee, ed., *Past Meets Future*, 16.

6. William J. Murtagh, *Keeping Time: The History and Theory of Preservation in America* (Pittstown, NJ: Main Street Press, 1988), 30.

7. Hosmer, *Presence of the Past*, 57.

8. Ibid., 261; and Murtagh, *Keeping Time*, 32.

9. Hosmer, *Presence of the Past*, 263.

10. Randall Mason, "Historic Preservation, Public Memory, and the Making of Modern New York City," in Max Page and Randall Mason, eds., *Giving Preservation a History: Histories of Historic Preservation in the United States*, 133–39 (New York: Routledge, 2004).

11. Kammen, *Mystic Chords of Memory*, 563.

12. Murtagh, *Keeping Time,* 42–44.

13. Charles B. Hosmer, Jr., *Preservation Comes of Age: From Williamsburg to the National Trust, 1926–1949,* 2 vols. (Charlottesville: Univ. Press of Virginia, 1981), 1064.

14. Deborah Edge Abele and Grady Gammage, Jr., "The Shifting Signposts of Significance," in Deborah Slaton and William G. Foulks, eds., *Preserving the Recent Past 2, sec. 2:* 2–9 (Washington, DC: Historic Preservation Education Foundation, National Park Service, and Association for Preservation Technology International, 2000).

15. Hosmer, *Preservation Comes of Age,* 1045 and 1051.

16. James Marston Fitch, *Historic Preservation: Curatorial Management of the Built World* (Charlottesville: Univ. Press of Virginia, 1990), 2–3.

17. For example, see John Walton Caughey, "The Local Historian: His Occupational Hazards and Compensations," in Carol Kammen, ed., *The Pursuit of Local History: Readings on Theory and Practice,* 206 (Walnut Creek: Altamira Press, 1996).

18. Judith W. Wellman, "Local Historians and Their Activities," in Kammen, ed., *The Pursuit of Local History,* 49.

19. Mrs. Lyndon B. Johnson, foreword, in *With Heritage So Rich: A Special Report of a Special Committee on Historic Preservation under the Auspices of the United States Conference of Mayors with a Grant from the Ford Foundation,* vii (New York: Random House, 1966).

20, "Recommendations," in *With Heritage So Rich,* 208.

21. Murtagh, *Keeping Time,* 62.

22. Tomlan, "Preservation Comes of Age," 73.

23. The architectural historian was Alison Hinson (Catherine Bishir—member of the North Carolina SHPO at the time of the "sea shell" nomination—in an email to Keith A. Sculle, Oct. 10, 2007). The industrial archaeologist was Brent Glass (per his telephone interview by Keith A. Sculle, Oct. 30, 2007).

24. Marc Wagner, "Three Models for Roadside Preservation," *Material Culture* 32, no. 2 (2000): 30.

25. The member of the New York SHPO was Doris Vanderlipp (formerly Manley; letter to Keith A. Sculle, Oct. 12, 2008); and the active preservationist, later the New York State Historic Preservation Officer, was Julia Stokes (letter to Keith A. Sculle, Nov. 16, 2008).

26. Catherine Howett, "Integrity as a Value in Cultural Landscape Preservation," in Arnold R. Alanen and Robert Z. Melnick, eds., *Preserving Cultural Landscapes in America*, 197 (Baltimore: Johns Hopkins Univ. Press, 2000).

27. Tersh Boasberg, "A New Paradigm for Preservation," in Lee, ed., *Past Meets Future*, 150.

28. Arnold R. Alanen and Robert Z. Melnick, "Why Cultural Landscape Preservation?," in Alanen and Melnick, eds., *Preserving Cultural Landscapes in America*, 7.

29. Charles A. Birnbaum, "Protecting Cultural Landscapes: Planning, Treatment and Management of Historic Landscapes," *Preservation Briefs* 36 (Sept. 1994): 2.

30. Alanen and Melnick, "Why Cultural Landscape Preservation?" 5.

31. Regarding NAGPRA, see Hester A. Davis, "Archeology in the Next 25 Years," in Lee, ed., *Past Meets Future*, 182. Also see Dean B. Suagee, "Keepers of the Native Treasures," Lee, ed., *Past Meets Future*, 189–95.

32. Christopher Tilley, "Introduction: Identity, Place, Landscape and Heritage," *Journal of Material Culture* 11, no. 1/2 (2006): 8–13.

33. See John A. Jakle and Keith A. Sculle, *The Gas Station in America*, 33; John A. Jakle, Keith A. Sculle, and Jefferson S. Rogers, *The Motel in America*, 14; John A. Jakle and Keith A. Sculle, *Fast Food: Roadside Restaurants in the Automobile Age*, 6; and John A. Jakle and Keith A. Sculle, *Motoring*, 6.

34. John R. Gillis, "Remembering Memory: A Challenge for Public Historians in a Post-National Era," *Public Historian* 14 (Fall 1992): 95–96.

35. See Frances Griffin, *Old Salem: An Adventure in Historic Preservation* (Winston-Salem, NC: Old Salem, [1970]).

36. For concise reviews of the preservation movement's birth in Charleston, see Robin Elizabeth Datel, "Southern Regionalism and Historic Preservation in Charleston, South Carolina, 1920–1940," *Journal of Historical Geography* 16 (Apr. 1990): 197–215; and Robert R. Weyneth, "Ancestral Architecture: The Early Preservation Movement in Charleston," in Page and Mason, eds., *Giving Preservation a History*, 257–87.

37. Paul W. Ivory, "Gas Station Architecture," copy of the typescript in authors' possession.

38. For example, see Carleton Knight III, "Roadside Riches," *Preservation News,* Sept. 1978): 7; "Gone, but Not Forgotten," *Preservation News,* Dec. 1978, 2; David Gebhard, "The Delights of Drive-ins," *Preservation News,* June 1985,

15; and "D.C. Designates 'Slip Covered' Bus Station a Landmark," *Preservation News,* Mar. 1987, 6. Also see "I'll Take that Diner to Go!" *Preservation (*July/ Aug. 2008): http://www.preservationnation.org/magazine/2008/july-august/ reporter-diner.html (accessed Dec. 16, 2008); and Ann Beattie, "Scenes from the Open Road: America's Fabled Route 66 in Black and White," *Preservation* (Mar./ Apr. 2008): http://www.preservationnation.org/magazine/2008/march-april/ feature2.html (accessed Dec. 16, 2008).

39. Richard Longstreth, "When the Present Becomes the Past," in Lee, ed., *Past Meets Future,* 215.

40. Ibid., 217, 224.

41. Ibid., 222, 224.

42. See Beth L. Savage, "Disappearing Ducks and Other Roadside Relics," *CRM* 16, no. 6 (1993): 23–25; and Richard Longstreth, "The Significance of the Recent Past," *CRM* 16, no. 6 (1993): 4–7. Also see Robert Venturi, Denise Scott Brown, and Steven Izenour, *Learning from Las Vegas,* rev. ed. (Cambridge: MIT Press, 1997), 87–89.

43. See "Gas, Food, and Lodging" in Deborah Slaton and Rebecca A. Shiffer, eds., *Preserving the Recent Past,* sec. II: 25–52 (Washington, DC: Historic Preservation Education Foundation, 1995).

44. See Beth L. Savage, "Road-related Resources Listed in the National Register," 13–15; Carol Ahlgren, "The Lincoln Highway," 16–17; Dwayne Jones, "What's New with the Pig Stands?--Not the Pig Sandwich!" *1*8–20; Jeff Winstel, "Petroliana and the Cultural Landscape: Preserving a Gas Station in a Historic Canal Town," 20–22; and Dennis Montagna, "The Early Passing of an Architectural Landmark," 23–24, all in *CRM* 19, no. 9 (1996).

45. W. Ray Luce, "Kent State, White Castles, and Subdivisions: Evaluating the Recent Past," in Slaton and Shiffer, *Preserving the Recent Past, sec. II:* 16–17.

46. Deborah Slaton and William G. Foulks, introduction, in Slaton and Foulks, eds., *Preserving the Recent Past 2,* 1.

47. Meredith Arms Bzdak, "From the Big Bear to the Big Box: Twentieth-Century Supermarkets in New Jersey," 35–42; and Nathalie Wright, "In Search of Tiki," 185–91, both in sec. 2, Slaton and Foulks, eds., *Preserving the Recent Past 2.*

48. Ronald E. Schmitt, "The Ubiquitous Parking Garage: Worthy of Preservation?," in Slaton and Foulks, eds., *Preserving the Recent Past 2,* sec. 2: 2–193.

49. Kammen, *Mystic Chords of Memory,* 37–38.

50. Richard Longstreth, "Integrity and the Recent Past," in Slaton and Foulks, eds., *Preserving the Recent Past 2*, sec. 2: 2–5.

51. Deborah Edge Abele and Grady Gammage, Jr., "The Shifting Signposts of Significance," in Slaton and Foulks, eds., *Preserving the Recent Past 2*, sec. 2: 9–10.

52. For SCA's manifesto, see "Concerning SCA," *SCA News Journal* 1 (Sept. 1978): 3.

53. For examples of interest in the roads themselves, see Arthur Krim, "Mapping Route 66: A Cultural Cartography," 198–208; Jan Jennings, ed., *Roadside America: The Automobile in Design and Culture* (Ames: Iowa State Univ. Press, 1990); Sara Amy Leach, "'Pines to Palms': A Drive along the Ocean Highway," *SCA Journal* 14 (Spring 1996): 28–32; Martha Carver, "The Dixie Highway and Automobile Tourism in the South," *SCA Journal* 16 (Fall 1998), 22–26; and Robert W. Hadlow, "The Columbia River Highway," *SCA Journal* 18 (Summer 2000): 14–25.

54. Glenn A. Harper, "Preserving the National Road Landscape," in Karl Raitz, ed., *The National Road* (Baltimore: Johns Hopkins Univ. Press, 1996), 381.

55. Michael Wallis, *Route 66: The Mother Road* (New York: St. Martin's Press, 1990); and Arthur Krim, *Route 66: Iconography of the American Highway* (Santa Fe, NM, and Staunton, VA: Center for American Places, 2005).

56. Peter B. Dedek, *Hip to the Trip: A Cultural History of Route 66* (Albuquerque: Univ. of New Mexico Press, 2007).

57. See Keith A. Sculle, "Missouri's Route 66 State Park: Showcasing the History and Mystique of the 'Mother Road,'" *SCA News* 11 (Summer 2003): 4–5.

58. D. Paul Marriott, *Saving Historic Roads: Design and Policy Guidelines* (Washington, DC: National Trust for Historic Preservation, 1998), 1.

59. Ibid.

60. From the 2004 conference, Dawn E. Duensing, "Hawaii's Historic Roads: A Glimpse into an Authentic Hawaii" and Robert W. Hadlow, "Obsolescence––The Columbia River Highway, 1922–1980" are especially relevant. Also useful are, from the 2006 conference, Richard Canale, Barbara Lucas, Dawn McKenna, Nancy Nelson, and Debbie Smith, "Finding a Twenty-First Century along an Eighteenth-Century Historical Legacy––the Battle Road" and, from the 2008 conference, Courtney Fint, "West Virginia Historic Turnpikes: Research and Survey Methods." Copies of these papers are in the authors' possession. For more information on the conferences and the papers presented at them, see the *Historic Roads* website: http://www.historicroads.org/.

61. Harpers Ferry Center, National Trails System Map & Guide, http://www.nps.gov/hfc/carto/nps-trails.htm (accessed Dec. 18, 2008). For an overview of the program, which was nearly thirty years old in 1997, see "CRM and the National Trails System," *CRM* 20, no. 1 (1997), an issue entirely dedicated to the program.

62. Scenic America, http://www.scenic.org/byways/national (accessed Dec. 18, 2008).

63. For a history of the program, see these professional papers archived on the Route 66 Corridor Preservation Program webite: Michael Romero Taylor and Kaisa Barthuli, "The Route 66 Corridor Preservation Program: How the National Park Service Is Working with Partners to Preserve Historic Properties along America's Most Recognized 20th Century Road" (2004), http://www.nps.gov/rt66/news/Port_Pres.htm; and Michael Romero Taylor, Kaisa Barthuli, and Andrea Sharon, "Interpretation Along Route 66" (2005), http://www.nps.gov/rt66/news/Charls_Pres.htm (both accessed Dec. 18, 2008). See also Kaisa Barthuli, "Route 66 Corridor Update," *Route 66 Magazine* 16 (Spring 2009): 5.

64. Barthuli, "Route 66 Corridor Update," *Route 66 Magazine* 16 (Spring 2009): 5.

65. For an example of the coequal faith in feeling, see Johnnie Meier, "A Guest Editorial—Writing the Route: 'It's more than concrete. It's a culture,'" *Route 66 Magazine* 16 (Summer 2009): 5. For examples of the popular media, see Russell A. Olsen, *Route 66: Lost and Found*, 2 vols. (St. Paul: MBI, 2004, 2006); and Russell A. Olsen, *Complete Route 66 Lost and Found* (Minneapolis: Voyageur Press, 2008).

66. Gillis, "Remembering Memory," 98.

67. For Rome, New York: H. P. Sears Oil Co., Inc., brochure in author's collection. For Mansfield, Ohio: John Merschdorf, telephone interview with Keith A. Sculle, Jan. 26, 2007.

68. Pat Best, "Piqua Lucky to Have Full Service Station," Feb. 23, 2005, clipping without page number or newspaper name from Kinsinger's personal album; "Local Service Station to No Longer Sell Gas," June 18, 2008, clipping without page number or newspaper name from Kinsinger's personal album; and Terry Kinsinger, letter to Keith A. Sculle, Aug. 28, 2008.

69. Mike Kertok, telephone interview with Keith A. Sculle, June 13, 2008; Mike Kertok, email to Keith A. Sculle, June 20, 2008; and Roger McKinney, "Fill 'er up with tourists," *Joplin* [Missouri] *Globe*, June 2, 2008, http://www.joplinglobe.com/local_story_233000104/resources-printstory (accessed June 2, 2008.)

70. Larry Cultrera, "Diner Hotline," *SCA Journal* 25 (Fall 2007): 36; and Larry Cultrera, "Diner Hotline," *SCA Journal* 21 (Fall 2003): 24–25.

71. Mella Rothwell Harmon, "The Biggest Little Diner: Landrum's Diner in Reno, NV," *SCA Journal* 18 (Spring 2000): 13.

72. Todd Bucher, telephone interview with Keith A. Sculle, Feb. 20, 2009.

73. "Delta Diner Site History" and "Our Original Diner Story," Classic American Diners—The Roadside Diner Experience at the Delta Diner, http://deltadiner.com/history.html (accessed Feb. 11, 2009).

74. Beattie, "Scenes from the Open Road."

75. Kevin J. Patrick and Keith A. Sculle, "The Lincoln Motor Court: Heritage Tourism and the Rise, Fall, and Preservation of a Lincoln Highway Landmark," *Pioneer American Society Transactions* 25 (2002): 5–7.

76. Ibid., 8–9 ; Brian A. Butko, "Historic Highway Preservation: Not a Dead End Street!" *CRM* 16 (1993): 36; and Brian A. Butko, *Pennsylvania Travelers' Guide: The Lincoln Highway* (Mechanicsburg, PA: Stackpole Books, 1996), 188–90.

77. Andrew F. Wood and Jenny F. Wood, *Motel America: A State-by-State Tour Guide to Nostalgic Stopovers* (Portland, OR: Collectors Press, 2004).

78. "Coral Court Motel, St. Louis, Missouri," BBC website, http://www.bbc.co.uk/dna/h2g2/A1309088 (accessed Feb. 11, 2009).

79. Shellee Graham, *Tales from the Coral Court: Photos and Stories from a Lost Route 66 Landmark* (St. Louis: Virginia Publishing, 2000), 35.

80. "Coral Court Motel," BBC website; and William O. Luton, Jr., "The History of Route 66 and Coral Court," http://www.isuzuperformance.com/bill/coral.html (accessed Feb. 11, 2009).

81. St. Louis Historic Buildings Commission, *Historic Buildings in St. Louis County* (Clayton, MO: St. Louis County Department of Parks and Recreation), 41.

82. Esley Hamilton, "A Gem of the Road, Coral Court," *SCA News Journal* 9 (Fall 1987): 3.

83. Esley Hamilton, interview with Keith A. Sculle, Feb. 17, 2009; and "Coral Court Motel," BBC website.

84. "Coral Court Motel," BBC website; and "Coral Court Closes," *SCA News* 1 (Winter 1993–94): 1.

85. "Coral Court Motel," BBC website.

86. Luton, "The History of Route 66 and Coral Court"; and "Built St. Louis: Coral Court", http://www.builtstlouis.net/coralcourt01.html (accessed Feb. 11, 2009).

87. Shellee Graham--Route 66 Photographer and Exhibitor, home.earthlink.net/~shelle66/sg.html; and "Built for Speed: The Coral Court Motel Store," http://www.cafepress.com/coralcourt (both accessed Feb. 19, 2009).

88. David Bonetti and Diane Toroian Keaggy, "Gone but Not Forgotten," *St. Louis Post-Dispatch,* July 27, 2008, F3.

89. For example, see American Diner Museum http://www.americandinermuseum.org/site/preservation.php (accessed Dec. 19, 2008); Route 66 News, "Motels" http://rwarn17588.wordpress.com/category/motels (accessed Dec. 19, 2008); Blair Tarr, "Nothing Could Be Finer Than a Valentine Diner," *Kansas Heritage* 11 (Summer 2003): 6–13; and William Neudorf and Kennedy Smith, *Better Models for Urban Supermarkets* (Washington, DC: National Trust for Historic Preservation, 2005).

90. Jeanne Lambin, *Preserving Resources from the Recent Past* (Washington, DC: National Trust for Historic Preservation, 2007), 1, 3.

91. Shannon Bell, "From Ticket Booth to Screen Tower: An Architectural Study of Drive-in Theaters in the Baltimore–Washington, D.C.–Richmond Corridor" in Alison K. Hoagland and Kenneth A. Breisch, eds., *Constructing Image, Identity, and Place,* Perspectives in Vernacular Architecture IX, 215 (Knoxville: Univ. of Tennessee Press, 2003).

92. Rebecca A. Shiffer, "Cultural Resources from the Recent Past," *CRM* 16, no. 6 (1993): 3.

93. Ibid.

94. Heather MacIntosh and Tomika Hughey, interviewed by Catherine Lavoie and Jamie Jacobs, "The Future Is Present: A Chat with Preservation's New Generation," *Common Ground,* Summer 2006, 45.

5. Historical Museums and Roadside America

1. Paula Findlen, "The Museum: Its Classical Etymology and Renaissance Genealogy," *Journal of the History of Collections* 1, no. 1 (1989): 60, 64, 69–70, 73; and James Steel Smith, "The Museum as Historian," *San Jose Studies* 2 (May 1976): 46.

2. Laurence Vale Coleman, *The Museum in America: A Critical Study,* vol. 1. (Washington, DC: American Association of Museums, 1939), 6–7.

3. Patrick H. Butler III, "Past, Present, and Future: The Place of the House Museum in the Museum Community," in Jessica Foy Donnelly, ed., *Interpreting Historic House Museums,* 33 (Walnut Creek, CA: AltaMira Press, 2002); Freeman Tilden's *Interpreting Our Heritage* (Chapel Hill: Univ. of North Carolina Press, 1957) has been taken as the first effort to identify and elaborate the principles of interpretation, but it gives far more philosophical principles that are less easily applicable by people in the field than does William T. Alderson and Shirley Payne Low's *Interpretation of Historic Sites,* 2d ed., rev. (Nashville: American Association for State and Local History, 1985). Tilden also addresses natural as well as historic sites, perhaps explaining why his work's principles are more general.

4. Alderson and Low, *Interpretation of Historic Sites,* x.

5. For a brief account of the period room in American museum history, see Gary Kulik, "Designing the Past: History-Museum Exhibitions from Peale to the Present," in Warren Leon and Roy Rosenzweig, eds., *History Museums in the United States: A Critical Assessment,* 12–17 (Urbana: Univ. of Illinois Press, 1989).

6. Butler III, "Past, Present, and Future," 28.

7. Edwin C. Bearss, "Historic Structure Report: Lincoln Home National Historic Site[,] Illinois," U.S. Department of the Interior, Denver, Colorado, July 1973, 38–39 (photocopy); and Timothy P. Townsend, "'The Site Adrift in the City': The Evolution of the Lincoln Home Neighborhood" (master's thesis, Univ. of Illinois at Springfield, 1995), 4.

8. Bearss, "Historic Structure Report," 39.

9. Ibid., 43.

10. Townsend, "Site Adrift in the City," 4; Bearss, "Historic Structure Report," 43; and Wayne C. Temple, *By Square and Compass: The Building of Lincoln's Home and Its Saga* (Bloomington, IL: Illinois Lodge of Research and the Masonic Book Club, 1984), 10.

11. Townsend, "Site Adrift in the City," 4.

12. Bearss, "Historic Structure Report," 51.

13. *Illinois State Journal,* Feb. 12, 1911, cited in Temple, *By Square and Compass,* 113.

14. Albert Eide Parr, "History and the Historical Museum," *Curator* 15, no. 1 (1972): 53–54.

15. Deed record, 80, 299, ms., Recorder of Deed's Office, Sangamon Co. building, Springfield, Ill., cited in Temple, *By Square and Compass*, 11.

16. Temple, *By Square and Compass*, 10–11.

17. Townsend, "Site Adrift in the City," 4.

18. Ibid., 5.

19. Bearss, "Historic Structure Report," 57–58, 74–79, 8–118; and Temple, *By Square and Compass*, 115, 117.

20. Townsend, "Site Adrift in the City," 83.

21. Ibid., 11.

22. Ibid., 42–63.

23. Neil Harris, "Expository Expositions: Preparing for Theme Parks," in Karal Ann Marling, ed., *Designing Disney's Theme Parks: The Architecture of Reassurance*, 19–20 and 24 (Paris: Flammarion, 1997).

24. Kenneth Hudson, *Museums of Influence* (Cambridge: Cambridge Univ. Press, 1987), 20.

25. James J. Flink, *The Automobile Age* (Cambridge, MA: MIT Press, 1988), 26.

26. Ibid., 129.

27. Kulik, "Designing the Past," 17.

28. For example, see Walter Muir Whitehill, foreword, in Hosmer, *Presence of the Past*, 14.

29. Thomas J. Schlereth, *Artifacts and the American Past* (Nashville: American Association for State and Local Press, 1980), 207.

30. Edward A. Chappell, "The Museum and the Joy Ride: Williamsburg Landscapes and the Specter of Theme Parks," in Terence Young and Robert Riley, eds., *Theme Park Landscapes: Antecedents and Variation*, 122 (Washington, DC: Dumbarton Oaks Research Library and Collection, 2002).

31. Hosmer, *Presence of the Past*, 212–13; Hudson, *Museums of Influence*, 147; and Warren Leon and Margaret Piatt, "Living-History Museums," in Leon and Rosenzweig, eds., *History Museums in the United States*, 66.

32. Richard Handler and Eric Gable, *The New History in an Old Museum: Creating the Past at Colonial Williamsburg* (Durham, NC: Duke Univ. Press, 1997), 15.

33. Ibid.

34. Hudson, *Museums of Influence*, 150; and Leon and Piatt, "Living-History Museums," 77.

35. Ibid., 66.

36. Eric Gable and Richard Handler, "Public History, Private Memory: Notes from the Ethnography of Colonial Williamsburg, Virginia, U.S.A.," in Amy K. Levin, ed., *Defining Memory: Local Museums and the Construction of History in America's Changing Communities*, 51 (Lanham, MD: AltaMira, 2007); and Edward A. Chappell, "The Museum and the Joy Ride: Williamsburg Landscapes and the Specter of Theme Parks," Young and Riley, eds., *Theme Park Landscapes*, 131–32.

37. Handler and Gable, *The New History in an Old Museum*, 129.

38. Murtagh, *Keeping Time*, 96–98.

39. Leon and Rosenzweig, *History Museums in the United States*, 67; Murtagh, *Keeping Time*, 98–99, 100; Kulik, "Designing the Past," 17–21; Leon and Piatt, "Living-History Museums," 67; and Richard S. Taylor and Mark L. Johnson, "A Fragile Illusion: The Reconstruction of Lincoln's New Salem," *Journal of Illinois History* 7 (Winter 2004): 254–80.

40. Thomas J. Schlereth, "Causing Conflict, Doing Violence," *Museum News* 63 (Oct. 1984): 45–52; Leon and Rosenzweig, eds., *History Museums in the United States*, 65 and 69; Gable and Handler, "Public History, Private Memory," 50; and Charles B. Hosmer, Jr., *Preservation Comes of Age: From Williamsburg to the National Trust, 1926–1949*, vol. 1 (Charlottesville: Univ. of Virginia Press, 1981), 74.

41. James Marston Fitch, *Historic Preservation: Curatorial Management of the Built World* (Charlottesville: Univ. of Virginia Press, 1990), 292.

42. Ibid.

43. Handler and Gable, *New History in an Old Museum*, 207.

44. Kenneth L. Ames, "Finding Common Threads: An Afterword," in Kenneth L. Ames, Barbara Franco, and L. Thomas Frye, eds., *Ideas and Images: Developing Interpretive Exhibits*, 314 (Nashville: American Association for State and Local History, 1992).

45. The Farmers' Museum—Collections, www.farmersmuseum.org/farmers'/collections (accessed Apr. 5, 2009).

46. Kulik, "Designing the Past," 12.

47. Ibid., 8.

48. Ibid., 21.

49. "The Magic of Progress," *American City* 54 (June 1939): 41.

50. Ibid., 40.

51. Phil Patton, *Open Road: A Celebration of the American Highway* (New York: Simon and Schuster, 1986), 120.

52. Tom Lewis, *Divided Highways: Building the Interstate Highways, Transforming American Life* (New York: Viking, 1997), 38–40.

53. See Theodore Hild, "Driving to Distraction," *Historic Illinois* 20 (Feb. 1998): 8.

54. Brochures in authors' collection.

55. Organization of American Historians, Ruth Heikkinen, "Becoming a Part of the National Park System," http://www.oah.org/pubs/nl/2005nov/heikken.html (accessed Apr. 6, 2009).

56. Illinois Department of Transportation, "The Lincoln Highway Association (LHA) Today," http://www.dot.state.il.us/il50/iha.html (accessed Sept. 23, 2008).

57. Carol Ahlgren, "The Lincoln Highway," *CRM* 19, no. 9 (1996): 17.

58. Angel Brownawell, "Lincoln Highway Battling for National Park Service Recognition," *Tribune Review*, Mar. 17, 2003, http://www.pittsburghlive.com/x/pittsburghtrib/s_123999.html (accessed Apr. 6, 2009).

59. Lincoln Highway Heritage Corridor, Ligonier, Pennsylvania http://www.ihhc.org/index.asp (accessed Feb. 27, 2008).

60. Story County, Iowa, "Lincoln Highway Corridor Study," http://www.storycounty.com/+index.aspx?DN=5798,5787,21,6,1,Documents (accessed Apr. 6, 2009).

61. Lyell Henry, "Iowa Roadside Complex Restoration Begins," *Society for Commercial Archeology News* 9 (Spring 2001): 1.

62. "Officials to Dedicate New Lincoln Highway Association National Office," Lincoln Highway Association press release, Apr. 16, 2007.

63. Michael Romero Taylor and Kaisa Barthuli, "Preserving Route 66: A Federal Perspective," *Forum Journal* 22 (Fall 2007): 16–23.

64. Route 66 Corridor Preservation Program, NPPress Release, "Route 66 Listed among World's and Nation's Most Endangered Places," June 14, 2007, http://www.cr.nps.gov/rt66 (accessed Apr. 21, 2008).

65. Margaret Foster, "Road Trip on Route 66," July 31, 2003, http://www.nationaltrust.org/magazine/archives/arc_news/073103p.htm (accessed Feb. 27, 2008).

66. Brochures in authors' collections.

67. Maurice Duke, "Motor Vehicle Museums," in Fred E. H. Schroeder, ed., *Twentieth-Century Culture in Museums and Libraries,* 159 (Bowling Green, OH: Bowling Green University Popular Press, 1981).

68. Joseph Corn, "Tools, Technologies, and Contexts: Interpreting the History of American Technics," in Leon and Rosenzweig, eds., *History Museums in the United States,* 239–47.

69. "Auto Legend: Home of 'Apogee of Style' Becomes a National Historic Landmark," *Common Ground,* Fall 2006, 14–16.

70. Jeff Price, "Lucky Star Shines on Packard Museum," *Lincoln Highway Forum* 3 (Winter 1995): 16–18.

71. Mike Davis, "Rise and Fall of Jennings Ford," *Ward's Dealer Business,* Apr. 2007, 30–31.

72. Pioneer Auto Show—Murdo, South Dakota, http://www.pioneerautoshow.com/history.htm (accessed Nov. 5, 2007); "Pioneer Auto Show and Prairie Town," *Murdo Coyote,* special centennial edition, June 8, 2006, 33; and Louis Wendt, "Former WNAX Oasis to Become Museum Exhibit," undated newspaper clipping from personal files of Dave Geisler provided to Keith A. Sculle.

73. See Joseph Corn, "Museum Exhibition Reviews," *Journal of American History* 76 (June 1989): 221–24.

74. Amy K. Levin, "The Camping Hall of Fame and Other Wonders: Local Museums and Local Histories," *Studies in Popular Culture* 19, no. 3 (1997) http://pcasacas.org/SPC?spcissues/19.3?levin.htm (accessed Nov. 21, 2008).

6. Experiencing the Past as Landscape and Place

1. Portions of this chapter previously appeared as John A. Jakle and Keith A. Sculle, "A Museum of the American Roadside: Isn't It about Time?," a paper delivered at Preserving the Historic Road, the Sixth Biennial Conference on Historic Roads, held at Albuquerque, New Mexico, in 2008. Conference papers were distributed to conference attendees by compact disc.

2. See Elizabeth Vallance, "Local History, 'Old Things to Look At,' and a Sculptor's Vision: Exploring Local Museums through Curriculum Theory," in Amy K. Levin, ed., *Defining Memory: Local Museums and the Construction*

of History in America's Changing Communities, 27 (Latham, MD: Rowman & Littlefield, 2007).

3. At least one attempt has been made to create a road- and roadside-oriented outdoor museum: the Museum of Roadside Culture proposed by the New York state legislature in the early 1990s for a location in the town of Southampton in Suffolk County on Long Island. The idea, however, did not get past its planning phase. One of the proposed exhibits was to have been Long Island's Big Duck, now located at Flanders, New York. J. Lance Mallamo, email to Keith A. Sculle, Oct. 18, 2007. Also see J. Lance Mallamo, "A Museum for Gas, Food, Lodging, and a Duck," *CRM* 16, no. 6 (1993): 43–44.

4. For discussion of how collective memory evolves in a society, see Paul Connerton, *How Societies Remember* (Cambridge, UK: Cambridge Univ. Press, 1989); and Michael Kammen, *Mystic Chords of Memory: The Transformation of Tradition in American Culture* (New York: Alfred A. Knopf, 1991). Especially insightful are two books by David Lowenthal: *The Past Is a Foreign Country* (Cambridge, UK: Cambridge Univ. Press, 1985) and *Possessed by the Past: The Heritage Crusade and the Spoils of History* (New York: FreePress, 1996).

5. Many books that treat roadside relics as a disappearing breed have been written for a popular audience. One of the more thoughtful is John Margolies, *The End of the Road: Vanishing Highway Architecture in America* (New York: Penguin Books, 1981).

6. Edward T. McMahon, "Let's Save the Landscapes, Not Just the Landmarks," *News and Observer* (Raleigh, NC), June 16, 1991, 7J.

7. Peirce F. Lewis, "The Future of the Past: Our Clouded Vision of Historic Preservation," *Pioneer America* 7 (July 1973): 8.

8. Ibid., 15.

9. Robert Venturi, "Thoughts on Preserving the Recent Past," in Deborah Slaton and William G. Foulks, eds., *Preserving the Recent Past 2,* 1 (Washington, DC: Historic Preservation Education Foundation, National Park Service, and Association for Preservation of Technology International, 2000).

10. John Brinkerhoff Jackson, "By Way of Conclusion, How to Study the Landscape," in Helen Lefkowitz Horowitz, ed., *Landscape in Sight: Looking at America,* 314 (New Haven: Yale Univ. Press, 1997).

11. Ibid., 315–17.

12. For elaboration, see John A. Jakle and Keith A. Sculle, *Motoring: The Highway Experience in America* (Athens: Univ. of Georgia Press, 2008).

13. For discussion of material culture as historical evidence, see Thomas J. Schlereth, *Cultural History and Material Culture: Everyday Life, Landscapes, Museums* (Ann Arbor: UMI Research Press, 1990).

14. For an introduction to museum curatorship, see Kenneth Hudson, *Museums of Influence* (Cambridge, UK: Cambridge Univ. Press, 1987); Robert Lumley, *The Museum Time Machine* (London: Routledge, 1988); Daniel Sherman and Irit Rogoff, eds., *Museum Culture: Histories, Discourses, Spectacles* (Minneapolis: Univ. of Minnesota Press, 1996); Gaynor Kavanagh, *History Curatorship* (Leiscester, UK: Leicester Univ. Press, 1996); and Amy K. Levin, ed., *Defining Memory: Local Museums and the Construction of History in America's Changing Communities* (Latham, MD: Rowman and Littlefield, 2007).

15. Critical assessments of America's outdoor "village" museums include Michael Wallace, "Visiting the Past: History Museums in the United States," in Susan Porter Benson, Stephen Brier, and Roy Rosenzweig, eds., *Presenting the Past: Essays on History and the Public*, 137–61 (Philadelphia: Temple Univ. Press, 1986); Barbara Burlison Mooney, "Lincoln's New Salem; or, the Trigonometric Theorem of Vernacular Restoration," *Perspectives in Vernacular Architecture: The Journal of the Vernacular Architecture Forum* 11 (2004): 19–39; and Jay Price, "The Small Town We Never Were: Cowtown Museum Faces an Urban Past," in Levin, ed., *Defining Memory*, 93–108.

16. For a discussion of the historic district concept, see Charles A. Birnbaum, *Protecting Cultural Landscapes: Planning, Treatment and Management of Historic Landscapes,* Bulletin 36 (Washington, DC: National Park Service, 1994). Also see Pratt Cassity, *Maintaining Community Character: How to Establish a Local Historic District,* Information Series No. 58 (Washington, DC: National Trust for Historic Preservation, n.d.). Early case studies embracing the historic district idea include Arthur P. Ziegler, Jr., *Historic Preservation in Inner City Areas* (Pittsburgh: Allegheny Press, 1971); Robert F. Tournier, "Historic Preservation as a Force in Urban Change: Charleston," in Shirley B. Laska and Dauphine Spain, eds., *Back to the City: Issues in Neighborhood Renovation* (New York: Pergamon, 1980); and Robin Elizabeth Datel, "Southern Regionalism and Historic Preservation in Charleston, South Carolina, 1920–1940," *Journal of Historical Geography* 16, no. 2 (1990): 197–215.

17. At this writing various websites describe heritage corridor activities along the old Lincoln Highway and former U.S. 66, including http://www.lhhc.org and http://www.cart66pg.oth/DC/index.htm (both accessed Sept. 3, 2006), with those on the Lincoln Highway being the work of private organizers and the former U.S. 66 sites sustained by the National Park Service. For discussion of the historical resources along the Lincoln Highway, see Drake Hokanson,

The Lincoln Highway: Main Street across America (Iowa City: Univ. of Iowa Press, 1988); Joanne Zeigler, "Preserving the Lincoln Highway: Pennsylvania's Lincoln Highway State Heritage Park," *Lincoln Highway Forum* 1 (Fall 1993): 22–25; and Brian A. Butko, *The Lincoln Highway: Pennsylvania Traveler's Guide* (Mechanicsburg, PA: Stackpole Books, 1996). For Route 66, see Arthur Krim, *Route 66: Iconography of an American Highway* (Santa Fe, NM, and Staunton, VA: Center for American Places, 2005).

18. "Reed/Nyland Corner: Where the Past Meets the Present," promotional brochure issued by the Colo Development Group, circa 2009.

19. John H. McDowell and Trevor J. Blank, "The Warren E. Roberts Virtual Outdoor Museum of Early Indiana Life," *Pioneer American Society Transactions* 31 (2008): 17–25.

20. Edward A. Chappell, "The Museum and the Joy Ride: Williamsburg Landscapes and the Specter of Theme Parks," in Terence Young and Robert Riley, eds., *Theme Park Landscapes: Antecedents and Variations*, 143–44 (Washington, DC: Dumbarton Oaks Research Library and Collection, 2002).

21. Kenneth Hudson, *Museums of Influence: The Pioneers of the Last 200 Years* (Cambridge, UK: Cambridge Univ. Press, 1987), 167.

22. Diane Barthel, *Historic Preservation: Collective Memory and Historical Identity* (New Brunswick, NJ: Rutgers Univ. Press, 1996), 8.

23. Edward M. Bruner, "Abraham Lincoln as Authentic Reproduction: A Critique of Postmodernism," *American Anthropologist* 96 (June 1994): 399–401. For further discussion of New Salem, see Mooney, "Lincoln's New Salem," 19–39.

24. David Lowenthal, "Authenticities Past and Present," *CRM Journal* 5 (Winter 2008): 6–7.

25. Ibid., 7.

26. Thomas J. Schlereth, *Material Culture Studies in America* (Nashville: Association for State and Local History, 1982), 5; and Stephen E. Weil, *Making Museums Matter* (Washington, DC: Smithsonian Institution Press, 2002), 66.

27. Schlereth, *Material Culture Studies in America*, 5.

28. David Thelen, "Memory and American History," *Journal of American History* 75 (Mar. 1989): 1125–129.

29. For a fuller discussion of place-product packaging, see John A. Jakle and Keith A. Sculle, *The Gas Station in America* (Baltimore: Johns Hopkins Univ. Press, 1994), 1–3.

30. See Keith A. Sculle, "Oral History: A Key to Writing the History of American Roadside Architecture," *Journal of American Culture* 13 (Fall 1990): 79–88.

31. These ideas have been more fully developed in John A. Jakle and Keith A. Sculle, *Motoring: The Highway Experience in America* (Athens: Univ. of Georgia Press, 2008).

32. Precedence exists. At the Saugus Iron Works in Saugus, Massachusetts, initial restoration of a seventeenth-century iron-making village was funded by a trade organization from within the iron and steel industry. Today the site is administered as a National Historic Site by the National Park Service.

33. J. Lance Mallamo email to Keith A. Sculle, Oct. 18, 2007; and J. Lance Mallamo, "A Museum for Gas, Food, Lodging, and a Duck, CRM 16, no. 6 (1993): 43–44.

7. The Road Continues

1. The argument is put succinctly in David Lowenthal, "The Heritage Crusade and Its Contradictions," in Max Page and Randall Mason, eds., *Giving Preservation a History: Histories of Historic Preservation in the United States*, 19–43 (New York: Routledge, 2007). See also David Lowenthal, *The Heritage Crusade and the Spoils of History* (Cambridge, UK: Cambridge Univ. Press, 1997).

2. Lowenthal, "The Heritage Crusade," 19–20.

3. For an introduction to current preservation practice, see Ned Kaufman, "Moving Forward: Futures for a Preservation Movement," in Page and Mason, eds., *Giving Preservation a History*, 313–28; and Norman Tyler, *Historic Preservation: An Introduction to Its History, Principles, and Practices* (New York: W. W. Norton, 2000).

4. See Charles A. Birnbaum and Mary V. Hughes, eds., *Design with Culture: Claiming America's Landscape Heritage* (Charlottesville: Univ. of Virginia Press, 2005).

5. See Catherine Gutis, *Buyways: Billboards, Automobiles, and the American Landscape* (New York: Routledge, 2004).

6. Peirce F. Lewis, "The Future of the Past: Our Clouded Vision of Historic Preservation," *Pioneer America* 7 (July 1975): 1.

7. For detailed case studies, see John A. Jakle and Keith A. Sculle, *Lots of Parking: Land Use in a Car Culture* (Charlottesville: Univ. of Virginia Press, 2004).

8. Lewis, "The Future of the Past," 3.

9. Ibid.

10. Hamilton Morton, Jr., "Update on United States Rehabilitation Tax Credits and the Transfer of Development Rights (TDR)," 1, http://www.international.icomos.org/publications/93 (accessed June 3, 2009).

11. Kevin Park, "Historic Preservation Tax Credit and Beyond," Rhode Island Tax Policy Council, discussion paper, July 2007, 1, http://www.nedc.com/files/EPC_07KevinPark_HistoricTaxCredit.pdf (accessed June 3, 2009).

12. National Register of Historic Places Official Website, http://www.nps.gov/nr/about.htm (accessed Feb. 27, 2008).

13. Douglas S. Noonan and Douglas J. Krupka, "Making—Or Picking—Winners: Evidence of Internal and External Price Effects in Historic Preservation," IZA, Bonn, Germany, Forschunginstitut zur Zunkunft der Arbeit, discussion paper 4110, Apr. 2009, 1.

14. Ibid.

15. Ibid, 5. See also Robin M. Leichenko, N. Edward Coulson, and David Listokin, "Historic Preservation and Residential Values: An Analysis of Texas Cities," *Urban Studies* 38 (2001): 1973–87; and Akram M. Ijla, "The Impact of Local Historic Designation on Residential Property Value: An Analysis of Three Slow-Growth and Three Fast-Growth Central Cities in the United States," master's thesis, Cleveland State Univ., 2002.

16. Donovan D. Rypkema, "The Economic Power of Preservation," paper presented at the Restoration and Renovation Conference, Washington, DC, Jan. 15, 2001, http://busdev3.odoc5.odoc.stateok.us/pls/portal30/occs/FOLDER/CWER/MAINSTREET/THE+ECONOMIC+POWER+OF+PRESERVATION>DOC (accessed June 3, 2009).

17. Town of Amesbury [Massachusetts], Preservation Plan, 2009, 1. http://www.ci.amesbury.ma.us/home.nfs?a=amesbury&s=special&1=;PROCEDURES;PRO (accessed June 3, 2009).

18. Ibid., 3.

19. "Scenic America: A National Voice for Preservation in America the Beautiful," www.scenic.org (accessed June 3, 2009).

20. See John A. Jakle and Keith A. Sculle, *Motoring: The Highway Experience in America* (Athens: Univ. of Georgia Press, 2008)

21. For recent reviews of the historic preservation movement in the United States, see Page and Mason, eds., *Giving Preservation a History;* Karolin Frank and Patricia Peterson, eds., translated by Hannah M. Mowat, Jeff Smith, and

Karolin Frank, *Historic Preservation in the USA* (Berlin: Springer, 2002); and Norman Tyler, *Historic Preservation: An Introduction to Its History, Principles, and Practices* (New York: W.W. Norton, 1999).

22. Lewis, "The Future of the Past," 8.

23. See Pete Davies, *American Road: The Story of an Epic Transcontinental Journey at the Dawn of the Motor Age* (New York: Henry Holt, 2002).

24. See R. Patrick McKnight, *Steamtown National Historic Site: The Nation's Living Railroad Museum* ([Scranton, PA]: R. L. Ruehrwein for the Steamtown Museum Association, 2001).

25. Scholarly writings concerned with automobility and its impact on American life, and especially the built environment in the United States, are plentiful. See, for example, Lewis Mumford, *The Highway and the City* (New York: Harcourt, Brace, 1953); James J. Flink, *The Car Culture* (Cambridge, MA: MIT Press, 1975); Stephen W. Sears, *The Automobile in America* (New York: Simon & Schuster, 1977); David L. Lewis, ed., "The Automobile and American Culture," *Michigan Quarterly Review* 19 (Fall 1980) and 20 (Winter 1981), both special issues; Gerald Silk, *Automobiles and Culture* (New York: Harry N. Abrams, 1984); Phil Patton, *Open Road: A Celebration of the American Highway* (New York: Touchstone, 1986); Jane Holtz Kay, *Asphalt Nation: How the Automobile Took over America and How We Can Take It Back* (Berkeley: Univ. of California Press, 1997); Tom Lewis, *Divided Highways: Building the Interstate Highways, Transforming American Life* (New York: Viking Press, 1997); and Peter Wollen and Joe Kerr, *Autopia: Cars and Culture* (London: Reaktion Books, 2002).

26. For example, see Peter Blake, *God's Own Junkyard: The Planned Deterioration of America's Landscape* (New York: Holt, Reinhart & Winston, 1964), and Ian Nairn, *The American Landscape: A Critical View* (New York: Random House, 1965).

27. See John A. Jakle and Keith A. Sculle, *Signs in America's Auto Age: Signatures of Landscape and Place* (Iowa City: Univ. of Iowa Press, 2004).

28. See Lisa Mahar, *American Signs: Form and Meaning on Route 66* (New York: Monacelli Press, 2002), and Catherine Gudis, *Buyways: Billboards, Automobiles, and the American Landscape* (New York: Routledge, 2004).

29. One insightful discussion of evolving place is William Leach, *Country of Exiles: The Destruction of Place in American Life* (New York: Pantheon Books, 1999).

30. See Harold F. Williamson, Ralph Andreano, Arnold R. Daum, and Gilbert C. Klose, *The American Petroleum Industry*, vol. 2, *The Age of Energy, 1899–1959* (Evanston, IL: Northwestern Univ. Press, 1963); Daniel Vergin, *The Price of Oil: The Epic Quest for Oil, Money, and Power* (New York: Simon & Schuster, 1991); Francisco Parro, *Oil Politics: A Modern History of Petroleum* (London: I. B. Tauris, 2004); and Antonia Juhasz, *The Tyranny of Oil: The World's Most Powerful Industry—and What We Must Do to Stop It* (New York: William Morrow, 2008).

31. Jakle and Sculle, *Lots of Parking*.

32. Thomas J. Schlereth, "Material Culture and Cultural Research," in Thomas J. Schlereth, ed., *Material Culture: A Research Guide*, 10 (Lawrence: Univ. Press of Kansas, 1985).

33. Ibid., 15.

34. Thomas J. Schlereth, *Cultural History and Material Culture: Everyday Life, Landscapes, Museums* (Charlottesville: Univ. of Virginia Press, 1992), 390.

35. Faith Davis Ruffins, "The Exhibition as Form: An Elegant Metaphor," *Museum News* 64 (Oct. 1985): 54–59.

36. Eric Gable and Richard Handler, "Public History, Public Memory: Notes from the Ethnography of Colonial Williamsburg, Virginia, USA," in Amy K. Levin, ed., *Defining Memory: Local Museums and the Construction of History in America's Changing Communities*, 35 (Lanham, MD: AltaMira Press, 2007).

37. Randolph Starn, "A Historian's Guide to New Museum Studies," *American Historical Review* 110 (Feb. 2005): 70–71.

38. The Disney Corporation stands today as the world's prime theme-park developer. For a discussion, see James Howard Kunstler, *The Geography of Nowhere: The Decline of America's Man-Made Landscape* (New York: Simon & Schuster, 1993), 217–27; and Marcia G. Synnott, "Disney's America: Whose Patrimony, Whose Profits, Whose Past?," *Public Historian* 17 (Fall 1995): 43–59.

39. Edward A. Chappell, "The Museum and the Joy Ride: Williamsburg Landscapes and the Specter of Theme Parks," in Terrence Young and Robert Riley, eds., *Theme Park Landscapes: Antecedents and Variations*, 122 (Washington, DC: Dumbarton Oaks Research Library and Collection, 2002).

40. Jules David Prown, "Style as Evidence," *Winterthur Portfolio* 15 (Autumn 1980): 208.

41. Timothy Davis, "Looking down the Road," in Chris Wilson and Paul Groth, eds., *Everyday America: Cultural Landscape Studies after J. B. Jackson*, 73, 76 (Berkeley: Univ. of California Press, 2003).

42. Keith A. Sculle, "History and Material Culture Studies," *Pioneer American Society Transactions* 32 (2009): http://www.pioneeramerica.org/currentpast/past2009artsculle.html (accessed Sept. 2, 2009).

43. Brian Ladd, *Autophobia: Love and Hate in the Automotive Age* (Chicago: Univ. of Chicago Press, 2008), 128.

44. Cotton Seiler, *Republic of Drivers: A Cultural History of Automobility in America* (Chicago: Univ. of Chicago Press, 2008), 41–42.

45. For a review, see Warren Leon and Margaret Piatt, "Living History Museums," in Warren Leon and Roy Rozenzweig, eds., *History Museums in the United States: A Critical Assessment*, 64–97 (Urbana: Univ. of Illinois Press, 1989).

46. Schlereth, *Cultural History and Material Culture*, 20–21.

47. Ibid., 313–414.

48. Richard Longstreth, "I Can't See It, I Don't Understand It: And It Doesn't Look Old to Me," in Deborah Slaton and Rebecca A. Shiffer, eds., *Preserving the Recent Past*, 1–16 (Washington, DC: Historic Preservation Education Foundation, 1995).

49. Kenneth Hudson, *Museums of Influence* (Cambridge, UK: Cambridge Univ. Press, 1987), 173.

INDEX

Pages numbered in **boldface** refer to topically-relevant illustrations.

Abilene, KS, 219, **220**
African-Americans, 24, 37–38, 138, 146, 204, 231
Agee, James, 2, 42–43, 46, 61
Alderson, William, 135
Alexandria, VA, 115
Alsop, Stewart, 67
Altizer, Bob and Debbie, 125
Amarillo, TX, **193**
American Assoc. of Highway Officials (AASHO), 32
American Scenic and Preservation Society, 99
American West, the, 21–24, 34, 40, 47, **144**, **145**
Amesbury, MA, 217
Anderson, Sherwood, 51
Annapolis, MD, **18**
Appleton, William Sumner, 99
architectural history, 100, 174, 177, 179, 212, 232
Arlington, TX, **190**, 191
Arroyo Seco Parkway (Los Angeles, CA), 113, **114**
Atherton, Lewis, 37
Auburn, IN, 163

automobiles, xvi, xviii, 4, 9–10, 13, 20, 26, 30, 59–61, 93, 95–96, 101, 104–5, 107, 128, 142–43, 168, 171, 174, 176, 178, 180, 212, 214, 217, 219, 221, 223–24, 231; convenience of, xvi, 9110, 13, 29, 51; ownership of, xviii, 7–9, 26, 36–38, 99, 142, 204, 214, 218; vintage, xv, xx, 133, 148, **149**, 165–66, 172, **173**, **174**, 225
automobile dealer garages, xviii, 53, 81, 163–64, **165**, 175, 186–87; America's Packard Museum (Dayton, OH), 163–64, **165**, 166
automobile industry, xviii, 6–7, 11, 20, 26, 218
automobile tourism, xx, 8, 10, 21, 23, 29, 33–37, 40–43, 58, 60, 77, 140, 143–44, 152, 155–56, 161, 167, 175, 183, 205, 218, 224
automobility, xv, xviii, xxi, 5–11, 24, 60–61, 63, 93, 96–97, 104, 133, 154, 169–70, 175, 183, 219, 231–32; defined, 4; gender issues, 6, 9, 24, 41–42, 98, 162, 170, 187, 204; impact on life in America, xv, xx, 4, 9–10, 13, 26, 168–69, 176–78, 206, 214, 217–18, 223–24, 226–27

Baerwald, Thomas J., 78–79
Barstow, CA, 160
Barthuli, Kaisa, 159
Basso, Hamilton, 37
Beagle, Peter S., 90–91
Belasco, Warren, 26
Benton, Thomas Hart, 25
Bement, Austin, 34
Bennett, J. M., 50–51
Blake, Peter, 65, 69
B. Lloyd's Pecan Service Stations, **47**
BP, plc (formerly British Petroleum), 118
Blue Ridge Parkway, 113
Breezewood, PA, **3**, 74
Bronx River Parkway, 33
Brookes, John, 57
Brown, Denise Scott, 70–71, 88, 110
Brunner, Edward M., 196
Bucher, Todd and Nina, 123–24
building codes, 19, 65, 221

Calgary, Alb, 182, **183**
camping and camp grounds, 42–43, **45**, 51
capitalism, xix, 11, 169, 221
Carpenter, Charles F., 142
Cecil, OH, 16
central business districts, 8, 38, 51, 55, 62, 82, 104, 214, 216, 222
Champaign, IL, **17**, 74, 76, 77, 85
change and changefulness, xv–xvii, 3, 11, 14–15, 19, 74–80, 111, 171, 177, 191–94, 204, 206, 209, 232; emphermality, xvi, xxi, 3–5, 9, 11, 13, 22, 27, 29, 74–75, 97, 134
Chaplin, Charles, 23
Charleston, SC, 105–6, **107**, **108**, **109**, 134–35, 216
Cherokee, NC, 210, **211**
Chesterhood House (Stockbridge, MA), 107
Chicago, IL, 85; automobity's impact on, v, xv, 2–4, 8, 11, 29–30, 48, 51, 53–55, 60–63, 88–91, 93, 104, 139–40, 222, 231; cities, 25, 93, 95; historic districting, 216; "strip-cities," 89
Cities Service Oil Co., 58, **59**
Clarks, NE, 158
Clay, Grady, 74–75
Cobb, Irvin, 46–47
Coffeyville, KS, **39**
Colo, IA, 138, 158–59, 185, **188**
Commerce, GA, **14**
commercial strips, xv, 2–4, 29–30, 40, 95, 103, 130–31, 139, **140**, 169, 175–77, 210, **211**, 213–14, 216, 228; at freeway interchanges, 73–74; dereliction along, 14, **16**, 85–86, **87**, 88; ephemerality of, 3, 13, 29, 54, 70–71, **75**, **76**, 77–78, **79**, 80, 86–87, 134, 210, 213, 217; homogeneity of, 15–16, 18, 24, 60, 73, 107; spatial configuration of, 11, 29, 52, 60, 65, 70–71, 96, 103, 221–22; "tax-payer strips," 86; "television roads," 92; "The Strip" (Las Vegas, NV), 53–54, 70, **71**, 88–89, **90**, **93**
Conner Prairie Museum (Noblesville, IN), 149
Constantine, MI, 84
Cooperstown, NY, 149–50
Coral Court (Marlborough, MO), **125**, 126, **127**, 128, **129**, 230
Coralville, IA, 77–78, 173–74
Corn, Joseph, 162–63
corporate brands, xvii, **3**, **14**, **15**, 23, 41, 58, 91, 199
Creekmur, Corey K., 23
Creston, IA, 118, **119**
Cross, Gary, 78
Crumb, R. ("A Short History of America"), 63, **64**
Cuba, MO 160, **161**
Curry, John Stewart, 2

Index

Daughters of the American Revolution, 36
Davis, Charles Henry, 36
Davis, Timothy, 86
Dayton, OH, 163–64, **165**, **166**, 187–88; Motor Car District, **188**
Dearborn, MI, 147–48, **149**, **165**, **169**, 182, 202
Deerfield, MA, 150
Delta, WI, 123, **124**
Dewart, PA, 35, **36**
Disney Corp., 25
Dogpatch Reptile Garden and Hillbilly Farm (Lake of the Ozarks, MO), 191, **192**
drive-in movie theaters, 23, 25, 80–81, 111, 165
Dupont Center, FL, **201**

Eagle, WI, 150, **177**, 180, 205
East Mystic, CT, 150, 160
Edison, Thomas, 148
"edge cities," 80
Eisenhower, Dwight, D., 32, 219–20
Eisenhower Museum (Abilene, KS), 219, **220**
Elk City, OK, 160
Evans, Walker, 25

Fairbanks, AK, **143**
Fairfax County, VA, 109
Faltermayer, Edmund K., 62–63, 86–87
Farm Security Administration, 25
Federal-Aid Highway Program, 31–32, 61; Highway Trust Fund, 32; highway acts of 1916, 1921, 1944, 1952 and 1956, 31–32
Federal Writers' Program, 143
Fisher, Carl Graham, xix
Fitch, James Marston, 100, 151
Flagg, James, 33–34, 46, 58
Flink, James J., 8
Ford, Henry, xviii, 7, 148, 155, 169, 182, 201, 214, 218

Ford Motor Co., xviii, 150, 200; Model T, xviii, 7, 142, 164
Fort Ticonderoga, NY, 152, **153**
Fortune, 2, 42–43, 61–63
franchising, 14, 1, 77–78
Franklin Grove, IL, 159
French, Daniel Chester, 107
Fuessle, Newton A., 36

Gable, Eric, 152
garages, xix, 34, 36–38, 51, 82, 183, **187**
Garreau, Joel, 80
gasoline stations, xv, xix, xx, 1, 3, 4–5, 12–14, **15**, 16, 23, 25–27, 40, **41**, **42**, 43, **44**, 46–48, 50–51, **52**, 54, 57–58, **59**, 65–66, 71, **72**, 73, 76–77, **81**, 82–83, **84**, **85**, 86, 88–89, 101, 104–6, **107**, 108, **109**, 110–11, 128, 130, 139–40, **145**, 172–73, **174**, 177, 184, **185**, **186**, **187**, 198, 200, 202
—building types, 82, **83**, 84, **85**, 120
—restored, 120–25, 154, 156, 184–85, 198; Magnolia station (Shamrock, TX), **186**, **187**; Phillips 66 Stations (Creston, IA, Cuba, Mo, Tulsa, OK), **118**, **119**, **123**; Sears Station (Rome, NY), **116**, **117**; Standard Station (Colo, IA), 158, 185, **188**; Terry's BP Station (Piqua, OH), 116, **121**, **122**; Texaco Station (Mansfield, OH), 118, **120**
Geddes, Norman Bel, 154
Geisler, A. J., 164
General Motors Corp., xviii, 154–55, 200, 203
gentrification, 104
geography, 9, 11–12, 35, 68, 103, 180, 183, 206–7, 213, 233; automobility's impact on, xv–xvi, 2–3, 10, 13, 96, 172–73, 178, 206, 214, 217–19, 221–22; as study of human spatiality, 179–80, 219, 227, 229, 232
George Washington Memorial Parkway, 113, 115

Getty, John Paul, xix
Gettysburg, PA, xvii, 175
Gieringer, Laurence and Paul, 155–56
Gila Bend, AZ, 51, **52**
Gilmore, Charles L., 41–42
Glacier National Park, 225
Gladding, Effie, 33–34, 46
Good Roads Movement, 30–31
Government-private partnerships, 213
Grand Island, NE, 150, 152
Great Depression of 1930s, 82, 143
Greenbelts, 217
Greyhound Corp., 200

Hamilton, Esley, 126–27
Handler, Richard, 152
Hartley, L. P., 19
Hazelius, Artur, 144
Henry Ford Museum and Greenfield Village (Dearborn, MI), 147, **148**, **149**, 165, 182, 200 205
heritage corridors, 159, 178, 183–91, 213, 218, 232: former Lincoln Highway, 157–58; former Route 66, 158–61
heritage vs. history, xxi, 19, 95, 125, 183, 210–11
Hess, Alan, 89
highway associations, 31–32
Highway Beautification Act of 1965, 68
highway construction and maintenance, 8, 30–32, 38, 40, 222; brick pavements, **7**; concrete pavements, **39**, 40
highways, xv, xviii, xix–xx, 6, 20, 26, 29–34, **35**, 36, 38–40, 48–50, 59, 61, 70, 74–81, 95, 107, 111–12, 144, 172, 183, 217, 226
—limited access roads, 8, 13, 25, 32, 32–33, 54–55, **56**, 57–59, 73, 95, 1000, 107, 113, **114**, 154, **155**, 212, 219
—named highways: Atlantic Hwy., 32; Dixie Hwy., **13**; 32, Jackson Hwy., 32;

Jefferson Hwy., 158; Lincoln Hwy., 3, **7**, 31–36, 45, 48, 74, 81, 125, 157–59, 183, 185–86, **188**, 219
—National Old Trails, 31, 36, 48, **50**, 81; Yellowstone Trail, 81; Old Spanish Trail, 31–32; Pikes Peak Ocean to Ocean Hwy., 32–33
—numbered roads: *I-55*, 139; *I-70*, **56**, 57; *I-75*, 13; *I-90*, 165; *I-494*, 78, **79**; *U.S. 6*, 7; *U.S. 25*, 13; *U.S. 30*, **3**, 48, 74, 158–61, 185; *U.S. 40*, 56–57; *U.S. 61*, **46**; *U.S 50*, 18, **39**; *U.S. 52*, 104; *U.S. 61*, **46**; *U.S. 65*, 158, 185; *U.S. 66*, xvii–xx, 15, 22, 58, 86, **112**, **113**, 114, 139–44, **145**, 158, 183–84, **185**, 186; *U.S. 80*, 164; *U.S. 83*, 164 *U.S. 93*, 225; *U.S. 150*, **41**
—relic roads, xix, 4, **7**, 74, **75**, 112, 213–14
—tollways: Merritt Parkway, 33; Pennsylvania Turnpike, 3, 33, 74, 125
Highway Trust Fund, 32
Hilton, Conrad, xix
Historic American Building Survey, 101
Historic Charleston Foundation, 106
historic districts, 96, 130, 138, **104**, **105**, 139–40, **141**, 178, 180, **181**, 182, 186–90, 212–16, 218, 232; Historic Williamsburg (Williamsburg, VA), **146**, **147**, 152; Lincoln Neighborhood (Springfield, IL), 135, **136**, **137**, 138, **139**, **140**; Old and Historic Charleston (Charleston, SC), 105–6, **107**, **108**, 109, 134–35, 216; Old Salem (Winston-Salem, NC), 14, **105**, **106**, 181–82; Sherbrooke Village (Sherbrooke, NS), **181**, 182
historic preservation, xv, xvi, xx, 1, 86–87, 93, 95–131, 157–58, 171–72, 175–76, 180, 210–28, 232; Historic Preservation Act of 1966, 96, 100–101, 108, 138, 211–12; "grass roots: preservation, 115–26; Special Committee on Historic Preservation, 100–101

Historic Roads Conferences, 113
history, xxi, 17, 19–20, 93, 99–100, 124, 169, 175–78, 180, 190–92, 194, 206, 209–14, 219, 226, 232; local history, 100, 129, 173–74, 176; oral history, 203–4; scholarly writing of, xvi–xvii, xx–xxi, 179, 192, 207, 230–31
history museums, xvi, xx, 19, 93, 104, 115, 131, 133–56, 163–69, 172, 175, 180–82, 186–87, 190, 204, 210, 214, 218–19, 220, 222–23, 228, 230–32
—archival holdings at, 200–201
—authenticity in, 194–97, 222, 228, 230
—automobile- and/or roadside-related, 142, 145, 149, 150, 154–70, 186–87, **222**; America's Packard Museum (Dayton, OH), 163–64, **165**, **166**, 187–88; Auburn, Cord, Dusenberg Museum (Auburn, IN), 163; Antique Car Museum (Coralville, IA), 173, **174**;
Henry Ford Museum (Dearborn, MI), **149**, 165, 205; National Museum of Transport (St. Louis, MO), **222**; Pioneer Auto and Antique Town (Murdo, SD, 164–66, **167**; Studebaker National Museum (South Bend, IN), **173**
—aviation-related, 169
—history of, 134–38
—house museums, 134–38
—"living history" interpretations, 46–47, 201, 214
—maritime-related: Mystic Seaport (East Mystic, CT), 150, 160
—outdoor (open air) museums, xx, 19–20, 93–134, 144, 145, 147–53, 172, 178, 179–223, 228, 231; Farmer's Museum (Cooperstown, NY), 149, 152; Fort Ticonderoga (Fort Ticonderoga, NY), 152, **153**; Greenfield Village (Dearborn, MI), 147–48, **169**; 182, 205; Heritage Park (Calgary, Alb), 182, **183**, 205;
Lincoln's New Salem State Park (Petersburg, IL), 150, **195**, 196, 205; Old Sturbridge Village (Sturbridge, MA), 157, 200–201; Old World Wisconsin (Eagle, WI), 150, **177**, 180, 205; Plimoth Plantation (Plymouth, MA), 150; Shelbrooke Village (Shelbrooke, NS), **181**, 182, 205; Stuhr Museum of the Prairie Pioneer (Grand Island, NE), 150, 152; Warp's Pioneer Village (Minden, NE), 151, **152**
—predominant historical themes in outdoor museums, 133, 135, 150, 174–76, 196, 226: influential persons, xviii, 135–38, 150, 162, 170, 195; pastoralism/agrarianism, 67, 150–54, 174, 179–80, 226; pioneering, 144, 145, 150–52, 195; political / military events, xvii, 153; village and small-town landscapes, 136, 147–49, 155–56, 174–78, 181–84
—railroad-related, 160, 164; National Museum of Transport (St. Louis, MO), 160, 164, 205, 219–20;
—"virtual museums" (through electronic simulation), 189–90, 203
Hopkins, Alden, 191
Hopper, Edward, 25
Horowitz, Richard P., 77–78
horse-drawn vehicles, 7, 29, 31, 64
hotels, 34, 36, 38, 42, 52, 80, 88, 94, 124
Houston, TX, 87–88, **89**
Hudson, Kenneth, 194, 196, 232
Hulbert, Archer B., 36
Humble Oil and Refining Co., 15, 23

Illinois Historic Preservation Agency, 101, 196; Historic Sites Advisory Council
Izenour, Steven, 70–71, 88, 110

Jackson, John B., 2, 52, 68–70, 73, 177–78, 229

Jacobs, Jane, 15
Jakle, John A., 1, 74, 76, 101–2, 236
Johnson, Claudia Alta ("Lady Bird"), 101
Joy, Henry Bourne, xiv, 164–66
journey-to-shop, 8, 60, 77, 224
journey-to-work, 8, 11, 60, 77, 231

Kansas City, Mo, 36, 56
Kerouac, Jack, 22
Kertok, Mike, 119–20
Keystone Film Co., 23
King, Mary, 27
Kingtree, SC, **45**
Kissinger, Terry, 118–19, **122**
Kroc, Raymond Albert, xix
Kouwenhoven, John A., 66–67
Kulik, Gary, 153
Kuralt, Charles, 25

Ladd, Brian, 231
Lake of the Ozarks, Mo., 191, **192**
landscapes, xvi–xvii, 2, 4, 9, 11–20, 27, 40, 50, 57–59, 62–63, 67–71, 95–97, 99, 102–4, 110, 130, 133, 136, 139–40, 147, 165, 169–71, 175, 177–78, 183, 196–97, 207, 209, 212–14, 219–20, 223, 226–27, 232; as built environment, xix, 1–2, 11–12, 15, 25, 60, 62, 93, 96, 111, 176, 217–19, 222, 230; consumerist-oriented, xix, 60, 63–65, 169, 209, 224, 224; defined, 11–12, 69–70, 73, 136, 197, 211; learning to "read," 1, 172, 176–77, 211; scale of, xx–xxi, 4, 130–31, 176, 178–79, 184, 189, 223, 229; "twilight," 5; vernacular, 73, 100, 103, 108
landscape visualization, 11–12, 24–25, 40, **44**, 56–58, 68, 90–96, 103, 172, 175–78, **226**, 229–30; roadside aesthetics, 10–11, 21, 63–70, 91–92, 99, 224; "speed reading," 80, 90, 223

landscaping, 50, 67, 88, 102, 138, 191, 196; along highway margins, 50,–51, 68
Las Vegas, NV, 53–54, 70, 110; "The Strip" (Las Vegas Boulevard), 53–54, 70, **71, 72,** 88–89, **90, 91, 93, 94,** 110–11
League of American Wheelmen, 33
Lee, Robert E., 176
Leroy, IL, **41, 42**
Larimer, George H., 45
Lewis, Peirce F., 66, 175–76, 214–15, 219
Lewis, Sinclair, 21, 40, 45–46
Liebs, Chester H., 80, 82, 236
Ligonier, PA, 158
Lilly, Eli, 149
Lincoln, Abraham, 135, 137–38, 142, 157, 170, 196
Lincoln Highway Association, 31–32, 34, 164; current organization, 125, 158–59
Lincoln, NE, 7
Lincoln, Robert Todd, 137
Livery stables, 37, 183
Lloyd, Harold, 23
log cabins, 145, 156–57, 178, 190
Longstreth, Richard, 77, 108, 110, 232, 236
Lookout Mountain, TN, 96
Los Angeles, CA, 54, 77, 113, **114**
Louisville, KY, **74, 75**
Low, Shirley, 135
Lowenthal, David, 19, 210
Lynch, Kevin, 18–19
Lynd Robert and Helen, 9

Mac Donald, Maurice and Richard, xix
"machine space," 73
Mansfield, OH, 118, **120**
Marlborough, MA, **125,** 126, **127,** 128, **129,** 230
mass transit, 8–9, 11, 29–30, 51, 54, 62, 64, 93

Mattson, Richard L., 74, 76
Marriott, Daniel Paul, 112–13
Marriott, J. Willard, xix
material culture, xvii–xviii, xix, xx, 4, 42, 103, 124, 171, 174, 194, 197, 209, 211, 219, 223, 228–31
McDonald, Kent, 91–92
McMahon, Edward, T., 175–76
McMurtry, Larry, 57
memory, xvi–xvii, xix, xxi, 11, 16–20, 99, 133, 187, 205–6, 209–11, 214, 219, 228; as storytelling, xix, xx–xxi, 17, 40, 210, 232; collective (public) memory, xvii, xx, 17, 20, 128, 204, 227; through built environment, xvii–xix, 160, 180, 187, 228
Merschdorf, George, 120
Minden, NE, 151, **152**
Mid-Continent Petroleum Co., **44**
Minneapolis, MN, 78, **79**
modernity, 9, 23, 72–73, 167–68, 220–21, 228
Moon, Least Heat, 58
Moorcroft, WY, **144**
Moriarity, NM, **145**
Moses, Robert, xix
motels, xvi, xix, 3–5, 12, 14, 22–23, 25–26, 40, 43, **45**, **46**, 52–54, 58, 65, 73, 80, **86**, **87**, **88**, 110, 124–26, **127**, 128, 130, 140, 177, 193, 200
—cabin courts, xix, 40, **45**, **125**, 126, 165; Coral Court (Marlborough, MO), **125**, 126, **127**, 128, **129**; Pueblo Court (Amarillo, TX), **193**
—franchise chains: Holiday Inn, 165; TraveLodge, 14
—restored motels: Lincoln Motor Court (Tulls Hill, PA), **125**
motorcycles, 24, 73, 90–91

motoring, xv, 2, 4–7, 9–10, 16, 21, 26, 29–31, 33–38, 40–43, 57–58, 60, 62, 68, 71, 73, 77, 165, 171, 174, 177–78, 199–200, 204, 217, 221, 224, 231; described in literature, 20–21, 33–36; difficulties in, 33, 34; speed in, 115, 177, 223
Mount Vernon Ladies Association, 98
Mumford, Lewis, 9
Muncie, IN, 9
Murdo, SD, 164–65, **167**

Nabokov, Vladimir, 22
Nairn, Ian, 65–66
National Museum of Transport (St. Louis, MO), 128, **222**, 230
National Register of Historic Places, 100–102, 109–10, 127, 129, 212; historical significance as defined by, 98–99, 102, 109, 114, 129–30, 157, 212–13, 215–16
National Scenic Byways, 7, 113, 213–14, 217
National Trails System, 113
National Trust for Historic Preservation, 99–100, 102, 107–8, 113; Main Street Program, 216
Native Americans, 103, 114, 143, 168, 210, **211**
Nelson, Willie, 26
Newburgh, NY, 97–98
New Mexico Heritage Preservation Alliance, 159, **161**
New Salem State Park (Petersburg, IL), 139
New York City, NY, 99
New York Council on the Arts, 206
night lighting, 2, 51, 89, 224, 227
Nodelman, J. N., 21
Nora, Pierre, 17
Norman, OK, 119
Norris, Darrell, 4–6, 73
Norsk Folk Museum (Oslo, Norway), 145

North Carolina Historic Preservation Office, 102
North Hollywood, CA, 53
nostalgia, xxi, 20, 106, 125, 135, 150, 168, 174, 210; roadside-directed, 124–25, 174

"odology," 70
Ola, AR, 198
"open road" myth, 26–27, 29, 204, 221
Ogden, IA, 158
Old National Road, 36, 81, 111
Oldroyd, Osborn, 136–37
"old road" versus "new road," 57
Old Salem, Inc., 104–5
Omaha, NE, **5, 6, 7**
Oscar II, King of Norway, 144
Oslo, Norway, **145**
"other-directed" buildings, 69–70

parking, xviii, 8, 29, 51, 54, 63, 71, 81, 87, 95, 104, 110, 139, 142, 181, 183, 197, 221
Pasadena, CA, 54, **55**
past(ness), xv, 1, 4, 17–20, 27, 93, 133–34, 171–72, 176, 183, 191–94, 197, 210, 215, 228–29, 231–32; recent past, xiii, 19, 93, 109–10; sense of past as history, xv, xvii, 19
Patton, Phil, 78
Pearl Harbor, HI, xvii
Perry, FL, 87
Petersburg, IL, 150, **195**, 196, 205
petroleum industry, 218, 221–22, 227, 231
Pew, Thomas W., 58
Philadelphia, PA, 71
Phillips, Frank and Lee Eldas, xix
Phillips Petroleum Co., 118–19, 123, 125, 162
Piqua, OH, 118, **121, 122**
Pittsburg, CA, 51, **53**
Pittsburgh, PA, 74
place, xvi–xvii, xix, xx, 2, 4, 9, 11–20, 27, 30, 40, 56, 58–59, 62–63, 68, 70, 73, 95–97,
101, 110, 172, 175–78, 183–84, 187, 207, 209, 212–13, 217, 219–21, 223, 227, 230, 232;
—common or ordinary, xvii, 5, 16, 68, 111
—defined, 11–12, 70, 73, 171; as behavior setting, 12, 68, 73; as social construct, 70
—outdoor museums as type of, 167–68, 178, 182, 196, 231
—visualized, 11–12, 16, 21, 24–25, 30, 56, 175–76
placelessness, 16, 60, 68
place-product-packaging, 43, 45, 78, 92, 199
Plymouth, MA, 150
Polson, MT, **225**
Pontiac, IL, 160
popular culture, 20, 66–67, 202–3, 221, 227
postcards, 201–3; Detroit Publishing Co., 201
Preservation and *Preservation News*, 108
Priestly, J. B., 47–48
Primeau, Ronald, 21
private versus public space, 221, 227
Prown, Jules David, 229
Public history, xvi, 197, 230
Pure Oil Co., 102
Pushkarev, Boris, 63, 65

Quality Oil Co., **81**, 102

railroads, 10, 30, 38, 46, **50**, 52, 147, 160, **164**, 219–20, 226
Relph, Edward, 16, 68
Reno, NV, 122
road maps, 33, 45, **59**
roadside America, xv–xxi, **2**, 3–4, 9–10, 13, 18, 20–27, 29–30, 40–55, 59–70, 73–82, 90–93, 96–97, 102–3, 113–15, 128, 130, 134–35, 144, 155–56, 166, 172–78, 191–92, 198, 200–206, 209–14, 216, 219, 224, 226–27, 230, 232

Index

—change over time, xv–xviii, xx, 16, 60, 70–74, **75**, **76**, 77–78, **79**, 80, 96–97, 111–12, 171, 177, 192–94, 198, 206, 209, 213, 217–19, 230

—criticism of, xx, 5, 47, 51, 61–79, 169, 176–77, 221–22

—defined, xv, 2, 12

—description of: in cinema and television, xvi, xx, 20, 23–26, 91–93, 115, 175, 202, 207; in literature, xvi, xx, 5, 20–26, 114, 175, 202, 207; in painting and other visual graphics, xx, 12, 20, 25, 114; in song, xvi, xx, 21, 33–36, 40, 45, 202; in still photography, xx, 25, 33, 80–81, 114, 125, 128, 175, 202; in travel diaries, xvi, 21, 33–36, 40, 45, 202

—land use in, xvii, 2–3, 5, 9, 29–30, 51, 64–65, 78–79

—relic architecture along, xv, xviii, 5, 18, 81, **84**, 85, **86**, 128, 131, 171, 175, 218

roadside architecture, 2, 4, 12, 14–15, **17**, 18, 29, 37, 53–54, 72, 78, 80–94, 110–11, 115–30, 177, 184, 199–200, 211, 221

—architectural styles, 1, 80, 82, 126, 128

—design of, xix, 2, 12, 29, 53, 62, 65, 69; "decorated sheds," 72, 81–82, 111, 224; "ducks," 29, 71–72, *81*, 82, 102, 106, 110–11, 200, 206, 210, **211**, 224, 227

—lighting of, 2, 53, 224, 227

—restored, **116**, 117, **118**, 119, **120**, **121**, 122, **123**, 124, **125**, 126, 184–85, **186**, **187**, **188**, 189

roadside blight, 5, 14, **16**, 48, **49**, 54, 62–63, **64**, 65–66, 70, 86–87, 175, 217; roadside litter, 45, 48, 50

roadside outdoor museum: speculation on, xx–xxi, 156–57, 170–75, 186–297, 218–31, 233–36

roadside restaurants, 3, 13–14, **16**, **17**, 23, 24, 36, 38, 41–43, 46–48, 50, 53–54, 110–11, 139, 175, 199–200, 202

—franchise chains: Howard Johnsons, **3**, 90; McDonalds, 78, 91, 110, 165, 199; Subway, 78; Wendy's, 91, 110; White Castle, 110

—diners, xix, 65, 120, 122–23, 165; Landrums's Diner (Reno, NV), 122;

—restored diners: Delta Diner (Delta, WI), 123, **124**; Niland Corner Café (Colo, IA), 158, 185, **188**

roadside commerce, xv–xvi, xix, 2–3, 5, 39–30, 36–38, 40–48, 50, 55, 61, 63, 81–82, 92, 143, 199–200, 221; auto-convenient and auto-oriented stores, xviii, 2–3, 9, 43, 68–80; discouraged along limited access highways, 57–58

roadside signs, xix, 5, 10, 13–15, **17**, **18**, 29–30, 33–, 37, 47–48, **49**, 52, 54, 56, 58, **64**, 72, 80–81, 92, 104, 130, 165–66, **169**, 199–200, 220–21, 224, 227; billboards, 48, **49**, 50, 52, 54, 62, 65–60, 68–70, **71**, 80–81, **86**, 88, **106**, 165–66, 175, 177, **193**, 198–200, 217; "heraldic" versus "locational" signs," 70; ordinances controlling, 221

roadside stands, 191, **192**, **201**, **202**

roadside tourist attractions, 224–25: Eskimo Museum and Gift Shop (Fairbanks, AK), **143**; Longhorn Ranch (Moriarity, NM), **145**; Miracle of America Museum (Polson, MT), **225**; Roadside America (Shartlesburg, PA), 155, **156**; Sod House Museum (Moorcroft, WY), **144**

Roberts. Kenneth L., 48

Rockefeller, John D., xix, 148–49

Rogers, Jefferson, 236

Rome, NY, **116**, **117**

Rowe, Peter G., 80

Route 66 Corridor Preservation Program, 114

Route 66 and *Route 66 Pulse* (magazines), 115

Route 66 (television program), 24–25
Ruscha, Edward, 25

Sanders, Harland, xix
St. Louis, MO, 48, 112, 126, 128, 160, 164, 205, 219–20, **222**, 230
Salem, MA, 146
Santa Rosa, NM, **15**
Saratoga Springs, NY, 102
Scenic America, 217
Schlereth, Thomas, 150, 223
Scranton, PA, 160, **164**
Sculle, Keith A., 1, 101–2, 135, 195, 236
Sears, H. P., 117
Sennett, Max, 23
sense of place, xvii, 20, 42, 40, 68, 97, 104, 130
Shamrock, TX, 184, **185, 186, 187**
Shartlesburg, PA, 155, **156**
Shelbrooke, NS, **181**, 182, 205
Shelburne, VT, 150
Shell Oil Co., 199
shopping centers and shopping malls, xviii, 5, 8, 52, 54, 62–63, 77–78, 80, 85–86, **88**, 127, 169, 202, 216
Skansen Open-Air Museum (Stockholm, Sweden), 144
Sloan, Alfred, xviii
Sloan, John, 25
small towns, xv, xviii, 2–4, 25, 29, 36, 41, 47, 51–52, 73–74, 213; main streets of, 29, 36–37, **38, 39**, 51, **52**, 54, 128, 133, 174, 185–86, 213; museum recreations, 182, **183**, 184
Smithsonian Institution, 153
Snow, Todd, 57
social values, xviii–xix, xxi, 5–6, 9, 17, 35, 38, 66–67, 69, 134, 204, 218, 227–28; change as progress, xvii, 9, 27, 84; convenience, 10, 18, 58–60, 69, 177, 209, 224; freedom/liberty, xx, 6, 9, 20, 27, 204, 209, 221, 231; individualism/independence, 9–10, 20, 25, 67, 178, 218, 221; mobility/speed, xxi, 5, 9–10, 20, 48, 58–60, 177–78, 218, 224, 227; patriotism, 98; utilitarianism functionalism, 48, 60, 69
Society for Commercial Archeology, 5, 111, 122, 225
Society for Industrial Archeology, 111
Society for the Preservation of New England Antiquities, 99
Solberg, Erling D., 54
Sondheim, Stephen, 1
South Bend, IN, 159, **173**
Springfield, IL, 135–42; Historic Site Commission, 140; Lincoln Home, 135, **136**, 137–41, **142**; Lincoln Tomb, 139; Old State Capitol, 135; Race Riot of 1908, 138
Standard Oil Co.: Indiana, 43, 144, **188**; Kentucky, **14**; New Jersey (Humble Oil and Refining Co.), 15, 195, **145**; Ohio, **3**, 118, **121, 122**
Starn, Randolph, 228
Steamtown National Historic Site (Scranton, PA), 160, **164**
Steinbeck, John, 22, 24–25, 42, 56
Stevenson, Adlai, 138
Stewart, George R., 56–57
Stieglitz, Alfred, 25
Stockbridge, MA, 107
Stockholm, Sweden, 144
"stranger's path," 6, 10–11, 13, 22, 27, 41–42, 57, 204
Studebaker Corp., 173
Sturbridge, MA, 150, 157, 200–201
suburbs and suburbanization, xv, xviii, 5, 8, 11, 25, 60, 62–63, 67–68, 74, 110, 169, 176, 216, 231; development along freeways, 78, **79**, 80

Suffolk County, NY, Department of Parks, 206
supermarkets, 52, 66
symbolic interaction, 17

Taft, William Howard, 137
taxes and taxation: abatements, credits and deferments, 215; Federal Rehabilitation Investment Tax Credit Program, 215–16; gasoline, 32; property, 216–17; tax-increment financing districts, 215
Taylor, Michael Romero, 159
Terry's BP Station (Piqua, OH), 118–19, **121**, **122**
Texas Co., the, 119
time and temporality, xv, 12, 71, 73, 170–71, 213
theme parks, 190–92, **228**; Six Flags Over Texas (Chaparral Antique Car Exhibit), **190**, 191
Times Beach, MO, **112**, **113**
Townsend, Tim, 138
trade journals, 201–2
traffic and traffic regulation, 5–6, 8–9, 29–30, 54, 56, 104, 126, 181, 199–200, 221; counts, 77; restricted areas, **147**, 181; rush-hour, 6, 51, 77
trailer parks, 52, 144
Troy, IL, **50**
Troy, MO, **46**
Tulls Hill, PA, **125**
Tulsa, OK, **123**
Trucks and trucking, xv, 6–8, 13, 30, 51, 60, 65, 73, 93, 133, 172, 178, 180, 231
Tulsa, OK, 86, **123**
Tunnard, Christopher, 63, 65

Updike, John, 22
Urbana, IL, 74, **76**, 77

urban renewal, 95, 100–102, 139, 154
used car lots, 52, 54, 66, 87–88, 203
utility poles and wires, 30, 33, 36, 48, 50, 63, **64**, 70, 198, 217
U.S. Bureau of Public Roads, 31–32
U.S. Environmental Protection Agency, 84
U. S. Federal Housing Administration, 61–62
U. S. Federal Works Agency, 32
U. S. National Park Service, 68, 102–3, 109, 111, 113, 137–38, 140, 157–58, 163, 205, 216, 219; Route 66 Corridor Preservation Program, 159
U. S. Office of Public Roads and Rural Engineering, 31
U. S. Office of Road Inquiry, 31
U. S. Postal Service, 31
U. S. Public Roads Administration, 32

Vale, Thomas and Geraldine, 57
Venturi, Robert, 70–71, 88, 110–11, 177

Wadena, MN, 37, **38**
Warhol, Andy, 25
Warp, Harold, 150–51
Washington, DC, 74, 135, 137
Washington, George, 97
Whitaker, Craig, 74
Whyte, William, 61–62
Williamsburg, VA, **146**, **147**, 152, 191
Williamstown, KY, **13**
Winston-Salem, NC, 81, 104–9; Old Salem, 104, **105**, **106**, 181–82
Wolfe, Tom, 53
World's Fair, automobile-related exhibits: Columbian Exposition, 1893 (Chicago), 141; Century of Progress Exposition, 1933 (Chicago), 148–50, **157**; Ford Rotunda, 149, **150**; New York World's Fair, 1939, 154–55; General Motor's "Democracy," **155**

World War I, 38, 82

World War II, 2, 5, 8–9, 55, 67, 93, 110, 120, 139, 154, 193, 219–20

Zion National Park, **226**

zoning, 15, 72–73, 87–88, 215, 221; enterprise zones, 215; historic district zoning, 102, 180–81, 216; strip zoning, 63

Remembering Roadside America was designed and typeset on a Macintosh computer system using InDesign software. The body text is set in 9.5/15 Mercury and display type is set in Savoye ITC. This book was designed and typeset by Chad Pelton.